THE NEW SPIRIT OF CREATIVITY

The New Spirit of Creativity

Work, Compromise, and the Art and Design University

SAARA LIINAMAA

UNIVERSITY OF TORONTO PRESS
Toronto Buffalo London

ISBN 978-1-4875-0280-5 (cloth)   ISBN 978-1-4875-1606-2 (EPUB)
                                   ISBN 978-1-4875-1605-5 (PDF)

Library and Archives Canada Cataloguing in Publication

Title: The new spirit of creativity : work, compromise, and the art and
   design university / Saara Liinamaa.
Names: Liinamaa, Saara, author.
Description: Includes bibliographical references and index.
Identifiers: Canadiana (print) 20220180822 | Canadiana (ebook) 20220180962 |
   ISBN 9781487502805 (cloth) | ISBN 9781487516062 (EPUB) |
   ISBN 9781487516055 (PDF)
Subjects: LCSH: Art – Study and teaching – Canada. | LCSH: Art schools – Canada. |
   LCSH: Creation (Literary, artistic, etc.) – Social aspects – Canada. | LCSH: Art and
   design – Social aspects – Canada.
Classification: LCC N331.C3 L55 2022 | DDC 707.1/171–dc23

This book has been published with the help of a grant from the Federation for the
Humanities and Social Sciences, through the Awards to Scholarly Publications
Program, using funds provided by the Social Sciences and Humanities Research
Council of Canada.

We wish to acknowledge the land on which the University of Toronto Press
operates. This land is the traditional territory of the Wendat, the Anishnaabeg, the
Haudenosaunee, the Métis, and the Mississaugas of the Credit First Nation.

University of Toronto Press acknowledges the financial support of the Government of
Canada, the Canada Council for the Arts, and the Ontario Arts Council, an agency of
the Government of Ontario, for its publishing activities.

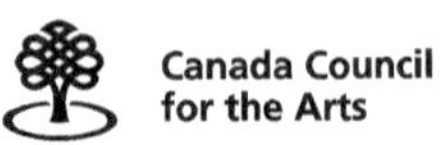

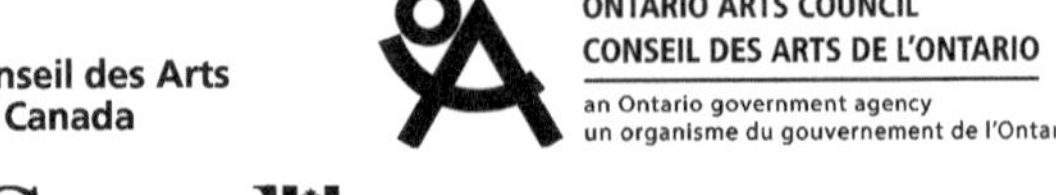

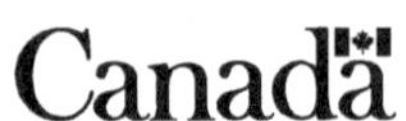

For my creative, exuberant, and loving family. Without you, this book would have been finished so much sooner. Thanks for the extra time with my ideas.

Contents

Figures

Acknowledgments

As I put the final touches on this manuscript, part of me still does not believe this book will ever be done. This process has left me with a new sense of appreciation – wonder, actually – for the endurance test of the book-writing process from start to finish. I apologize for previously taking the many books that have passed through my hands for granted. Here, I express my gratitude for the deep time and labour of all the authors whose research and ideas have fed into this book. Overall, I would like to acknowledge the time and support of the many people required to see this project through to completion.

I am very appreciative of the funding I received during the life of this project. First, funding from the Social Sciences and Humanities Research Council (SSHRC) was crucial at every point, starting with my SSHRC Postdoctoral Fellowship. This fellowship allowed me the time and space to explore and develop research and ideas central to this book. But more importantly, this fellowship allowed me to stay in academia after completing my PhD – this SSHRC funding made all the difference. Second, this book has been published with the help of a grant from the Federation for the Humanities and Social Sciences, through the Awards to Scholarly Publications Program, using funds provided by SSHRC. Third, I was delighted to receive a Harrison McCain Emerging Scholar Award while I was a faculty member at Acadia University. This award provided crucial funds for research travel and the hiring of research assistants. Finally, having moved to a position at the University of Guelph during the revision stages of this book, I am thankful for the research money the university provided to cover publication-related costs such as indexing.

This book's completion depended on an academic infrastructure devoted to supporting and circulating research. I would like to thank the art and design universities where I conducted my field research. I am indebted to NSCAD for hosting me as a postdoctoral fellow, especially the division of Art History and Contemporary Culture. Without the time, assistance, and support of many individuals at NSCAD, this research would not have been possible.

In particular, I would like to recognize the generous intellect and enthusiastic support of Sandra Alfoldy when I started my fellowship. I am so sorry to hear of her death – what a loss for NSCAD and Canadian craft scholarship. Additionally, I must recognize Bruce Barber for his vibrant insights and expansive intellect as my postdoctoral supervisor at NSCAD – so many thanks! I would also like to express sincere gratitude to the staff in a range of roles at all three schools who helped in my quest for documents and in clarifying information; thank you so much for your time and attentive replies to various queries. This sort of assistance was crucial. Two research assistants, Samantha Teichman and Katie Zimmer, also provided valuable help; thank you so much for your careful work. A big shout out to the skillful copy-editing of Samantha Rohrig; thank you for enduring my many errors. And much thanks to Patti Phillips for the meticulous index. Finally, I would like to thank the University of Toronto Press for their professionalism, insights, and support, especially Doug Hildebrand for initially supporting this project and Meg Patterson for her care and patience in bringing this book to publication. The expertise and recommendations of the reviewers for this book strengthened the final version immensely; thank you so much for your intellectual generosity during the revision process.

This book has benefitted immensely from the insight and support of many colleagues and friends. While working at Acadia University, I had the pleasure of everyday intellectual conversations, support, and much need advice on how to make this book a reality from Claudine Bonner, Lesley Frank, Sarah Rudrum, and Amanda Watson. I miss working with you all so much! However, I am delighted to now be working alongside so many brilliant and supportive colleagues in the Department of Sociology and Anthropology (SOAN) at the University of Guelph. I appreciate their patience while listening to my dilemmas around the final stages of this process, especially Karine Gagné and Erin Nelson. Further, this book benefited from the steadfast advice and early career support provided by SOAN Department Chairs Elizabeth Finnis and Vivian Shalla. I would like to thank my good friends from the Canadian Network for Critical Sociology for their careful reading and sharp insights on some earlier versions of chapters; Jesse Carlson, Michael Christensen, Laura Eramian, Matthew Hayes, Mervyn Horgan, Fuyuki Kurasawa, Peter Mallory, Marcia Oliver, Elisabeth Rondinelli, Phil Steiner, Steve Tasson, and Cathy Tuey – your feedback was crucial to setting the stage for the direction and focus of this book. Thanks especially to Marcia for always reassuring me that I was up to the task, and to Liz for responding to every panicked text message on writing dilemmas with a solid solution. I also have three academic mentors to whom I am deeply indebted: Zelda Abramson, Fuyuki Kurasawa, and Janine Marchessault. Each of you has made an invaluable contribution to my work and my ability to navigate the academic world. Without your guidance and patience over the years, this book would not have been possible.

Finally, I have to thank my creative and talented family. Thank you to my mother Lynda, from whom I get my intellect and curiosity, and to my sister Maija, from whom I get unconditional encouragement and sentence structure advice. Thanks so much to my children, Kaija, Will, and Finny, for making sure I don't take myself too seriously. Every day I am reminded of the necessity of taking the time to play, laugh, and do household chores. I save my last thank you for my partner in life and work, Mervyn Horgan. Mervyn, where do I start? Thank you for reading drafts and sections, even when you had more pressing work to do, for managing the various crises of uncertainty during the writing process, and for fixing sentences that were well past the line of readability. This acknowledgment seems insufficient, so I hope my everyday love and gratitude can help bridge the gap.

Abbreviations

ECUAD Emily Carr University of Art + Design
NSCAD Nova Scotia College of Art and Design University
OCAD Ontario College of Art and Design University

THE NEW SPIRIT OF CREATIVITY

The New Spirit of Creativity

"You compromise, compromise, compromise." This is how Dominic, an accomplished artist well regarded for his contributions to contemporary art in Canada, matter-of-factly summarized his decades of experience at Imagination University. Dominic is known for his critical and conceptually oriented works exploring a range of social themes, but compromise, he explained, was crucial to his career as an artist and educator within the institution. Across the fifty-four interviews with artists and designers that I conducted for this book, compromise was a recurring theme that surfaced within diverse descriptions of everyday work and creative activity. Yet, if compromise is as essential as Dominic and others claimed, its arrangements and effects should not be taken for granted: compromise and creativity are deeply entwined.

Popular discourse valorizes the uncompromising creative self – the artist who is unyielding in their passion and determination. These characteristics, we are told, are crucial to both aesthetic and, if desired, market success. Well-intentioned advice about ways to better access and develop this exacting creative vision abounds. Yet, when artists and designers speak about their creative practice and paid work arrangements, their descriptions are full of stories about compromise. Compromise here can be most simply defined as the ways in which an artist and that artist's creative activities are able to coexist, to some degree or another, in the world. Compromises can either strengthen or erode creative practices. Thus, to understand the multifold logics, values, and entanglements of compromise and contemporary creativity, I situate this investigation within a setting explicitly dedicated to advancing creativity.

Artistic Creativity and the Art School

This book is a study of artistic creativity and its formal organization within a dedicated art/higher education institution, the art and design university. I employ the term *artistic creativity* to focus on specialized aesthetic practices in art, craft, media, and design.[1] My investigation rests on the argument that we are currently witness to a "new spirit" of creativity, one that both converges with and diverges from key aspects of artistic creativity. This new spirit champions a creativity-driven reshaping of concepts of identity, work, and consumption, while underscoring the pivotal role creativity plays within a voracious and adaptable contemporary capitalism (Boltanski and Chiapello 2007; Du Gay and Morgan 2013; Sennett 2007). This spirit may be glimpsed in the vigorous production of self-help manuals on creative self-exploration, in the surfeit of TED Talks on activating one's creative potential, in key recommendations from management texts on cultivating a creative workforce, and in public policy and programming on creativity-led economic development. Accordingly, creativity centred discourse has become common place, a product of the successful institutionalization of creative values and principles across worlds of work and leisure (Mould 2015; Reckwitz 2017; Ross 2004, 2009). Yet this spirit, in its many guises, too often advances a thin version of creativity in order to uphold a robust version of austerity. A new centrepiece of success is to do more with less via creative solutions.

To analyse this new spirit of creativity, I employ "spirit" in its sociological sense; it is a way to disentangle taken-for-granted representations that provide social practices with meaning. I scrutinize how shifting conceptions of creativity are established, navigated, and contested within an art school, a site that is expressly dedicated to creative practices – specifically, its contemporary incarnation in Canada as the art and design university. In contrast to many popular images of creativity as daring and innovative, my account unpacks the everyday work, organization, and administration of creativity. Consequently, the chapters are organized around two interrelated concerns:

(1) The potential for creativity to be an inequitably recognized and rewarded resource within an institution. Who gets to be creative? How is it evaluated? How does this align with existing fault lines of difference? When creativity is labelled as an asset, institutional dynamics, policy, and administration can serve to reinforce practices that result in unevenly distributed benefits and unintended consequences in the name of creativity.
(2) Meaning-centred analysis that examines how social actors genuinely strive to make sense of artistic creativity and interrelated questions of creative practice. Artists and designers express considerable creative integrity. They offer insightful critiques of existing arrangements and navigate often competing frames of reference that account for creative value and worth.

However, I do not to seek to affirm a binary of authentic–inauthentic artistic creativity – a recognizable trope in cultural analysis. Rather, I position a sociologically rooted understanding of creativity that underscores the centrality of both critical insight and compromise to the job of creativity within an art school. Critique and compromise are crucial to the everyday, often effortless work of social coordination (Boltanski and Thévenot 2006); in this case, they are an inroad to analysing the tension and uncertainty surrounding artistic creativity and cultural work.

In the coming chapters, I examine the organizational logics, everyday critiques, and forms of compromise that combine to support and maintain advanced artistic creativity within teaching, practice, and research. Compromise, at its core, is an ambivalent concept. It is celebrated as the key to cooperation, denounced as a signal of the betrayal of values, championed as a measure of goodwill, and disregarded as a weakness (Margalit 2013, 6). I subtly disagree with the prevalent assumption that compromise is necessarily a diminished or lesser option. Sociologically, compromise is part of everyday social coordination and exchanges, surfacing in a range of formal and informal ways, and often without a clear vision or hierarchy of best to worst options; day-to-day work requires and even thrives on compromise, which is why distinguishing between compromise as a social relation and compromise as a political or legal arrangement (e.g., Wendt 2018) is central to better understanding organizational contexts.

Drawing on different associations with the term *compromise* and its mix of both positive and negative connotations, I identify three forms of compromise relations between work and creativity at Imagination University: compromise as recombination, compromise as mutual concession, and compromise as vulnerability. The first form of compromise I locate, *recombination*, is a compromise between different things, a hybrid; for example, a novella instead of short story or novel, a moped instead of a bicycle or motorbike. In the context of this research, this type of compromise is grounded in forging alternatives – hybrid arrangements of creative practice and organization to meet academic–artistic contexts. The second form, *mutual concession*, refers to the mutual giving up required to reach accord. This is its usual meaning within binding agreements or legal proceedings: "an intermediate state between conflicting alternatives reached by mutual concession."[2] This type of compromise is the formal domain of collective agreements, but I use it to refer to the routine work of finding common ground during everyday operational, policy, and planning activities. The final form of compromise, *vulnerability*, describes a situation of endangerment – to be compromised or vulnerable; for example, an immune system compromised due to illness. This version of compromise between work and creativity is a way to discern complex organizational practices and their unevenly distributed impacts. The mix of vulnerability and enrichment that marks the organizational life of artistic creativity thus comes into focus through these compromise relations. Yet to consider compromise also invites the question of critique – without critique, there would be no need to forge compromises or develop alternatives. Thus, alongside compromise, this book examines the fate of artistic critique – what I term institutional-artistic critique – within the contemporary art school.

A Critical-Interpretive Sociology of Creativity

This book adopts a critical-interpretive framework that seeks to augment the sociology of creativity by connecting shared interests within the sociology of art, cultural sociology, cultural studies, and critical theory. This framework attends to both the constitution and consequences of organizational activities that inform artistic work and identity, and how individuals make sense of these practices and discourses against competing narratives and imperatives. Chan argues that the "construction of a *sociology* of creativity has not been given the attention it deserves" (2011, 135). The vast literature on creativity is generally dominated by business and psychological models, and while in this vein of work there is some validation of the importance of social contexts and environments to supporting creative processes and experiences (Amabile 1996; Csikszentmihalyi 1996), too much focus on individual-level talent or personality characteristics impoverishes a more rigorous understanding of the social situatedness of creative practices, social structures, and meanings. The wider study of creativity often prioritizes agency over structure. The sociology of creativity as an area of study is often only weakly identified or understood, mixed into many labels and disciplinary boundaries (Reuter 2015). Yet there are many influential texts within the discipline that explore creativity sociologically (e.g., Becker 1982; Bourdieu 1984, 1993; Durkheim 1995; Joas 1996; Wolff 1981), and there is evidence of a growing contemporary current (Burns, Corte, and Machado 2015a, 2015b; Fine 2004, 2018; Reckwitz 2017; Reuter 2015; Wohl 2021). The approach to the sociology of creativity that I develop here draws on overlapping lineages of cultural sociology and sociology of the arts (e.g., Alexander 2011; Alexander and Bowler 2014; Born 1995, 2005; Childress 2017; Chong 2020; Gerber 2017; Griswold 1987, 2000; Heinich 1996, 2015; Zolberg 2015), as well as critical variants of cultural studies attuned to everyday practices of power, ideology, identity, and representation (e.g., Banks 2007, 2017; McRobbie 2015; Hall 2018; Saha 2018). While at its radical edge critical theory positions creativity as a rich and unruly provocation that capitalism's endless formations seek to constrain and exploit (Deleuze and Guattari 1987), critical cultural studies carefully recognize how everyday creative subjectivities become instituted through the subtle arrangements of social and institutional power while still leaving space for transformative practices (McRobbie 2015).

Existing lineages for the sociology of creativity carve out key questions around collective meaning, social action, and constraint. For example,

Durkheim's (1995) classic study of ritual and religious belief understands collective meaning and signification as both organized and improvised. This influential approach has grounded later explorations of social creativity and "the imagination as social practice" within global cultural processes (Appadurai 1996, 31). Joas's *The Creativity of Action* develops a theory of social action that places creativity at the centre and seeks to resolve the inherent contradictions within existing rational and normative theories of action. His alternative is "to regard creativity as an analytical dimension of all human action" (1996, 116). Such a model is valuable for its rigorous theorizing of social creativity, but this ambition turns away from the specificity of artistic creativity, something that other sociologists have actively engaged. For example, Bourdieu's (1993) extensive legacy centres on his careful dismantling of notions of artistic autonomy and aesthetic genius by recognizing cultural contingency and social context, elucidating the subtle dynamics of power and status. Cultural conceptions of creativity are inseparable from questions of status, elitism, and gatekeeping; the work of taste and distinction are telling markers of "the social conditions of the constitution of the mode of appropriation that is considered legitimate" (Bourdieu 1984, 1). Similarly, Becker's classic study, *Art Worlds*, demystifies the creativity associated with art and artists by treating art as "not so very different from other kinds of work, and treating people defined as artists as not so very different from other kinds of workers" (1982, x). Becker pinpoints some now widely researched themes including cooperation and networking, symbolic boundaries, organizational constraints, and market demand. Becker's attentiveness to art worlds validates the dynamic character of artistic work that is dependent on the specificity of the art scene, social organization, and practices. Wolff's defining text on the social production of art locates the importance of social structures to any notion of creativity and innovation and argues that artistic creativity is deeply connected to other types of creativity. By refusing the presumed opposition between structure and creativity, where art is either regarded as individual genius and expression or reduced to "social, economic and ideological coordinates" (1981, 2), Wolff demonstrates how "practical activity and creativity are in a mutual relationship of interdependence with social structure" (9).

More recently, Childress models how to trace the entire life of the novel across the fields of creation, production, and reception, calling for new attention to the "relationship between fields as well as how inter-field relations affect intra-field activities and practices" (2017, 9). As part of this, he identifies "creativity as social collage" (21) to account for the relationships, communities, resources, and institutions that support the creation process, while mapping it alongside the other fields. Fine's (2004) influential work on self-taught artists and the art world's search for and commodification of creative authenticity, as well as his more recent ethnography of the distinct culture of MFA graduate student training (Fine 2018) has carefully demonstrated the importance of social organization to artistic production and the contingency of creative values. Fine deftly sums this up as follows: "Groups, networks, organizations, and institutions shape how creativity is defined, how objects and performances are produced, and how workers come to think of themselves as creative" (2018, 220). Similarly, Wohl's ethnography of the New York art world, *Bound by Creativity*, situates the creative process within the contemporary art world as a "whole organism" (2021, 5) with an emphasis on how aesthetic judgment is formed and negotiated, taking "a production-focused, temporal, and relational approach to analyzing aesthetic judgments" (8). These contemporary currents indicate how the sociology of creativity is well equipped to examine the creativity of everyday life, communication, and organization, as well as specialized domains of artistic creative practice. It is this combination of trajectories that supports the sociology of creativity's relevance and diversity as a sub-field – one that builds upon and extends the contemporary relevance of the sociology of the arts (Zolberg 2015).[3]

While the character of artistic cultures and processes of stratification are central within many of the texts named above, often with Bourdieu as a common reference, recent scholarship further nuances the dynamics of cultural production by exploring the interpretive issues – especially in terms of valuation and evaluation – that the sociology of creativity invites. As Beljean, Chong, and Lamont (2015) argue, despite the many excellent studies that have been produced using a Bourdieusian framework, the reification of economic and aesthetic oppositions in the field and the ahistorical application of Bourdieu's work has constrained analytical possibilities inherent in his work on culture. Drawing on Lamont's considerable contributions to the sociology of evaluation (Lamont and Thévenot 2000; Lamont 2009, 2012), Beljean, Chong, and Lamont carve out directions more attentive to the dynamics of valuation-evaluation of culture – namely, standards of evaluation in the field, self-concepts of evaluators, and the agency of objects in evaluation (2015, 39). Similarly, Gerber (2017) develops a multidimensional model for understanding how artists position value and worth in their practices; she combines Bourdieu with Boltanski and Thévenot to analyse accounts of creative value within artistic practice. Likewise, Georgina Born advocates for an approach to the sociology of art that welcomes more interdisciplinary breadth. She notes Bourdieu's only "sporadic attention to the character of institutions" (2010, 179), something that her own ethnographic studies of cultural institutions seek to overcome (Born 1995, 2005). Born develops an "analytics of mediation" that grounds an interdisciplinary methodology able to address the temporality, agency, inventiveness, and multiplicity of cultural production (2010, 182). Taken together, I draw on these critical and interpretive insights from this inclusively defined sociology of creativity to understand artistic creativity as everyday paid work for salaried employees within a complex art institution devoted to advanced art and design teaching, research, and practice.

Themes in Cultural Work

By studying the job of artistic creativity within the art school, this research engages with dilemmas surrounding cultural work and creative professions. The alliance between art and work has never been straightforward. Dominant ideas about professions and the value of labour mean that art production is regularly dismissed as unviable or unproductive work. Artists must develop various strategies to deal with the "uncertain environment" of art worlds (Becker 1982, 123). Bryan-Wilson identifies the "special power and flexibility of the term *art worker*" and its recourse to historically rooted confrontations over meaning (2009, 2). Artists have steadily identified themselves as workers since the 1960s and more widely participated in labour organizing and activism to address questions of art markets, working conditions, and remuneration. They have looked to various models of work to guide their practices, fashioning themselves as everything from manual labourers to lab technicians to corporate entrepreneurs (Jones 1996). With this, the idea of art as a profession – alike yet different from other professional systems (Abbott 1988) – also becomes possible. Credentials and training become an important part of professionalization, and so does more active engagements with art institutions, to various effects (Fine 2018; Kunst 2015a; Möntmann 2006). Artists' disenfranchisement from art institutions becomes a more focused target of critique once they start to play a stronger role within them, but this focus too often leaves questions of mutual security and everyday working relationships within such institutions less well examined.

Recent research considers the fragile arrangements of creativity, labour, and commerce within the cultural industries (Banks 2007, 2017; Banks, Gill, and Taylor 2013; Conor, Gill, and Taylor 2015; Gerber 2017; Hesmondhalgh and Baker 2008, 2011; McRobbie 1998, 2015; de Peuter 2011, 2014a, 2014b). The existing literature on cultural work broadly attends to the following key themes, which I will briefly summarize here: autonomy, aesthetics, inequality, solidarity, and professional identity. Together, these themes indicate how the analysis of cultural work often finds itself tripped up in both/and scenarios, where it is both similar to other forms of work and employment and distinct in its orientation to time and production. Or, it offers diverse pleasures and freedoms, and it is a path towards legitimating insecure work and lessening social supports. This book maintains that studying a (relatively) stable institution of teaching, research, and professional practice adds more layers to our understanding of creativity and cultural work within clearly defined paid employment arrangements. While my argument is a broader contribution to the sociology of creativity, it also responds to Canadian focused studies of cultural work, where there are currently many critical academic voices engaging in these dialogues (e.g., Bain 2013; Campbell 2013; Cohen 2016; Cohen and de Peuter 2018; Druick and Deveau 2015; Léger 2010; Liinamaa and Rogers 2020; Murray and Gollmitzer 2012; Stephens 2015).

The first theme, autonomy, identifies how cultural work has often troubled conceptions of work–life as well as production–consumption; this makes autonomy important and challenging to position. The appeal of creative freedom and labour independence is what draws many workers into the field, and those in creative positions often confirm that they enjoy considerable freedom in decision-making compared to other types of work (Hesmondhalgh and Baker 2011). Creative autonomy cannot be dismissed outright as rhetoric but can bring some progressive changes to workers' experiences (Banks and Milestone 2011). It is often a fine line between, as Ben Woo puts it, the "leisure and labour" of creativity-based work (2015, 57). Importantly, those who are successful do often have an enviable combination of creativity, autonomy, and dignity within their work arrangements (Stahl 2013; Thornton 2009). At the same time, the question of autonomy can be another way of phrasing economic insecurity, where positioning and measuring art as work comes with a difficult lineage (Menger 2001). Intermittent work patterns of drought or flood, hard to predict contracts, and the unpaid labour of constant opportunity-seeking are normalized experiences in the creative fields (Banks 2007, 2017). The rhetoric of creative autonomy is a way to successfully repackage disadvantageous labour conditions (Gill and Pratt 2008). Under the logic of creative autonomy, celebrations of creative work are often labour management guides in an alternate guise, providing "companies the conceptual tools with which they might better capture the fruits of their employees' creativity" (Szeman 2010, 19). Autonomy, when cast as a trendy and desirable feature of cultural work, is used to justify the higher levels of employment insecurity required in the industry (Neff, Wissinger, and Zukin 2005). Yet autonomy is not a clear-cut position; as Gerber and Childress argue, the tension between art and market has shifted such that artists, through activities such as teaching, find "pathways to autonomy through market activity" (2017, 1533).

The next theme, aesthetics, draws on the multidimensionality of the term's meaning. Aesthetic labour is relevant to many types of work (e.g., the service industry), but assumes distinct dimensions within cultural work as the centrepiece of creative activity, one that often relies on high levels of embodiment and performativity (Hracs and Leslie 2014). Aesthetics, like autonomy, represents another tension in scholarship: how much or how little does this aesthetic component shape and distinguish labour experiences and contexts? On the one hand, a recurring point is that we need to address cultural work as we would any other type of work; in order to strengthen an interconnected labour politics, we need to correct the tendency to insist on its uniqueness. As Stahl argues, minimizing differences between cultural and other types of work "can give us theoretical and critical leverage in our examination of cultural labor as a component in the social division of labour" (2013, 15). Yet, at the same time, it is crucial to take seriously how cultural work provides aesthetic pleasures and rewards. As Banks reminds us, "that work *is* actually the source of much of our personal happiness and self-respect should not be lightly discounted" (2014, 247). Cultural workers characterize the aesthetic process as "pleasurable absorption" that provides a key source of work satisfaction; pleasure from creative time and decision-making provides a sense of dignity that can also offset some of the less positive features (Hesmondhalgh and Baker 2011, 132–6). Or, Siciliano uses "aesthetic enrollment" to describe the aesthetic base of job satisfaction for even those tasked with routine and less creatively rewarding positions in the cultural industries (2016, 691–2). This aesthetic component is an important dimension and source of satisfaction; research continues to indicate that cultural workers find their work meaningful in ways not reducible to concepts of self-exploitation or alienated labour (Campbell 2013; Cohen 2016).

The next theme, social inequality, examines the social hierarchies and inequities at the core of cultural work and production. This involves even more attention in the field to issues of, as Banks calls it, "distributive justice," such as "who receives the most prestigious cultural education, the highest pay and the best (or indeed any) kind of cultural industry job" (2017, 2). With concepts of tolerance and openness knit into the creative class thesis (Florida 2004), the task of understanding cultural work's relationship to social regulation and discrimination has fallen to critical cultural theorists (McRobbie 1998, 2015). The youthful, dynamic status of the cultural industries as "cool, creative and egalitarian" (Gill 2002, 70) remains an animating assumption about the creative economy, even when diversity statistics readily contradict such claims (Banks and Oakley 2016; Saha 2018). There are all too familiar patterns of gendered labour disparity, as well as new forms of emerging disparity specific to the culture of creative work (Conor, Gill, and Taylor 2015). With widespread recognition of how social and cultural capital work to uphold mechanisms of belonging or exclusion (Banks 2017; Lee 2011), the psychosocial demands and affective impacts of inequities in the cultural industries are generating more attention (Gill 2014a; Hesmondhalgh and Baker 2008), and the prominence of sexual harassment and violence remains understudied and poorly addressed (Hennekam and Bennett 2017). Research has identified how dominant representations of creativity can naturalize the exclusion of women and racialized workers as "less" creative (Taylor 2011; Taylor and Littleton 2012). Social exclusion within the production of cultural representations and knowledge has clear impacts on the socio-cultural constitution of difference. With much work in this vein focusing on the gendered dynamics of work, continued exclusions around racialization and ethnicization, age, and ability have been less robustly researched (Finkel et al. 2017). There is ample attention paid to how cultural objects mediate representations of social identities, but much less attention given to how racialization and ethnicization shape cultural work and production (Saha 2013, 2018; Yuen 2017). As Tatli and Özbilgin demonstrate, "ignorance of the white middle-class bias" is striking, and, from an employment equity perspective, more attention to the place of gatekeeping in terms of race and ethnicity as well as religion is especially required (2012, 261). Recently, Alacovska and Gill (2019) addressed the Western-centric nature of most scholarship and argue for an "ex-centric" perspective that can productively disentangle embedded assumptions in the field and pursue case studies outside of Western contexts.

Deeply related to the above, the next theme, solidarity, points to some of the most promising directions in terms of implementing change and cultivating a collective orientation towards equity and social justice. There is growing interest in understanding how cultural workers are organizing around insecure and unjust conditions and developing strategies for managing difficulties in both formal and informal ways. Consider the international multi-city research project Cultural Workers Organize and its compilation of examples of collective organizing within education, work, and policy. In this project, researchers pinpoint how co-working spaces, cooperatives, unions, and professional associations in the cultural industries mobilize different ways of coming together and locate large- and small-scale issues and solutions (de Peuter and Cohen 2015; de Peuter, Cohen, and Brophy 2015). As de Peuter and Cohen explain, there is a need in the study of cultural work for "deeper engagement … with efforts to organize, agitate and resist precarity" (2015, 305). Cultural workers are mobilizing around conditions, remuneration, job security, and discrimination, from the fields of visual arts to film and television to journalism and publishing, often foregrounding different models for organizing and collectivizing resources (Bodnar 2006; Boyle and Oakley 2018; Cohen and de Peuter 2020; Coles 2016; McRobbie 1998; Sandoval 2016). Further, studies of cultural work policy are emphasizing the role labour policy and "flexicurity" within social security measures can play in enhancing labour protections for cultural workers, and where the successful realization of these measures requires the concerted organizing of academics, workers, and policy analysts (Murray and Gollmitzer 2012). Deuze and Lewis confidently foreground the capacity of cultural workers "to determine their own destiny and create an identity by inventing new institutions on their terms, perhaps uniting in more informal and international contexts" (2013, 174). Alacovska (2018) argues for a reconsideration of the place of hope in cultural work, and in a way that challenges many assumptions about the nature of this work as necessarily precarious. The debates about how to makes sense of what is distinct to cultural work without overstressing its uniqueness remain important here too; solidarity can be limited if cultural work is elevated above regular work, but research on processes specific to cultural work are vital to dissecting how labour hierarchies do function and how they might be changed. The question is how to nurture collective solidarity and collective action, not only among cultural workers but also between cultural workers and those in other sectors.

The final theme, professional identity, often pulls in features of the other themes. The bleed between work and non-work identity is especially pronounced in cultural work, and the centrality of passion to ideas of creative identity can displace other modes of understanding cultural production as work (McRobbie 2015). The difficulty here is in effectively positioning identity as both inside and outside paid employment. Studying cultural work in terms of only paid employment excludes the range and diversity of creative labour, including many unpaid activities; at the same time, it is important to understand how professional identity is cultivated within labour markets, and in ways that can shape, cultivate, or minimize opportunities. Many artists express considerable uncertainty around how or when to identify as a professional artist, and identification may or may not align with work experiences (Lena and Lindemann 2014). For example, someone might declare themselves a professional artist, but this declaration is not dependent on proof (except maybe for tax purposes) of a certain level of income. Or, an artist or designer might embrace or minimize the place of teaching in their professional identity for a range of reasons, even if the bulk of their paid employment comes from teaching. As Fine (2018) argues, artistic identity is especially complicated because of the uncertainty around value that accompanies a creative career, in no small part because of the uneven remuneration of labour. As Taylor and Littleton's research on aspiring creatives establishes, it is a "complex, effortful process to negotiate and reconcile culturally established and local meanings concerning, for example, what it means to make creative work" (2012, 39); it requires navigating and accounting for your past history and achievements while responding to the demands of the present. There is marked interest within creative identities and cultural work scholarship on student and youth articulations as they strive to carve out sustainable career trajectories (Ashton 2011, 2013a, 2015; Campbell 2013; Noonan 2013; Taylor and Littleton 2012, 2013). Further, the analysis of professional identities intersects with dynamics of inclusion/exclusion discussed above, as some are more readily able than others to occupy a creative identity according to authorized social scripts of creativity.

Together, these themes in cultural work unfold in this study against a wider context of higher education debates and restructuring both in Canada and elsewhere, where the consequences of neo-liberalization continue to take shape and move towards yet uncertain ends (Côté and Allahar 2007, 2011; Newfield 2011; Peters 2011; Slaughter and Rhoades 2004). This research explores what are pressures from multiple sides. The art and design university is a leading example of a stable workplace compared to the wider field, but where ideas around creativity, work, and value from the cultural field shape and direct institutional life. Yet, it is a university type that is distinctly vulnerable due to its size and subject matter, situated as it is within a university system increasingly tempted by the playbook of disaster capitalism (Letizia 2016; Klein 2008).

The Art and Design University in Canada

I conducted the fieldwork for this research at three art and design universities in Canada (Emily Carr University of Art + Design; Nova Scotia College of Art and Design University; Ontario College of Art and Design University); together, they are referred to as Imagination University throughout this book. These schools house art, craft, media, and design expertise of all sorts, and this concentration of creative activities is one of their most defining features – where else we can find the same diversity and range in a single place? Within Canada's almost exclusively public university system, the independent art and design university is an uncommon type. All were past art schools, then art and design colleges, and now all are uniquely specialized outliers, with only four such universities in Canada.[4] The art and design university is even more vulnerable to the changing tides of government, policy, funding, and public discourse than comprehensive universities due to its small size (all with fewer than 5,000 students), its relatively new university status, and poor public understanding of its mandate. In the recent past, these schools have both experienced greater recognition and struggled to keep pace with demands and expectations that are part of the university system overall and specific to this university type. There is very little academic scholarship on these schools in Canada.

The themes in cultural work discussed above play out in different ways at the art and design university, particularly when studying permanent employees who do not have to struggle with labour insecurity and the uncertainty of project-based work. Within the Canadian art and design university, permanent faculty teach within their areas of expertise and have considerable autonomy in terms of aesthetic decision-making; they are largely free to pursue their creative practice (e.g., commercial, non-commercial, or both) as they see fit.[5] But this creative autonomy and flexibility brushes up regularly against institutional, bureaucratic organization, which is the cost of secure employment. Occupational identity translates to the university in a way that stresses creative practice and teaching, but not administration or bureaucracy; participants in this study did not enthusiastically describe themselves as "artists in offices" (Adler 1979).

Universities do hold a different relationship to recognition compared to the larger art world and its markers of commercial success. As Fine explains, "the institutional pressure within universities is to gain a reputation: to become known, not to become rich" (2018, 207). Here, social inequities inherent to institutions of higher education and cultural work intersect. Reproduction of dominant culture, habitus, and cultural capital are certainly at play, but key opportunities are less tied to social networking and informal ties than the wider cultural gig economy and more structured by the hybrid art–academic field. There are formal equity and diversity policies in place, however imperfectly they are often put into practice, and faculty are unionized with active faculty associations. So, rather than striving to piece together new forms of solidarity and collectivism for cultural work, the art and design university in Canada is a site where formal solidarity exists in terms of labour contracts and bargaining rights. In the literature specific to higher education and the cultural industries, art schools are featured as the training ground for future cultural workers, with attention to debates over pedagogy, employment prospects, and educational outcomes (Ashton and Noonan 2013; Oakley, Sperry, and Pratt 2008). However, these schools themselves are rarely treated as central cultural employers and workplaces; they are left out of the literature on cultural work because of its focus on the dynamics of insecurity and flexibility within contract work.[6] Yet the art and design university does not just prepare students as future cultural workers – it also represents a key cultural work trajectory (Gerber and Childress 2017). Gill (2014a) makes an appeal for a more robust critical lexicon of cultural labour studies that recognizes academics as cultural workers amidst intensifying demands and increasing precariousness. The complicated figure of the teaching artist who already troubles many assumptions about the meaning and value of labour is an excellent place to start mapping alignments between cultural work and academia.

Together, this book centres on an overlooked cultural workplace and a marginalized area of higher education. The art and design university remains poorly understood and recognized within higher education, and in ways that hinge on how creativity and artistic labour are valued, yet the understanding I develop here is not exactly fit for the next recruitment campaign. Instead, in the chapters to come, I elaborate on the bureaucratic, day-to-day workings of an intensely creative institution, where being creative is something managed, cultivated, and contested at all points by faculty and administration at Imagination University.

Notes on Methods and Methodology

I will briefly address methods and methodology here, with a more detailed description to be found in the Methodological Appendix. I am committed to methodological pluralism within qualitative research. This approach, as Lamont and Swidler explain, is well suited for collecting data "about representations, classification systems, boundary work, identity, imagined realities and cultural ideals, as well as emotional states" (2014, 157). There are a number of methodological principles embedded in my critical-interpretive framework. First, I borrow a recognition found within different qualitative lineages, from feminist studies to cultural sociology: we are all participants in the social world, and, when asked, individuals can account for their experiences and world views with considerable insight; contradictions within everyday accounts are not a sign of unreliability or ignorance but derive from the fact that identity and subjectivity are messy. The research task is to identify and understand the multiple meanings at work and at stake within a given context, and with varied implications. The second principle, drawing on mixed trajectories of cultural studies found within both the humanities and social sciences, recognizes that culture is not secondary to social or economic structure, but an active agent in our ordering and understanding of the world. We need to be attentive to the centrality of meaning within social life and the instituting qualities of culture. This brings me to my third point: there is much complexity to how the micro and macro dimensions of this social world as co-constituted and meaning-laden intersect. It is not a one-size-fits-all scenario, and this research seeks to paint a dynamic portrait of these exchanges within a specific site and context. Appropriately, these above principles are why I cannot argue that creativity is now a totally bankrupt or empty discourse; this would dismiss the rich ways creativity is threaded throughout Imagination University. Rather, what I have is an analysis of moments when debates over meaning and value surface, the different ways these are put to use to justify practices, and the mixing of both positive and negative effects.

I conducted fifty-four in-depth, semi-structured interviews with university faculty members and administrators, plus follow-up and informational interviews. The number and cross-section of participants sought to mirror the size and scale of the smallest university in this research (NSCAD) with its lean organization of fifty or so permanent full-time (tenured or tenure-track) faculty members and key upper-level administrators. This design purposefully focuses on those most responsible for everyday operations and the three-fold responsibilities of teaching, service, and research/practice; these are the permanently employed, well-salaried artists and designers who have yoked their careers to the university. In addition to interviews, I draw on participant observation, policy and planning documents, recruitment and advertising campaigns, and popular press stories. Between 2013 and 2017, I spent many hours on these university campuses, watching everyday interactions in hallways, hanging out in studio spaces, attending events, and chatting with people in informal ways. That said, the absence of student voices is a limitation that I wish to explain. I did not interview students, and thus when the topic arises, the account is clearly one-sided. What I have is faculty and administrators talking about their perceptions of student experiences and attitudes; and I include references to recruitment brochures and institutionally produced literature attempting to reach an audience of students. Student outcomes and experiences are important; I do not want readers to take my silence on the issue as dismissal. Student-centred studies are a valuable part of the larger puzzle, but one that is already better developed in the existing research (see chapter 1). This study complements this research by examining the art and design university as a cultural workplace, and the analysis I develop identifies and explores themes that were evident across all three universities.

The first full draft of this manuscript included pseudonyms and quotations from all participants, with varying details around their artistic careers and backgrounds and many constraints on presenting relevant information; the number of upper administrators is a very small group of players in the national scene, and I had concerns that many of the artists and designers, as public figures, could be too easily identified. This was especially a concern for faculty who are members of under-represented groups, where the lack of diversity within these universities also heightened concerns around potential loss of privacy. Thus, in this early version I felt that participants' insights and experiences were not well captured. I tackled this dissatisfaction by adopting a composite approach to representing participants and interview data. Apart from providing brief histories of the three universities included in this study (chapter 2), I take a composite approach to the presentation of the university, Imagination University, and participants. Composite constructions are sometimes misunderstood as a qualitative method and raise questions around the relationship between data and its representation (Markham 2012); however, all qualitative work involves trusting the researcher to responsibly organize and interpret the data, and composites are no different (Willis 2019). In this case, a composite approach brings a number of interpretive strengths in terms of capturing participants' insights into their work experiences at Imagination University while minimizing the loss of privacy risk for participants. So, while all quotations, paraphrasing of positions, and observational details come directly from interview transcripts and observations, this method allows me to present a more coherent sense of different perspectives via seventeen composite profiles.

Argumentation Snapshot

Hayot's guide for academic writers calls chapter descriptions in the introduction "usually one of the most boring things in the universe" (2014, 100). I take this insight to heart, so I will not provide full summaries but rather a succinct overview of how I develop my argument and map out the relationships between chapters to guide the reader.

This book is organized into two sections and seven chapters. The first section consists of two chapters that are designed to provide concepts and context for the research and analysis to come. Chapter 1 starts with a description of the new spirit of creativity as an analytic category, where I map out principles and conflicts between it and artistic creativity. Bridging literatures from sociology to art history, I discuss how the new spirit of creativity invites new tensions and debates over the nature of artistic creativity and critique. Accordingly, I bring these to the study of the art school and develop institutional-artistic critique as a concept that captures the dilemmas of paid creative work within art institutions. Next, I locate the art school as a creative and contrary institution and explain why artistic critique is such a resilient yet ambiguous concept in the contemporary context. In chapter 2, I provide a brief account of the art and design university in Canada and each art school included in this research. I identify how both elevation and dismissal accompanies the development of the art and design university and touch on its uneasy relationship with the wider system of higher education.

In the second section, I analyse five key changes that emerged in my research, each of which underscores dilemmas of artistic creativity, everyday work, and institutional transformation at Imagination University as the new spirit of creativity takes hold: (1) the growth of artistic research culture; (2) the rise of audit culture; (3) new demands placed on creative identity at the service of the institution; (4) changing perceptions of employment security and creative currency; and (5) multiplying institutional uncertainties. I explore how each change intersects with day-to-day struggles such as increased workloads and administrative duties, ambiguous evaluation procedures, pressures to secure research funding and grants, expanding commercialization initiatives, and planning amidst many unknowns. While such demands are generally in line with shifts in higher education overall, they raise issues specific to creative work and practices at Imagination University.

In chapters 3 to 7, I trace how artistic creativity and the new spirit coexist and diverge through examples where tensions erupt around how to organize and value creativity. In chapter 3, I examine how the growth of artistic research and the rise of research planning at Imagination University is an example of how the new spirit advances the professionalization, commercialization, and credentialization of creativity, and in ways that can exclude artistic practices that do not easily sit within these discourses. Yet at the same time, the embrace of artistic research remedies some previous exclusions and provides more room for diverse practices. In chapter 4, I address the dilemma of evaluating artistic creativity, and the procedures and paperwork that have flourished as the new spirit's key principles intersect with the demands of audit culture. While faculty and administrators express a genuine commitment to creative excellence, formal and informal types of evaluation invite creative hierarchies and exclusions.

In chapter 5, I explore the institutional performativity of creativity as the new spirit places a higher premium on creative identities at the service of the university; in this case, untenured women and racialized faculty express their difficulties navigating the demands placed on their identities for institutional image and gain. In chapter 6, I examine how the new spirit's embrace of flexibility and creative currency impacts how insecure work is justified and explained at Imagination University by faculty and administrators. Permanent faculty express nostalgia for their creative past while on contracts, while administrators present contract work as a desirable fit between the university's needs and talented instructors who desire work flexibility. Finally, in chapter 7 I analyse participants' descriptions of institutional uncertainty. These accounts point to multiplying uncertainties within the new spirit of creativity and feared erosions of artistic creativity and community; further, this uncertainty troubles conceptions of institutional time (past, present, future) and artistic value.

Throughout each of these chapters, I map out the interplay between critique and compromise that accompanies the new spirit's embeddedness within Imagination University. Based on this, I am able to theorize the relationship between artistic creativity and the new spirit of creativity as one grounded in multifold artistic critiques and in compromises of different orders and consequences for the artists and designers who work at the university. This is what a creative career within an art/higher education institution looks like in the contemporary moment: flashes of brilliance amidst constellations of compromise.

SECTION I

Creativity, Critique, and the Art School

Chapter One

Our New Spirit and the Dilemmas of Artistic Critique

The past two decades have seen a great expansion of the arts in higher education, with the consequence that artists are increasingly likely to find themselves (as least for some periods in their lives) working as employees of large bureaucratic organizations.

– Adler, *Artists in Offices* (1979), xiv

The team comes in with, like, clipboards and a PowerPoint presentation with miserable graphics. Uh, really? We are going to reimagine our creative future in a claustrophobic room with people talking at us about creativity?

– Nate, study participant

It has been a transitional period at Imagination University. The art school has undergone many changes in the recent past. Changes like, as Nate explains above, having a team of consultants come to the school to lead discussions about institutional identity and strategic vision. According to those with deep institutional memory, the recent transition has seemed more intense and more sweeping than previous ones, starting – but not ending – with the move to university status. Marked by many uncertainties and some new opportunities, it has been a mixed bag of struggle and achievement.

Studying transitional moments within organizations foregrounds dilemmas and debates that would usually go unrecognized. I regard such moments as a time when the scaffolding of cultural repertoires and meaning is either absent, unclear, or not as readily available within the organization; it is the uncertainty that sits at the crossroads of what Swidler (1986) refers to as "settled" and "unsettled" times. Instead, what emerges are diverse efforts by actors to assemble strategies, stabilize meaning, and establish justifications for actions, be it through new principles, combinations of new and old, or re-entrenchments of past conventions. Uncertainty breeds more intense critiques and disagreements, and, consequently, organizational life requires more conscientious efforts of negotiation and compromise. This does not just mean that more time is spent debating planning objectives, policy, or funding allotments – it also translates into amplified ambiguity around professional and personal identities and the constellations of work and life that intersect with these changes. The transitional moment in this study – the big change that this book identifies – centres on changing ideas around artistic creative competencies and value. Certainly, the wider landscape of uncertainty is representative of shifts in both education and work overall, but there is also something more specific to contemporary art and design work, art schools, and disputes over creativity and creative practices.

In this chapter, I examine the emergence of creativity as a key pillar in a contemporary lexicon of potential – especially, for the purposes of this research, in terms of cultural work and higher education. So, to draw on McRobbie (2015), I am pointing towards the widespread call to "be creative." I use the phrase "the new spirit of creativity" to capture the simultaneous entrance of creativity into business and the economy, public imagination, policy, and institutions. Many of the artists and designers in this study expressed concerns about how to survive, creatively, in a moment that claims to embrace the vibrancy of artistic creativity but often champions something else – something that does not resemble well their own creative activities and teaching practices. Throughout this chapter, I locate resources from sociology, art history, and cultural studies that align with the interpretive-critical framework discussed in the introduction. By developing the new spirit of creativity as an analytic category, I disentangle tensions between artistic creativity and the new spirit of creativity, and I return to the thorny issue of artistic critique within this contemporary dynamic.

Positioning the New Spirit of Creativity

In the title of this study is used the somewhat pretentious phrase the *spirit* of capitalism. What is to be understood by it? The attempt to give anything like a definition of it brings out certain difficulties which are in the very nature of this type of investigation.

– Weber, *The Protestant Ethic and the Spirit of Capitalism* ([1904] 2003), 53

Weber said it well. Substitute creativity for the word capitalism, and my employment of such a "pretentious phrase" is laid bare; yet there are a number of dimensions to my use of "the new spirit of creativity" as a central reference point in this study. On one level, it is shorthand for diverse contemporary mobilizations of creativity. This version broadly captures the rise of creativity-driven discourses and the reorientation of existing practices. However, the second level of meaning brings more analytical and interpretive weight to the concept.

The term *spirit* is a reference to a history of intellectual wrangling around the analysis and interpretation of culture and value in the social sciences. This version is a way to recognize and invite questions around the value-laden nature of creativity into my study while acknowledging the specific genealogies of creativity at work in contemporary Western culture (Reckwitz 2017). Finally, with this phrase, I am teasing out a thread within recent academic scholarship that returns to spirit to describe the expansiveness of late capitalism and its restructuring of work, time, and employment relationships; this vein of scholarship uses spirit to ground a sociology of critique that accounts for processes of cooptation and compromise characteristic of contemporary capitalism. Here, creativity features as a way to neutralize discontents over the constraints of work and minimize the visibility of diminishing employment security and quality working conditions. In sum, creativity anchors the rearrangement of social life and practices in telling ways, and spirit is an inroad for disentangling its roots in social meaning. I draw on the new spirit of creativity as an analytic category that captures this reorganization. From this perspective, spirit is not a clear-cut case of either recovering an authentic creativity or documenting a more restrictive one. It is not that there is an entirely "good spirit" (a friendly ghost?) or an entirely malevolent one (a haunting spectre?). Instead, what I document is an emerging normative imperative and the uncertainties and contestations over value and meaning that emerge as this new spirit takes hold.

It is reasonable to ask the following: is there a difference between the new spirit of creativity versus the new spirit of capitalism or the creative spirit of capitalism? Let me briefly explain. Capitalism has always been inseparable from creativity and the endless inventiveness of the market and bourgeoisie in search of the new, or at least the illusion of the new (Benjamin 2002). However, capitalism is not the focus of this study but a backdrop. Creativity, on the other hand, is my central concern, but I am not merely substituting the word creativity for capitalism. With the new spirit of creativity, I grant more autonomy to creativity itself as an ethos, rather than making it secondary to the political economy of values and organization. This is in line with directions in cultural sociology that stress the autonomy of culture, affect, and meaning rather than their dependence on external social structures and roles in the reproduction of social relations (Alexander 2006). The argument I make here about spirit offers a different way of conceptualizing what McRobbie refers to as the creative *dispositif* (2015, 11), which she positions largely in a Foucauldian sense (see Foucault 1980), meaning, the multifold arrangements and exercises of power that inflect subjectivity and its possibilities. Similarly, Reckwitz's compelling account around the "invention" of creativity also draws on *dispositif*, but develops "social affectivity" alongside it to recognize how emotions and attachments are central to contemporary creativity's coercive features (2017, 3). As part of my critical-interpretive approach, I use analytic tools from cultural sociology to examine creativity's distinctive arrangements of control and agency via every-day assemblages of meaning and accounts of value and justification.

The suggestion that there is a new spirit of creativity raises questions of time and history: is there an old spirit of creativity to speak of? In this sense, I am not proposing a tidy set of oppositions or a straightforward account of old versus new. Instead, this study examines tensions, expressed both in interview accounts and supporting institutional documents, between what I term artistic creativity and an emerging, more capacious version of creativity tethered to wider social and economic discourses and institutional arrangements. Based on my analysis of different descriptions of creativity in the empirical data, the core concepts and associations set out in fig. 1.1 describe the two orders of creativity.

These terms do not operate as binary oppositions; they do not have absolute counterparts and there are many ways these ideas are combined and exchanged. Importantly, there are shared concerns that animate principles within both orders, and this is what enlivens the affinities and contradictions

ARTISTIC CREATIVITY		NEW SPIRIT OF CREATIVITY
	O R I G I N A L I T Y	
Autonomous *freedom of practices and ideas; independent*		**Instrumental** *rational agency; goal oriented*
Aesthetic *rooted in aesthetic principles, affect, and knowledge*		**Flexible** *key values/principles adapted according to the situation*
		Entrepreneurial *product development, commercialization, and markets*
Experimental *new techniques, approaches, and open exploration; boundaryless*	**A G E N C Y**	
Critical *questions existing practices and authority; challenges taken-for-granted knowledge*		**Professional** *knowledge and approaches legitimated by professional expertise and credentials*
Individualistic *freedom of self-expression; non-conformity*	**F A B R I C A T I O N**	**Expansive** *far reaching; connected to every domain of work and life*
Crafted *time intensive practice; acquired skill through mentorship; artisanal labour*		**Technological** *technology driven production; technical skill and applied problem solving*

1.1 Artistic creativity and the new spirit of creativity

between them. These shared concerns are situated in the middle: agency, originality, and fabrication. For example, creative agency is a central concern within both orders. With artistic creativity, participants described agency in terms of autonomy (freedom of ideas and practices) and the ability to minimize or reject constraints on the creative process. The new spirit of creativity also foregrounds agency, but this creativity is described in more rational and instrumental terms – creativity is a catalyst for contemporary success. Similarly, creative agency is cast as central to processes of experimentation as well as critical thinking within artistic creativity, but it is described as crucial to the realization of entrepreneurial visions and for responsiveness and flexibility under the new spirit. Originality is another shared principle, where both orders value the production of original content, be it conceptual and/or formal. However, while artistic creativity locates originality mostly within aesthetic experience or experimental newness, or with daring and non-conformity with expectations, the new spirit of creativity mostly associates originality with fresh perspectives on creative entrepreneurialism and tangible products, especially market-oriented innovations in design and technology. Or fabrication is a shared concern across both orders, but within artistic creativity this is described in terms of experimentation with forms and aesthetic perceptions, or craft and the time-intensive skill development of artisanal labour. The new spirit emphasizes fabrication in terms of professional knowledge, technology-driven production, and applied problem solving.

Yet these shared concerns are central to a blurriness between the two versions. In order for the new spirit to take hold, it must both draw on and reframe principles from artistic creativity. In order to be effective, this new spirit addresses some of the long-standing critiques of artistic creativity's inward focus, elite character, and rigid commitment to aesthetics. For example, participants expressed discomfort with the idea of creativity as individual genius, elevated self-expression, or enlightened aesthetic appreciation. No one willingly described their activities as elite, self-centred, or distant from the world. The idea that creativity is now more inclusive and relevant is threaded throughout the new spirit, and through the language of creative agency as a shared concern. The new spirit's expansiveness capably addresses such previous objections to artistic creativity. Similarly, if artistic creativity is considered too rigid in its adherence to an aesthetic vision, the new spirit makes flexibility the name of the game to champion a responsive and adaptable creativity. Or the complaint that many critical and experimental artistic practices are incomprehensible, if not outright indulgent, is addressed by prioritizing instrumental approaches and technologically driven problem solving. And legitimation is drawn from the language of professionalization: it is not social, political, or artistic critique but specialized creative expertise and credentialed knowledge that justifies action. These overlaps mean, too, that terms from artistic creativity feature in the new spirit, but to seemingly more superficial ends. So, for example, while craft is part of the definition of artistic creativity, it features in the new spirit as well, but is celebrated for its applied value in a way that is easily separated from an aesthetic and embodied skill developed over time. Or, during interviews, I was provided with many examples of when, despite claims to embrace experimental practices, Imagination University did not wholeheartedly welcome or understand the potential risks and failure of artistic creative experimentation. If art markets and economic gain were cast as secondary to non-economic values in artistic creativity, the new spirit actively centres and promotes the many art-commerce intersections, past and present, to champion the creative entrepreneur.

Taken together, what emerges is that artistic creativity exists throughout the institution, but artistic creativity is both invited and constrained under the new spirit. It is these principles of artistic creativity that inform the artistic critiques of this new spirit that I examine in the coming chapters. What develops throughout is how uncertainty takes shape between artistic creativity and the new spirit as artistic practice, professional identity, creative value, and evaluation come under heightened scrutiny.

Capitalism, Creativity, and the Artistic Critique

To speak of "spirit" invites ambiguity – one that circulates around a number of interpretations in the social sciences, starting with the German *Geist* and its translation as "mind" or "spirit" (Hegel [1807] 2017). We have the spirit as ghost – perhaps a haunting, a spectre (Marx and Engels [1848] 2012), and, not unrelated, we have the spirit as divine, the all-encompassing. Spirit is the domain of the immaterial that becomes, at times, available to the senses, but which poses a challenge to the social science toolkit. When one speaks of spirit, the question of evidence is necessarily at play. Weber's argument in *The Protestant Ethic and the Spirit of Capitalism* is canonical and contested (Barbalet 2010; Ghosh 2014; Greenfeld 2003). By Weber's assessment, Calvinism was ideologically fertile ground to sustain the spirit of capitalism, where ideas such as predestination, the prosperity of the chosen ones, vocational calling, and self-denial cultivated the regimes of productivity and accumulation necessary for the smooth integration of capitalist economics into society. Something so elusive as spirit provides coherence to a range of practices and beliefs. "Spirit," as he explains, is "a complex of elements associated in historical reality which we unite into a conceptual whole from the standpoint of their cultural significance" ([1904] 2003, 56); thus, the definition of spirit must be qualified by history, research process, and standpoint. Weber turns to "provisional description" as a way to explain the character of capitalism and how it unfolds into procedures of authority and bureaucracy, themes throughout his work. My study, too, is one that stresses the interconnection of these realms, where any such notion of spirit (whether of capitalism or of creativity) is also deeply, banally bureaucratic. Weber recognizes the need to weave back and forth between social structure and social meaning – that is, between the objective organization of social institutions and the intersubjective, meaning-oriented actions and interpretations that people bring to social situations; it is in this to-and-fro that spirit crystallizes. Here, I am underscoring Weber's significance to understanding culture (Scaff 1989; Schroeder 1992), especially the importance of organizational studies and institutional logics approaches attuned to culture (e.g., Friedland and Alford 1991; Thornton, Ocasio, and Lounsbury 2012). This lineage of institutional logics has something to offer our understanding of cultural professions and organizations, such as book publishing, symphonies, architecture, and museums (DiMaggio 1991; Glynn and Lounsbury 2005; Jones and Livne-Tarandach 2008; Thornton 2004).

In their influential study, *The New Spirit of Capitalism*, Boltanski and Chiapello (2007) return to the concept of spirit in the social sciences to account for the dynamics of critique and legitimation that together uphold capitalism's durability and justificatory logics.[1] Based on a comparison of leading management textbooks from the 1960s and 1990s in France, they demarcate phases of capitalism's spirit. The new spirit reorganizes work according to project-based contracts and flexible time, profitably incorporating the most powerful social and cultural critiques of capitalism and undergirding capitalism's dominance even amidst worsening social and economic conditions for many. The effectiveness of this sort of critical manoeuvring is not a straightforward act of absorption but represents complex adaptations and appeals to various conceptions of justice and the social good to be successful. Boltanski and Chiapello advance a sociology of critique able to examine such processes and better account for the more subtle and diverse forms of contemporary labour exploitation that are typical of contemporary work arrangements. If, as they argue, "capitalism has not only survived, but ceaselessly extended its empire, it is because it could rely on a number of shared representations – capable of guiding actions – and justifications, which present it as an acceptable and even desirable order of things: the only possible order, or the best of all possible orders" (2007, 10). Their approach builds on the above Weberian tradition and nuances Boltanski and Thévenot's earlier work, *On Justification*, and its development of specific terminology to explain the taken-for-granted nature of social accord, equivalence, and justification: "social coordination requires a continuous effort of comparison, agreement on common terms and identification"(2006, 1).[2] At issue is not just how justifications of worth emerge according to guiding principles and objects of value specific to each order (inspired, market, domestic, fame, industrial, civic) but how critiques are absorbed and how compromises emerge through appeals to a common good that can justify an object's worth in a mutually compatible way. For example, Boltanski and Thévenot provide the example of "techniques of creativity" as a compromise object that can be justified as a common good across the inspired and industrial worlds (278). However, they position any such compromises as fragile. It is important to note here that another backdrop to their book is Chiapello's (1998, 2004) own research on arts organizations and management strategies and the contemporary convergence of art values with management directives.[3] These ideas are not just being applied to the arts but were developed out of empirical research on the arts, and for two key reasons: art's unstable relationship to questions of worth and value, and its significance to practices of critique.

I turn to Boltanski and Chiapello (and related works) as a resource for understanding critical operations, one especially well-suited for organizational analysis; it is not a coincidence that the empirical data of *The New Spirit of Capitalism* examines management texts. To be clear, I am by no means replicating their study and its elaborate methodology, argumentation, or linguistic approach to data analysis. Here, I follow Willmott's assessment: "It is not as a critique of contemporary capitalism, nor as a contribution to the revival of critique, but as a sociology of critique that [*The New Spirit of Capitalism*] offers something distinctive" (2013, 99). As a key text of the French school of pragmatic sociology, *The New Spirit of Capitalism* orients away from the dominance of Bourdieusian critical sociology by stressing the everyday coordination of social action and meaning rather than prioritizing structures of domination and oppression (see Boltanski 2011; Du Gay and Morgan 2013; Susen and Turner 2014). A distinguishing feature of this pragmatically oriented sociology is how it conceives of social actors. The idea is to adopt the perspective of ordinary actors in order to discern the insights they bring to their activities rather than position them as oblivious to, or mere victims of, their circumstances, incapable of critical analysis (Boltanski 2011). This approach understands that it is difficult to reject overarching frameworks that supply everyday structure and meaning. Rather, we need to understand how people deal with uncertainty and change while recognizing that it would be "utter folly to demand for themselves changes in their life that presuppose a radical transformation of this framework" (32). Thus, Boltanski argues that studying operations of critique employed by social actors in everyday contexts avoids the dilemma of critically oriented research that provides accounts of the world that are either "too grim" or "too rosy" (27), and instead allows us to access the nuanced and often contradictory ways the world actually operates. In this respect, *The New Spirit of Capitalism* identifies two key modes of critique that have offered the most to platforms for progressive change, and which have been most effectively reformulated in the pursuit of unencumbered economic growth: the social critique and the artistic critique. The stakes are high if we turn to the big picture; we need a revival of critique and platforms for meaningful change in order to counteract a world that has become surprisingly tolerant of social inequality and dramatic discrepancies in quality of life.

The artistic critique grounds one of the most vigorous denouncements of the prioritization of the economy over humanity. This critique is one rooted in the "invention of a bohemian lifestyle" (Boltanski and Chiapello 2007, 38), and it is primarily concerned with two realms; on the one hand, capitalism's alignment with disenchantment and inauthenticity, and, on the other, its various constraints on "freedom, autonomy, and creativity" (37). While the social critique centres on the social dimensions of scarcity, class, and inequality (particularly poverty, working conditions, and labour exploitation), the artistic critique is in many ways the search for a different version of life altogether. It is rooted in the Baudelaire-inspired vision of the dandy who rejected "any form of subjection in time and space and, in its extreme forms, of any kind of work" (38). This artistic critique is traditionally positioned in opposition to formal work and instead prioritizes the authenticity and autonomy found outside economic and market demands. It is cast as a response to some of the key failures of capitalist modernity; or, put differently, the artistic critique recognizes that creativity is a way of restoring meaning, restoring value, against the work of standardization and commodification, and does so in ways that trouble conventional associations between production and value. Yet expanding interest in creativity under the new spirit of capitalism represents the careful absorption of these critiques to different ends. As Boltanski and Chiapello explain,

> The demand for creativity ... has received greater recognition than could have been hoped for thirty years earlier, when it became obvious that an ever growing share of profits derived from the exploitation of resources of inventiveness, imagination and innovation developed in new technologies, and especially in the rapidly expanding sectors of services and cultural production. (326)

Critique, they make clear, is always incomplete; critique must "share 'something' with what it seeks to criticize" (40). Accordingly, I bring forward that this shared concern with creativity between the new spirit and artistic creativity produces considerable ambiguity within contemporary organizational contexts. Curiously, however, despite the centrality of the artistic critique to Boltanski and Chiapello's argument, it has not received the same amount of academic attention as the social critique, which has been considerable (Du Gay and Morgan 2013).

With some exceptions (Murphy and Fuente 2014; Roberts 2012), the artistic critique is generally cast as less compelling than the social critique, in part, as Lazzarato (2007) argues, because distinctions made between the social and artistic are easily muddied. In social science scholarship on art and culture, the relevance of Boltanski and Chiapello's theorization of artistic critique tends to be acknowledged as valid but quickly dispensed with (e.g., Banks, Gill, and Taylor 2013; McRobbie 2015; Mould 2015; Tinius 2015). Reckwitz sums it up as follows: "The tradition of artistic critique thus seems to have been rendered superfluous by becoming an omnipresent reality in the economy" (2017, 5). Additionally, empirical studies of cultural workers' experiences note the relevance of the artistic critique but find it does not seem to match their interview data in the way they expect (Oakley 2009, 288). Still, the scholars who nod to this version of the artistic critique make a case for more forceful and critical alternatives to the status quo – for more robust and organized practices of critique – even as the exact role of cooptation and compromise remain unresolved questions. Thus, by better elaborating upon the new spirit of creativity, we can glean a stronger conceptualization of why the artistic critique matters: it remains one of the most important ways to build more just arrangements of work and life. It continues to call attention to crucial issues, especially those surrounding artistic creative work and organizations. Identifying and analysing its presence generates discussions around the value of art and non-economic values and priorities, which are aesthetic, cultural, and intellectual, and that easily fold into the social. Further, the above discussion demonstrates a desire for more empirically grounded research that can refine and augment our understanding of how artistic critique both thrives and falters within social life.

The following chapters in this book explore the question of how artistic critique and its counterpoint – compromise – function under the new spirit of creativity at Imagination University. The art school supports a range of artistic creative practices and research centred on critique, yet the contemporary character of institutional administration and organization also, at times, champions aspects of this critique as well. Vibrant forms of critique inform many employees' day-to-day understanding and creative practices while artistic critique is repackaged within the new spirit's approaches to policy, planning, and branding, often with a neo-liberal dexterity that upholds discourses of economic innovation and self-reliance. To build on this context, I bridge this sociological version of artistic critique with perspectives from art history and cultural studies by developing the concept of "institutional-artistic critique" to describe the tension between compromise and critique specific to everyday work within art institutions.[4] This term combines insights from the well-known genre of conceptual art practice and art criticism known as institutional critique (e.g., Alberro and Stimson 2011) with dimensions of the pragmatic sociology of artistic critique sketched out above. I use the term institutional-artistic critique to account for the status of artistic critique within the everyday work and organization of the art school. How does this critique factor into everyday arrangements of work, planning, and decision-making? It describes a critical mode that identifies and analyses how everyday artistic institutional work – the difficulties, debates, and pleasures – takes shape at Imagination University.

This term takes a cue from institutional critique but instead studies the wider institutional and social organization of artistic work beyond the art object.[5] Institutional-artistic critique is thus a sociological term I employ to account for the organization of employment within art institutions and the complex relationship this paid employment has to principles of artistic creativity, critique, and ultimately compromise alongside the new spirt of creativity.

Artistic critique is often *the* question at the heart of diverse traditions within cultural analysis. While there is a rich tradition of cultural studies scholarship on the complicated intersections of margin and centre, countercultural identity, and mainstream consumption (Dhoest et al. 2015; Hebdige 1991; Tasker and Negra 2008; Thornton 1996), there is also considerable work specific to artistic cultural production and institutions. There is ongoing critical interest in the institutional contexts that inform art and curatorial practices (Duncan 1995; Jackson 2011; Jones 2016; Kwon 2002), especially the uneasy relationship of art institutions to market, patron, and managerial power (O'Neill, Steeds, and Wilson 2017; Sholette 2011). The bind art institutions face is embedded in their evolving strategies; as McDonnell and Tepper explain, "they have supported the elevation of fine art as sacred and distinctive and appealing to sophisticated and enlightened patrons, while on the other hand, they have promoted access to the arts, community service, and education. Cultural non-profits have variously positioned themselves as both of the people and above the people" (2014, 21). As Kunst (2015b) argues, there are key alignments between the cultivation of diverse participatory practices in art institutions and audiences and the wider precarity of subjectivity under neo-liberal practices. These circumstances are in many ways a consequence of the entrenchment of "institutionalization" within arts policy, which DiMaggio explains as "nurturing arts organizations, preventing existing organizations from failing, encouraging small organizations to become larger and large organizations to seek immortality" (2000, 56). The more expansive organizational contexts that support artistic production make for more complicated alignments between creative practices, work, and institutions.

Institutional critique in contemporary art defines critique as a set of aesthetic strategies that artists bring to institutional settings. These techniques disrupt the stability of institutional knowledge (broadly defined) by exploring topics through a combination of artistic and social research and suggest alternative possibilities. As an example of critical practice, there are three valuable insights I draw from institutional critique. First, social critique and artistic critique combine in telling ways within the genre of institutional critique; for example, notable works by Hans Haacke, Fred Wilson, Andrea Fraser, and Mark Dion have long established the combined force of such intersections, but there are diverse examples of recent intersections as well (Tello 2020). This reluctance to draw clear boundaries between the social and artistic means the targets of critique can be more ambiguous or harder to recognize. Yet, if we follow the works of art, this resistance to rigidity or heavy handedness also lends nuance to, and disrupts the tendency towards, binary oppositions within critical thought. Second, the recognition that artistic practices are both part of and critical of institutional dynamics has long been part of the analysis and reception. So, for example, institutional critique often centres on practices of representation and gatekeeping within the museum or gallery, while at the same time, in order to develop such a critique, the artist is most often an institutional participant. This is recognized, albeit with a legacy of debate, not as mere hypocrisy or straightforward co-optation, but as a feature of the nature of critique. As artist Andrea Fraser astutely remarked, "Just as art cannot exist outside the field of art, we cannot exist outside the field of art, at least not as artists, critics, curators, etc. … the institution is inside of us, and we can't get outside of ourselves" (2005, 282). Critique never exists totally removed from its object of scrutiny and this tension is regarded as an impetus for critical engagement. Thus, I bring forward the idea that positioning the institution as more than just constraint opens up critical analysis and possibilities. Third, institutional critique has been named as one key aspect of the contemporary reinvention of critical artistic practices. For example, Raunig and Ray describe this "third phase" of critique as a "combination of social critique, institutional critique and self-critique" (2009, xiii). Artistic critique must better respond to current issues and conditions, including this heightened ambiguity between critical practice and institutions, and with a stronger sense of how art institutions can anchor progressive, even radical, changes.

The transformative possibilities of institutional critique are both debated and defended. So, while some artists emphasize the need to develop alternatives to the existing order, others emphasize that institutional critique "is not an effort to oppose or even destroy the institution, but rather to modify and solidify it. The institution is not only a problem, but also a solution!" (Sheikh 2009, 30). Further, the performance of critique by the institution has long been recognized as a feature of changing dynamics of the genre of institutional critique (Buchloh 1990; Fraser 2005). This is why, as Sheikh puts it, "institutionalized critique" is a way to better account for its current status and potential relevance "as an analytical tool, a method of spatial and political criticism and articulation that can be applied not only to the art world, but to disciplinary spaces and institutions in general" (2009, 32). Many contemporary art versions now push beyond the art world, with institutional critique taking on renewed relevance as radical social rebuilding, where artists not only "work in, and across, disparate sectors, [but] also abandon the walls and infrastructures of the artworld and create their own worldly, socially engaged institutions (Tello 2020, 636). Institutional-artistic critique is a way to place these insights from institutional critique alongside the sociology of artistic critique in order to clarify the nature of critique and compromise within the new spirit of creativity. So, what better way to ground this analysis then in an institution abound with creativity and critique?

Fond Memories of Rebellion

The failed consultation exercise, like the one cited at the start of this chapter, was a frequently shared story when I inquired about recent institutional changes at Imagination University. These stories of unsuccessful attempts to generate ideas about institutional identity or how to envision new directions provided more or less detail about what the process involved. Some participants made offhand (often derisive) comments about the forced nature of the exercise, while others tried to account in careful detail why it was ineffective, but the key point across the board was that consultants are poorly equipped to grasp the distinctiveness and creativity of Imagination University. Nate shared a detailed account of the consulting agency that was brought in to develop an institutional image that would "crystallize the school's personality" while we sat at a table near a busy student café and study space. He recounted how the consultants became increasingly frustrated trying to develop a clear vision: "These poor guys, they just about lost their minds ... they had nothing." He said he tried to intervene, to help them: "I said, 'Don't you understand? This is an art school. That's what these people do. They're not ... gonna rally around the flagpole. Your job is to say something totally off the map ... a moving target cannot be reduced to three, four-word bullet points.'" Nate explained how the standard culture of consultancy "won't work here" because it "confused the role of the artist and designer," meaning, he clarified, that artists and designers are accustomed to being at the forefront of ideas, but in this instance, they were supposed to be obedient subjects for "someone else's visions ... it's the wrong relationship." The team went away empty-handed, and administration subsequently backed off trying to organize such exercises. Nate used this example to explain how the wider "political and economic regime ... can't handle the mess, inconvenience, unpredictability of the art school." Mel put it more bluntly: "It was crap team building and collaboration stuff." Further, it didn't make sense to bring in consultants and other design firms when the school already had many experts in these areas. As she continued, "Why pay thousands of dollars for someone else to design our vision? ... We have the skills and deep knowledge here." This in-depth understanding of the school stands in contrast with the idea that consultants "trade in surface stuff." These conversations about failed consultancy gather around a type of critique that is identified by faculty as fundamental to the history of the school: the ability to reject current conventions in higher education. Faculty expressed that there is something about the school that will not be so readily captured in a website redesign, recruitment brochure, or strategic plan. Will the future of creativity be found gazing absent-mindedly at a PowerPoint presentation? Probably not.

Art schools have a lengthy history as rebellious institutions – as sites of provocation, activism, and dissent. As Tickner (2008) documents in her archival reconstruction of the 1968 student occupation of London's Hornsey College of Art, the art school is a potent site for protest and agitation.[6] Similarly, when CalArts' newly minted Feminist Art Program orchestrated the controversial Womanhouse installation and performance space in a dilapidated house in 1972, it effectively carved out an art world future for feminist creative practices (Fields 2012). More recently, art schools are rooting conversations around systemic racism within and beyond the cultural field in ways that dramatize the important role art and aesthetics have within wider social justice dialogues. Even within day-to-day operations, art schools have played a key role in debating and redefining, often through openly contentious means and practices, the meaning and value of art and expanding repertoires of teaching and learning (Adler 1979; Kennedy 2012). As of late, the history of art school resistance and student occupations is being fondly remembered against a current landscape of higher education constraint, with calls to "envision the 'beyond' of art education by remembering its historical contestations" (Hudson-Miles and Broadey 2019, 59). As one art critic quips about the contemporary art school, "now we have the Academy of Cool, schools that treat avant-garde rebellion as a learned occupation" (Solomon 1999, SM38).

Further, the academization of art has transformed ideas about art and artists. As Singerman's careful tracing of the shift from atelier training and apprenticeship models to university-based training demonstrates, "the practices of the art and the identity of the artist are fashioned in the discourse of the American university ... The artist, or artistic subjectivity, is the university's problem and its project" (1999, 5). Accordingly, it is not surprising that so many influential contemporary artists have devoted their experimental resources towards reimagining art education (Allen 2011). Yet while art schools hold a crucial place in our cultural imagination as sites of creativity and even transformation, the contemporary art school is at a crossroads. Madoff explains the dilemma as follows: "The factory of ideas, objects, practices, and pedagogies that constitute an art school today, as they will tomorrow, seems particularly restless, wanting more porosity, irritated by bureaucratic weight, impatient for new shapes, even for an ephemeral life" (2009, x). As contemporary responses to creativity change, so do the institutions charged with its cultivation, even if what the changes should be or how to achieve them is unclear.

In the wider scholarship on cultural work (see introduction), "training and education rarely occupy a central interest" (Ashton and Noonan 2013, 3). Further, higher education as a *site* of cultural work is usually overlooked with only a few exceptions, most of which focus on the dilemmas of the teaching artist.

At best, the art school is widely regarded as a training ground for future cultural workers – not itself a cultural workplace. When higher education contexts of cultural work are addressed, the research usually focuses on student experiences and outcomes, curriculum and pedagogy, and higher education policy and funding arrangements. Current scholarship demonstrates a keen interest in how students learn to become creative workers, their identity perceptions and shifts, and how well they adjust to the field after graduation (Ashton 2010, 2011, 2013b, 2015; Comunian and Gilmore 2016; Fine 2017, 2018; Oakley, Sperry, and Pratt 2008; Pollard 2013). Banks and Oakley (2016) adeptly capture the double-talk around art higher education as follows: art schools have been identified as important access points for working class students; however, at the same time, the creative economy and higher education contexts disadvantage these students despite this image of inclusiveness. Recent research places more attention on the art school as a site that reproduces social disadvantage that in turn impacts educational experiences and professional aspirations. In terms of art and design pedagogy, curriculum, and programs, there has been much debate around, for example, graduate degrees in art and design and the impacts of academicization (Buckley and Conomos 2009; Candlin 2001; Elkins 2009; Jagodzinski and Wallin 2013; Singerman 1999). Certainly, there is attention to how art schools are shaped by wider higher education and policy contexts, not only in terms of creative industries initiatives but also restructuring and funding of education (Banks and Oakley 2016; Beck and Cornford 2012; Ashton and Noonan 2013). These perspectives exist alongside sociological interest in the distinctive culture of the art school. For example, Fine portrays the art school as a sort of hidden kingdom: "To students and faculty, as well as to its public, the art school feels like a place apart, a cloistered, inward-looking arbiter of taste with distinct customs and standards" (2017, 1463).

While the literature is mainly student-centred, there is some research on the role of "industry practitioners," "teaching artists," and "teaching creatives" in higher education that recognizes their distinct creative career trajectories and work biographies (Ashton 2013a; Clews and Clews 2011; Gerber and Childress 2017; Rabkin 2012). There are many possible types of expertise in terms of teaching and creative professional practice that fall within this category of artist, designer, or media practitioner, and this impacts how expertise or specialization is communicated and understood. As Noonan (2013) notes, there are different pathways that include supplemental teaching alongside active careers versus a more permanent move into academia after a professional career. Yet the overriding issue remains: universities could do a better job of supporting professional activities outside of the university and valuing what creative practitioners contribute to student training inside the university (Clews and Clews 2011). Traditionally, teaching has been one of the most stable sources of income for artists. We are wise to take this avenue more seriously as a central, not just an incidental, feature of creative work. Yet teaching is often maligned in accounts of artistic practice. For example, Gerber's research identifies the scepticism artists who do not teach have about teaching artists. As she explains, "too much emphasis on credentialing is undeniably taboo; artists delegitimize practices they see as aiming toward commercial work or the tenure file" (2017, 90). There is always the suspicion that if an artist teaches full-time too soon, their own artistic practice does not develop. However, artists with university or college positions counter this negative image by identifying the plentiful opportunities for exploration; there is, for example, freedom to pursue ideas without the pressure of gallery sales (Gerber 2017, 45). For these artists, pursuing an MFA is not so much attractive because of the credential itself, but because it allows for greater development and exploration of practice.

There is a readiness to dismiss teaching artists' contributions both inside and outside of higher education, despite the emergence of more research on the significance of teaching to artistic careers. Across all levels of the education system, many arts alumni have worked at least part-time as arts educators in the course of their careers (Lena and Lindemann 2014). As Thornton explains, "actual professionals who practice within the fields of art and education … often are engaged with, or are confronted with, overlapping practices that standard professional labels do not always fully reflect" (2013, 131). How the growth of higher education programs and teaching positions impacts the artistic careers of practicing artists is less understood (Singerman 1999). Gerber and Childress's research demonstrates that the importance of teaching to art careers requires rethinking many assumptions about professionalization and values; teaching can allow for more freedom and autonomy in artistic practice (2017, 1536–7). Professions in the arts are hard to capture, often brushing up against out-of-date definitions of artistic practice and slipping through occupational descriptions that use primary source of income as measurement (Lena and Lindeman 2014, 73). Even here, the hybrid nature of work in the arts is clear. According to Canada's National Occupational Classification, participants in this study are classified under the banner of "fine arts professors" within the category of "university professors and lecturers"; only artists who teach privately are included in the category of "professional artists." Teaching at a university makes for a range of characterizations of one's professional status and artistic practice.

There are a number of interesting, earlier social science studies of the distinct environment of art schools, especially in terms of student trajectories and identities. For example, Getzels and Csikszentmihalyi's *The Creative Vision: A Longitudinal Study of Problem Finding in Art* (1976) is one of the first academic studies to take seriously the question of which students become professional artists and how. As a psychological study of students at the School of the Art Institute of Chicago, most of the research involved the application and analysis of standardized tests designed to measure aspects of intelligence and creative process; however, these quantitative results are mixed with some qualitative data that rounds out the study's findings on creative process and the likelihood of success. Although largely focused on individual-level process and characteristics, it does glance at features of wider social context; for example, young artists from affluent and supportive families "are more likely to survive in the competitive world of art" (169). Thus, in this book there is an interest in better assessing the nature of artistic creativity, and in a way that disarms an easy version of genius; however, it does so psychologically and not sociologically.

Another example, Strauss's "The Art School and Its Students" (1970), strives to understand social-institutional context and demonstrates its important relationship to identity formation. Strauss examines how art students seek a haven from life pressures and choices and identifies the permeable boundaries of professional identification. Art schools have traditionally been a place where students who do not fit well within conventional academic teaching and learning environments find a context in post-secondary education. As Frith and Horne's (1987) classic study, *Art into Pop*, makes clear, the productive relationship between art schools and popular music emerged out of a context supportive of creative experimentation and exchange; it was the overall creative scene and spaces at the art school that cultivated developments in popular music in the 1960s and 1970s. As Beck and Cornford more recently explain of this distinctive period of UK post-secondary art education, "it is this collision of tradecraft and high art experienced by an unprecedented socially diverse student body that produces the moment of the British art school as an engine of unforeseen cultural outcomes (2012, 61). However, such dynamic prospects seem now to be vanishing and unfulfilled within the "lost future of unregulated creative practice" (58). With so many recent changes impacting the goals and delivery of higher education, there is notable apprehension that something has irrevocably changed within the contemporary art school. To better comprehend this current landscape, I turn to Adler's *Artists in Offices: An Ethnography of an Academic Art Scene* (1979) as a prescient account of the contours of higher education and the employment of artists.

Adler studies the idealism and conflict of the early days of the California Institute of the Arts and its efforts to establish an alternative art school model (the bulk of the field research was conducted between 1970 and 1972). Adler's text firmly puts the labour of cultural production into the equation. Her book challenges the sociology of art's study of cultural products at the expense of recognizing the context of production and relevant organizational settings that inform and direct how artistic practices and objects become valued and understood; she rejects the "ideological determined reluctance to regard art as work" (xiii). By bringing paid work into the discussion, Adler foreshadows debates on autonomy, aesthetics, and professionalization specific to cultural work in the twenty-first century (see introduction). The book underscores that artists are subject to multiple demands including markets and institutions, patronage and government support, and the everyday banal requirements of employment. The institutional artist must be dedicated to rigorous creativity while also becoming an active participant in the labour economy and everyday life of bureaucracy. Her account of the tensions that surround the institutionalization of art and artistic careers within the university remains strikingly accurate; faculty artists find more autonomy and freedom from market pressures in their university posts, yet the effects of professionalization and bureaucracy inscribe upon them new constraints. In her research, what plays out is a dramatic tension between art scene and institution – the fluidity of the scene versus the formality of the institution – and with significant implications for recognizing as well as exploiting artistic identities and labour in the name of the new institution. In her assessment, the scene that was crucial to the art school's formation quickly dissolved. The artists themselves accommodated to new opportunities for salaried employment in academic bureaucracy, even when it regularly produced "chronic and demoralizing uncertainty among students and staff" (1). I build on Adler's sociological attention to processes and conflicts around artists' practices within higher education and the complexity of the academic art scene, recognizing that her book made an important early contribution to understanding the curious dynamics for artists who are employed within higher education.

More recent sociological scholarship also demonstrates the importance of situating art and design education within the wider context of creative economy and higher education debates. McRobbie's (1998) work directly queries the relationship between higher education and the art and design industries, and it connects the history of art education in Britain to debates over nationalism and cultural values that still influence the marginalized and gendered status of fashion in the art school system. At the beginning of her recent book on cultural work, she reflects on her position as a university professor and the uneasy relationship universities have to the wider field of cultural production. As she assesses of her years of interactions with students, "unfolding in front of my eyes … is a microcosm of the new creative labour market" (2015, 1). Likewise, Fine's (2017, 2018) examination of occupational imaginaries of MFA students is especially attentive to how students learn to navigate the structure of the art world within their graduate programs, and how networks and social groups generate this participation. Because of the pronounced uncertainties of an artistic career, Fine's research illustrates the role the university setting plays in advancing competing models of valuation and dilemmas of artistic identification: "Student outcomes are built on both structures within an institution (the university) and structures beyond (the art world). The reality that both fields are uncertain, and participants are ambivalent about market valorization or rejection makes difficult the choice of an artistic self" (2017, 1482). Similar themes emerge within Wilf's study of post-secondary music education – a related site. Wilf develops a multifaceted ethnographic portrait of the institutionalization of jazz in academic music programs, examining the creative paradox that emerges with "modern individuals' attempts to engage in creative practice within modernity's rational institutions" (2014, 4). Likewise, other related ethnographies of cultural institutions (besides art schools) constructively disentangle the idiosyncratic culture of art worlds and the role of everyday practices of administration, judgment, and evaluation (Born 1995, 2005; Bunzl 2014; Thornton 2009; Wohl 2021).

Navigating Creative Uncertainties

The first part of this chapter gathered academic resources relevant to understanding the new spirit of creativity as a central concept, one that aligns with the critical-interpretive sociology of creativity I sketched out in the introduction. The new spirit of creativity shares features with artistic creativity and revises some of its key principles. I mapped out distinctions and overlaps to capture the organizational uncertainty around creative meaning and legitimation that animate the chapters to come. In particular, using resources from cultural sociology, I stressed the nuanced insights that social actors bring to everyday circumstances and the ongoing work of justification, critique, and compromise that making sense of creativity involves, with a special emphasis on the concept of artistic critique, which is identified as an important and troublesome concept in literature across the arts and social sciences. Here, I provided a definition developed to account not for the production of conceptually oriented art works, but for artists' employment within art organizations: that of institutional-artistic critique. This term is a means by which to assess in the chapters to come the complicated ways that artistic critique features within the institutionalization of artistic creativity and work – something that is especially salient to the contemporary art school.

In the second part of the chapter, I have underscored the role of the art school as a principal mediator of creativity, yet this porousness between education and the cultural field is often not well captured in research. Given that most research centres on student experience or issues of teaching and pedagogy, the art school as a key cultural workplace – and the hybrid artist-teacher or creative practitioner as a secure employee – is not well recognized or considered, and it comes at the expense of better understanding contemporary creativity as paid work. The art and design university not only supports creativity-driven teaching and research but also many other activities that frame interest, dialogue, and public engagement, including exhibitions, workshops, public lectures, symposia, artists' residencies, and other forms of art patronage. Accordingly, the analysis of such an institution enables sharp insights into the rising star of creativity-driven values as well the status of artistic critique in light of its legacy of questioning organizational conventions. But before we dive into the analysis of Imagination University and the tensions between artistic creativity and the new spirit, the next chapter provides a brief history of and regional contexts for understanding the cultural and educational contributions of the art and design university in Canada.

Chapter Two

What Could Be More Creative Than an Art School? Canada's Art and Design Universities

"New" universities, with little economic or cultural capital, have less shelter from state policy but may be less constrained by established assumptions about their role.

– Parker and Jary, "The McUniversity" (1995), 320–1

What on earth am I here for? Good question. This plea for answers is written in red safety tape on a construction fence at Emily Carr University's new location at Great Northern Way campus (fig. 2.1). This sort of casual, creative intervention and its existential entreaty is a regular part of the art school landscape. It is unlikely (but not impossible?) that this sign was interrogating the role of contemporary art and design higher education, where the value and contributions of advanced art and design have certainly received their fair share of questioning and debate over the years. But when this appeal caught my eye during a campus visit, I found it hard not to take on this line of inquiry: what, exactly, is the art and design university here for?

With its exuberant buzz of creative activity, the art and design university is a model site for understanding the new spirit of creativity. In Canada, these institutions were previously art schools (or amalgams of such) that consolidated into publicly funded art and design colleges, and then formally recognized universities. They offer a range of undergraduate and graduate programs, and in NSCAD's case, have been granting degrees for over four decades (BFAs and MFAs since the mid-1970s). Faculty at these schools have been crucial players in the professionalization of art, media, craft, and design in Canada (Alfoldy 2005), not to mention their central role in advancing contemporary art and art pedagogy. However, as small institutions of an uncommon university type in Canada, these universities have experienced a mix of vulnerability and opportunity in the recent past.

This chapter surveys the changing contexts and perceptions of art and design higher education that have influenced the operation and organization of these

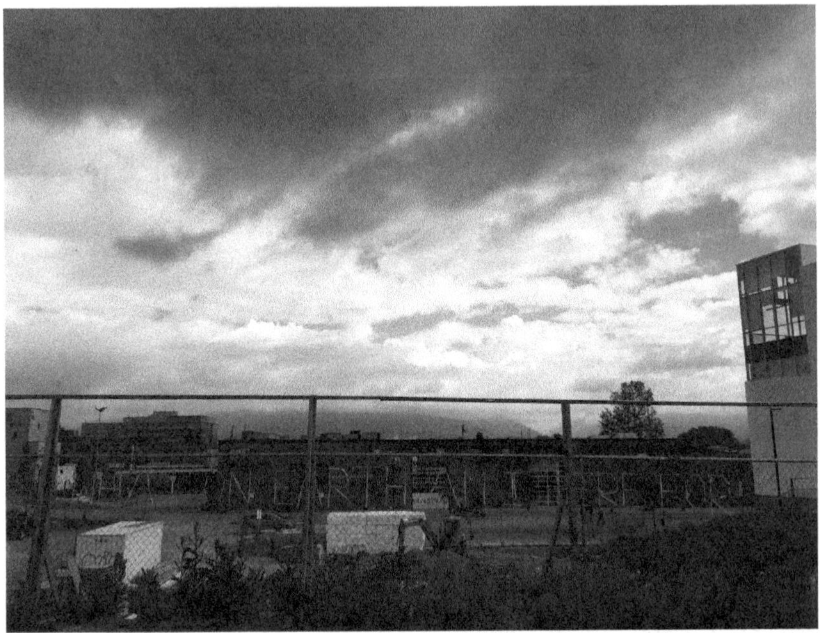

2.1 "What on Earth Am I Here for." Public intervention, ECUAD, Great Northern Way campus, Vancouver, BC, 2018. Photo credit: Author.

universities in Canada. It explores how the contemporary frame of creativity anoints the art and design university as an essential part of future progress and well-being, evident in catch phrases like "the MFA is the new MBA" that circulate in popular media (Bell 2008; Dupree 2008). Yet this shift in popular perception intersects with many changes from within. As one journalist comments, "Even the words art and artists are disappearing. These schools are places for creatives, emphasizing 'soft skills' and specializing in creativity" (Landry 2016, 142). Certainly, these schools have always been important sites for diverse and vigorous creative exploration, and in a society that has not always been so receptive to such activities. The art and design university, as a dedicated cultural institution, is a leading example of how many different and specialized practices of creativity come together under one organizational umbrella.[1] All cultural institutions incorporate education into their mandates, but most are primarily concerned with cultural products, while the art and design university places creative processes and cultural production at centre stage.

Together, this chapter captures the uneven status of the contemporary art university within the new spirit of creativity. The first section provides a short history of art and design higher education in Canada. I establish a brief account of each university's regional context and history and demonstrate the curious position of the art and design university within the Canadian system. Recent histories of these schools indicate the many demands and ideas attached to art and design education. Building on the general dilemmas of the art school discussed in the previous chapter, I here identify specific factors that shape how the art and design university in Canada is both admired and marginalized within current popular and academic contexts alike. Issues such as regional politics, government funding formulas, and social perceptions of art education set a context for understanding the everyday experiences and conflicts reported and analysed in the chapters to come.

Art and Design Higher Education in Canada

There is little dedicated literature on the history of art and design education in Canada. There has been some focused research on different provinces, institutions, or pedagogical influences (Barber 2006; Chalmers 1993, 1998; Henry 2001; Kennedy 2012; Stankiewicz and Soucy 1990), but only one book (Clark 1994) and one edited collection devoted to shared origins and distinctions across Canada (Pearse 2006). The scholarship specific to post-secondary art education is often mixed into wider historical overviews (Chalmers 2006; Stirling 2006a, 2006b). Much of the early history of Canadian art schools traces the models and modifications in Canada to existing influential approaches, such as widespread uptake of the South Kensington model from the UK. That said, the significance of the dedicated art school does occasionally surface within other histories of art and culture in Canada, such as Alfoldy's (2005) research on the professionalization of craft education, Whitelaw's (2017) book on the establishment of art museums in Western Canada, and the collaborative, multi-institutional research and travelling exhibition on the development of conceptual art in Canada (Arnold and Henry 2012). However, most of the literature specific to ECUAD, NSCAD or OCAD that is currently available is a patchwork of self-produced histories and exhibition catalogues, with notable exceptions such as Kennedy's *The Last Art College: Nova Scotia College of Art and Design, 1968–1978* (2012).[2] Thus, it is important to build on this existing work while also responding to the growing interest in art and design higher education and the need for more comparative analysis between national contexts (Ashton and Noonan 2013; Comunian and Gilmore 2016; Ladkin, McKay, and Bojesen 2016; Madoff 2009; Orr and Shreeve 2018). ECUAD, NSCAD and OCAD have a distinct context and history as independent public universities and share issues and concerns common to art, design, and media programs, departments, and faculties in comprehensive universities and colleges.

In recent mainstream media, reports stress both the cultural and economic assets of these institutions. OCAD is cast as an "international leader in the commercialization of art and design" (Coates and Morrison 2013, 116), while ECUAD has "limitless" potential: "There's a natural resource that's in play in this school that is far more valuable and far more sustainable" (Canadian Press 2013). And NSCAD is described as "one of Canada's oldest and most revered art schools" (Bradshaw 2011). This heightened esteem and interest within media and public discourse stems from interrelated factors: more government awareness of the cultural and creative industries, the reach of creativity narratives, the transition to university status, and more funding opportunities for creative technology and design areas. Against this context, the uniqueness of the institutional type becomes clearer.

Whereas universities are generally valued for their comprehensive offerings within Canada's extensive, publicly funded university system, art and design universities are unusually specialized.[3] Contrary to the trend elsewhere to eliminate or absorb art schools into pre-existing universities (Beck and Cornford 2012), the strategy of granting university status to Canada's main independent art and design colleges has been deemed "an intelligent and inventive way forward" (Buckley and Conomos 2009, 10). That said, this affirmation, however flattering, could be misleading – this was not the product of a concerted federal strategy. University accreditation is managed provincially, and thus each province has slightly different processes of oversight and designation. With provincial recognition, universities can apply to become a member of the national association, Universities Canada, that provides a number of services centred on advocacy and quality in higher education (Universities Canada 2016). These universities are also part of provincial or regional associations that compile data and represent their interests (Association of Atlantic Universities; Council of Ontario Universities; British Columbia Association of Institutes and Universities). British Columbia has a provincial Research Universities' Council (e.g., University of British Columbia, Simon Fraser University, and University of Victoria) in which ECUAD is not included, while neither Ontario nor Nova Scotia maintain this division at the provincial level.

A question shadowing the art and design university in Canada is how much or how little the university designation transformed the institution. Importantly, this is different in each case/province. Key features of institutional criteria, as outlined by Universities Canada, include course offerings in an array of undergraduate subjects to allow for degree breadth; specialized teaching expertise with advanced credentials and regularly peer-reviewed programs; research and teaching mandates; a board of governors and senate that supports transparency and participation in governance; and that the institution operates not-for-profit (Universities Canada 2016). So, transitioning to a university involves measures such as instituting bicameral governance (board of governors and senate), developing strategic research planning and research support, and conducting arms-length program reviews. However, the process as well as the interpretation of the criteria varies by province; for example, how breadth in course offerings is interpreted varies across these institutions. NSCAD's transition to university status in 2003 was relatively smooth because it had been degree granting for decades already; it was already performing in many respects like a university, but it did need to reorganize its governance structure. With OCAD, the changes were more significant because it did not have this history of degree-granting status and its provincial context, as the largest province with many universities, was more challenging to navigate. In order to start granting its own degrees in 2002, OCAD had to organize various changes, from course offerings to administrative structure and governance. ECUAD was somewhere in between, granting its own degrees since 1996 and obtaining university status in 2008. For ECUAD, it took considerable lobbying to get the province on board; former president Alan Barkley referred to this as "the degree saga" (1994, 14–15), which starkly differs from the ease with which NSCAD was able to award degrees (McLaughlin 2016).

While entrance into the category of "university" required a number of organizational changes, its symbolic value carried considerable weight. For example, these schools were not required to change their name to include "university," but all eventually did. As OCAD President Sara Diamond said of the approval of the name, "It's a vote of confidence … about the quality of education at OCAD" (as cited in Bradshaw 2010). Or, as ECUAD President Ron Burnett put it more bluntly, "For better or for worse, being a university is more attractive to students" (as cited in Lederman 2008). While these changes were not without debate at these institutions (see chapter 3), they did happen, and the strategic reasons were well recognized: the change to university designation firmly placed these schools on the same playing field as comprehensive universities with art and design programs, but now with a better chance of securing research funding, attracting high caliber faculty, and developing graduate programs.

The yearly data compiled by the Canadian Association of University Business Officers (CAUBO), a non-profit association that compiles financial data on Canadian universities, indicates some general characteristics and distinctions (CAUBO n.d.). The place of provincial funding within OCAD's finances has steadily declined since 2009. In 2009, provincial funding was 57.5 per cent of its overall operating budget. At year end in 2015, it was 36.8 per cent. For NSCAD, over half of its annual income was from the province, with some fluctuations.[4] For ECUAD, the annual figures have hovered between slightly over or slightly under 50 per cent of its annual income from provincial funding. Endowment and investment income is not strong at any of these schools compared to other institutions, but ECUAD ranks highest in terms of non-tuition–based sources of revenue.[5] However, with any of these numbers it can be hard to know exactly how budget lines are being defined and reported, and how other factors are impacting, for example, the percentage of provincial funding within the total income. So the reasons for changes can indicate funding

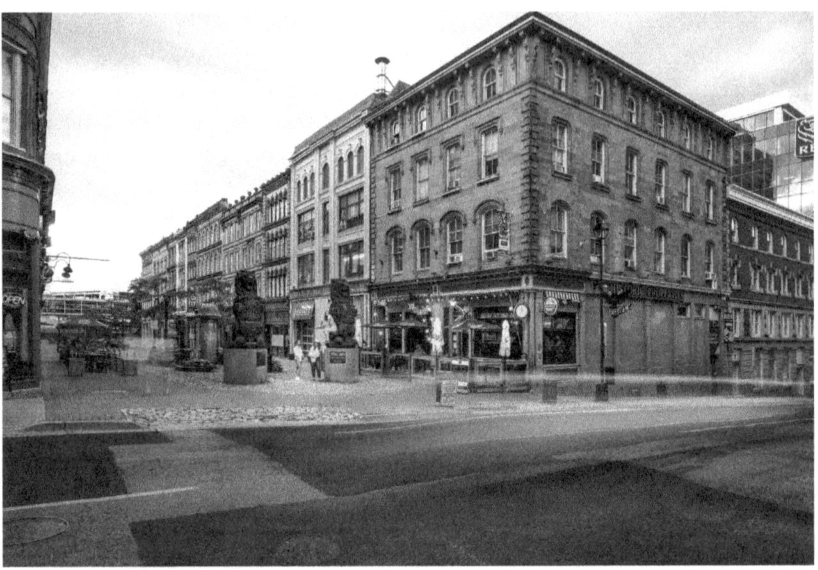

2.2 NSCAD University, Fountain Campus, Halifax, NS, 2020. Photo credit: Stephen Brookbank.

cuts as well increases in other revenue sources, namely tuition. As CAUBO warns at the outset of its annual reports, institutional definitions and practices of data collection vary, even year to year, and thus comparing years both among institutions and even within the same institution has its limits. That said, the numbers indicate the important role provincial funding plays in the overall finances of these universities, and the overall trend is towards government funding forming a smaller proportion of total income. As for student numbers, ECUAD's enrolments from 2009–15 have been fairly stable; with OCAD, student numbers have generally increased, while at NSCAD, student enrolments have generally decreased. With neither politics nor economy nor demographics suggesting that there will be opportunities for notable increases in government funding or enrolment, the overall climate is one of trying to hold steady.

The Art School, the Art College, and the Art University

The history of each of these schools is very similar in many respects. They all started out as art schools, consolidated into colleges of art, then into colleges of art and design, and finally into universities of art and design. This section will provide a brief sketch of each school's history and key issues in their recent pasts as well as issues of regional and provincial specificity.

Nova Scotia College of Art and Design University (NSCAD)

NSCAD University (fig. 2.2) has five main areas of instruction (Craft, Design, Fine Arts, Media Arts, and Art History and Contemporary Culture), with a choice of ten areas in which undergraduates can major, as well as graduate degrees in Design (MDes), Fine Arts (MFA), and, since 2019, Arts in Education (MA Ed). NSCAD is an appropriate place to start this discussion for a number of reasons. One such reason is its fairly turbulent recent past, which deserves examination; as an article in *Canadian Art* put it, "In the standard history of contemporary Canadian art, there is perhaps no chapter as essential or enigmatic as the legacy of the Nova Scotia College of Art and Design" (McLaughlin 2016). While I am not providing a full account, in the context of this discussion NSCAD represents an important conversation around survival strategies for art and design within higher education. As a key player in the "de-institutionalization of art education" during its historical heyday of the 1970s (McLaughlin 2016), NSCAD has engaged in a trenchant struggle with re-institutionalization on all fronts. With its legendary status as a model experimental art school of the 1970s (fig. 2.3), this "NSCAD myth," as one critic puts it, means that the contemporary school stands in contrast to "the apparently untarnishable aura of its conceptual art past" (Dault 2008, 84). Maintaining university enrolments remains a concern in the province overall, but NSCAD's stability depends on some constancy with student numbers. For example, enrolment in Fall 2008 was 1,046. By Fall 2016 it was at an unexpected low of 783. While starting to regain some ground, enrolment was still hovering below the 1,000 mark in 2021, a number mentioned to me during interviews as the minimum target for stability.[6]

Halifax, a former colonial military base settled on Mi'kmaq territory, had little infrastructure for the fine arts at the end of the nineteenth century. Its first art school, the Victoria School of Art and Design, was established in 1887 through the efforts of four dedicated woman: Anna Leonowens (immortalized in theatre and film productions of the *King and I* as the tutor for the King of Siam), Helen (Furniss) Kenney, and Ella and Eliza Ritchie.[7] From the start, the school boasted a varied repertoire of activities including training in the fine and industrial arts, art education classes for schoolteachers, and children's art classes. The school changed sites many times, but it started by occupying space in the Union Bank Building in 1887. Arthur Lismer, well-known in Canadian art history as a member of the Group of Seven, was the principal from 1916 to 1919; he helped to spearhead a renewal of the school during a low point that, by his account, was fuelled by an elitist version of art education. As he explained, "The school has been allowed to fall into disuse mainly on account of the lack of interest of its directors who regard art as an exclusive & cultured subject for the edification of the few – & the fewer the students the greater their pride in

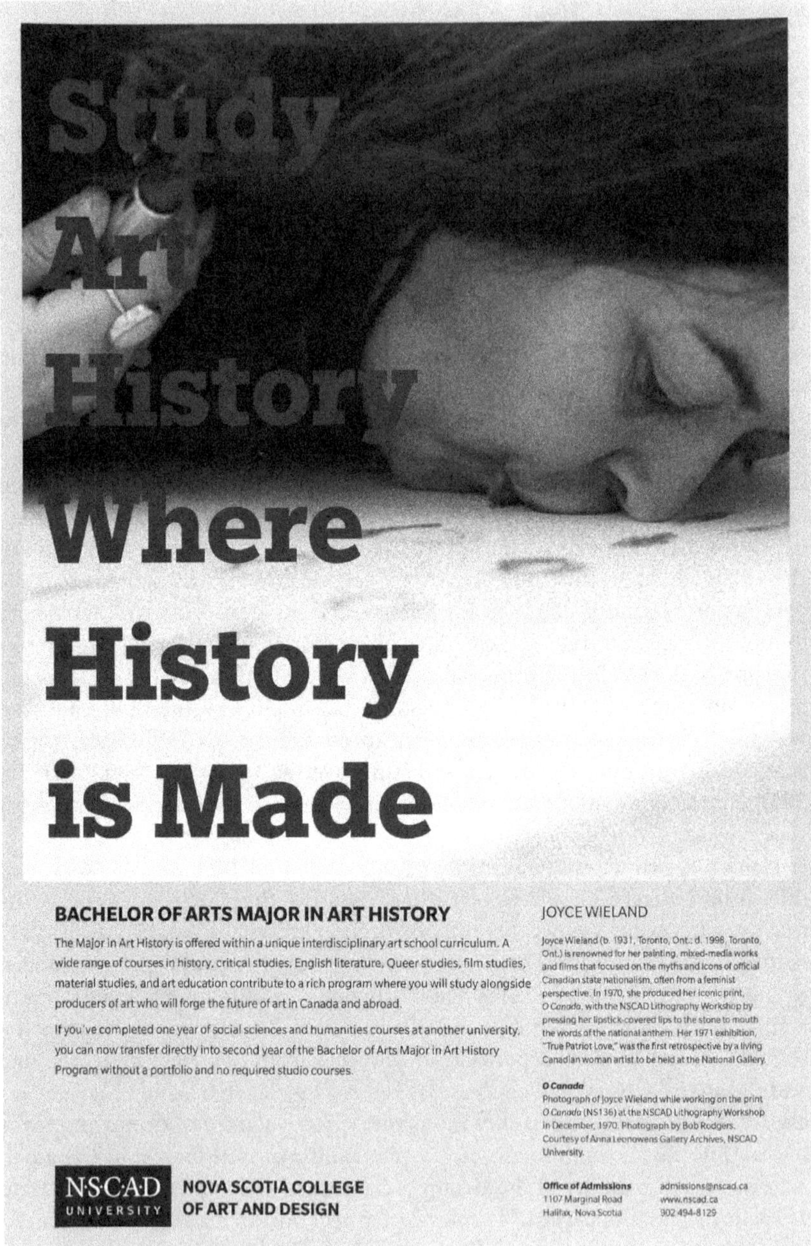

2.3 "Study Art History Where History is Made." Recruitment poster, NSCAD University, 2013. Poster features acclaimed Canadian artist Joyce Wieland producing one of her best-known lithographs at NSCAD in 1970. Photo credit: NSCAD.

their connection with it, & its exclusiveness" (as cited in Kelly 1982). In 1925, the school was renamed the Nova Scotia College of Art and was incorporated by provincial charter. In 1969, after considerable postwar growth, "design" was formally added to its name, but it was still a modest operation overall. The school had a mere 125 students and 9 faculty in 1967 (Kennedy 2012, xii). In 1978, after years of renovation, it moved to the historic buildings of its current main campus on Granville Street. After almost three decades of granting degrees, it became NSCAD University in 2003.[8]

Remarkably, NSCAD's contributions to the development of contemporary art in North America have exceeded its small institutional stature. The vibrant activities of the school are well recognized in Canadian art history and have been recently documented in *The Last Art College: Nova Scotia College of Art and Design, 1968–1978*. Edited by artist and former president of the school during this period, Garry Neill Kennedy, this book provides a multi-perspectival document of the "supercharged activity" (2012, ix) of NSCAD's past and documents the activities of significant players who passed through the school such as Vito Acconci, Carl Andre, John Baldessari, Joseph Beuys, Daniel Buren, Joseph Kosuth, Sol LeWitt, Yvonne Rainer, Martha Rosler, Micheal Snow, Joyce Wieland, and Kristof Wodicziko – to name a few.[9] There was also a companion exhibition and series of events dedicated to this period that ran at the Art Gallery of Nova Scotia from January to April 2016.

Artists have long voiced concern over the rigid and hierarchical nature of art education. As Kennedy recalled, "We used to talk in grad school about how art schools were terrible, so incredibly bureaucratic, and how to make a good one"(as cited in McLaughlin 2016). Halifax seemed surprisingly receptive to such a reimagining. Influential critic Lucy Lippard explained in the 1960s, "In Canada, maybe you can start from scratch and don't even have to mess with breaking down any barriers" (as cited in Kennedy 2012, xiii). Kennedy argues that NSCAD was well positioned to experiment, ironically, because of its backwardness and "marked absence of modernist practices in the visual arts ... this relative vacuum presented an opportunity for a fresh start" (xiv). NSCAD's ability to commit to creative experimentation is explained via its distance from the key cultural centres and discourses, something that changes as it gains broader recognition.

NSCAD's recent past has been marked by much uncertainty, starting with the provincially commissioned report (O'Neill 2010) on the fiscal health of Nova Scotia universities. The province's financial picture is especially complicated in a "have-not province"[10] struggling to maintain an above average concentration of universities (eleven) with a provincial population that hovers just under one million. NSCAD was particularly susceptible in this context; it was carrying deficits year-to-year, and while not the only university in the province to do so, the deficits were also increasing year-to-year. Further, the $9 million expansion to the Port Campus in 2007 was underfunded, which significantly added to the overall debt load of about $19 million (Windsor 2011, 5). As a small, only recently recognized university that is not well endowed, it was most vulnerable to external forces. As one newspaper article plainly stated, "NSCAD is hardly a fundraising powerhouse" (Bradshaw 2010). The school had to undergo a number of provincially imposed financial planning and debt reduction exercises. NSCAD, "storied but cash-strapped" (Bradshaw 2011), became featured in numerous media reports gambling on its chances of survival in a tough economic climate.

The province had a keen interest in making changes to NSCAD. The provincial report described NSCAD as being in an especially challenging position:

> Nova Scotia College of Art and Design (NSCAD) currently faces a significant cash flow problem in which there is no resolution short of a government intervention. However, even without its current deficit and debt problems, NSCAD has significant constraints on its capacity to expand its offerings or even to continue to offer the full range of current courses and programs. A significant portion of its existing space is not adequate for many of its programs, and it will ultimately require new infrastructure and new premises. (O'Neill 2010, 168)

This assessment of NSCAD was followed by the provincial government appointing Howard Windsor to direct restructuring at the school. The first paragraph of Windsor's report, *Time to Act*, describes NSCAD as "under a cloud of financial instability, its future is threatened," going on to note that the school is more dependent on government funding than any other university in the province (2011, 2). With a list of recommendations to ensure a viable solution (under heavy provincial supervision), the last recommendation provides a glimmer of recognition: "The Province should ensure that any collaboration agreements recognize and protect the NSCAD brand and the studio-based, multidisciplinary curriculum of NSCAD" (13). In response, NSCAD was required by the province to write a report that justified the university's programming and activities. This report rebrands NSCAD as a centrepiece of the creative economy. Its final assessment reads as follows:

> NSCAD is a niche university offering a full spectrum of fine arts programming. It is one of a kind east of Toronto. A fine arts university has a unique vibe and attracts a cohort of students who want a more creative and edgy environment ... As such, NSCAD is a key pillar in the development of the creative economy in Nova Scotia and crucial to securing the financial health of the province for years to come. (NSCAD 2013b, 28)

In this regard, the "niche university" with a "creative and edgy environment" finds a natural home in the new creative economy. This strategy was deemed successful – definitely more successful than the arguments the university made to the province that focused on its cultural values and contributions. As one upper administrator at NSCAD explained during an interview, with a note of irony in his voice, "The government was delighted by this proof we provided of our originality and specialization. It had not stood out to them like that." NSCAD's status as a niche institution protected it against concerns over program replication, something that was an issue given Nova Scotia's small population and high concentration of universities. As Garry Neill Kennedy explained of his time as president of NSCAD, "Nobody was worried in these days about what the College would look like on paper" (2012, xv). Ironically, in the recent past, how the school looked on paper has been crucial to its future – how to interpret the financial facts and figures in light of other types of evidence that attest to its value.

The debate about NSCAD's future was vigorous and public. A coalition of students, faculty, and supporters formed Friends of NSCAD to advocate for its survival and independence. While no one predicted the school's complete collapse, a foremost concern was the threat to NSCAD's autonomy through an enforced merger with another Halifax university (Dalhousie University). The public face of the dialogue focused mostly on the need to protect the unique, not to mention, critically acclaimed teaching and learning culture at the school, and the features particular to studio practice (e.g., greater space requirements, smaller classes). These dialogues made clear the need to value art and design outside of economic contributions, and not without a utopian tinge. As Haiven (2012) described it,

> At its best, NSCAD is a studio for developing the resources for a different world. It is a mine in which we can look to our youth for the raw, unpolished ore of social change. It is a work of art in and of itself – a solidification of the world's cooperation that, in turn, teaches the world how to cooperate in ways we haven't yet imagined.

Study participants portrayed this period as "exhausting," "demoralizing," and "dispiriting" during interviews; university communications to faculty, students, and staff included references to "difficulty and sacrifice" (O'Brien 2013) and sentiments such as the following: "We have experienced more than our fair share of uncertainty and unwelcomed and sometimes critical public scrutiny" (O'Brien 2012). In the final verdict, however, the financial benefits of a merger proved questionable. Through careful negotiations, NSCAD remained an independent art and design university through a vigorous cost reduction and debt repayment plan designed under government supervision. While the debt is slowly but steadily declining, it remains a worry. Even with extensive planning put in place, many concerns remain around government reductions to university budgets in Nova Scotia and across-the-board declines in enrolment.

A related dilemma is how to address ongoing spatial woes at NSCAD's main campus. The future of this campus – renamed the Fountain Campus in 2014 to honour the $3-million gift from Margaret and David Fountain – remains uncertain. These historic buildings make for a charming and central downtown location, but the maintenance costs are disproportionately high, and the space is not adequate for a full range of teaching and studio activities. Consequently, with the cost of renovating the campus estimated at around $25 million, NSCAD announced in 2015 that it would divest from this property and join the Art Galley of Nova Scotia (AGNS) at a new development on the downtown waterfront. However, while the AGNS has moved forward with this initiative, NSCAD's plans still remain unclear; in May 2021, NSCAD reportedly informed staff that it would not be part of this development (Mullin 2021). Other cracks have also surfaced with the Board of Governors' abrupt removal of the new president, Aoife Mac Namara, in June 2020 after only one year in office, which has left the university community shocked and concerned (Currie 2020).[11] Even more troubling is the suggestion that Mac Namara's dismissal was related to her efforts to lead new anti-racism and decolonizing initiatives and concern over how the potential sale of the campus was being negotiated by the Board (Peek 2020; Dafoe 2020). As the much acclaimed first independent degree-granting art school in Canada, the curious position of NSCAD as both highly revered and in jeopardy seems representative of the contradictory contemporary terrain faced by these schools.

Ontario College of Art and Design University (OCAD)

Founded in 1876, OCAD University (fig. 2.4) predates NSCAD's formation by a decade. Known as the Ontario School of Art, it was established through the efforts of the Ontario Society of Artists, Canada's longest standing nonprofit artist's society, founded in 1872. It started with a mere fourteen students and moved to many locations across the city of Toronto as it grew. In 1912, it became the Ontario College of Art (OCA) and started to receive an annual grant from the provincial government. By 1921, when it bought its first building and moved to the Grange campus, it had over 300 students and seven regular instructors. Arthur Lismer, after his stint at NSCAD, was named vice-principal of the school in 1920, with artist G.A. Reid as principal. OCA offered training in professional fine and commercial arts, with more design curriculum being incorporated since the 1950s. Design was officially added to the school's title in 1996 (Ontario College of Art and Design), and OCAD was recognized as a

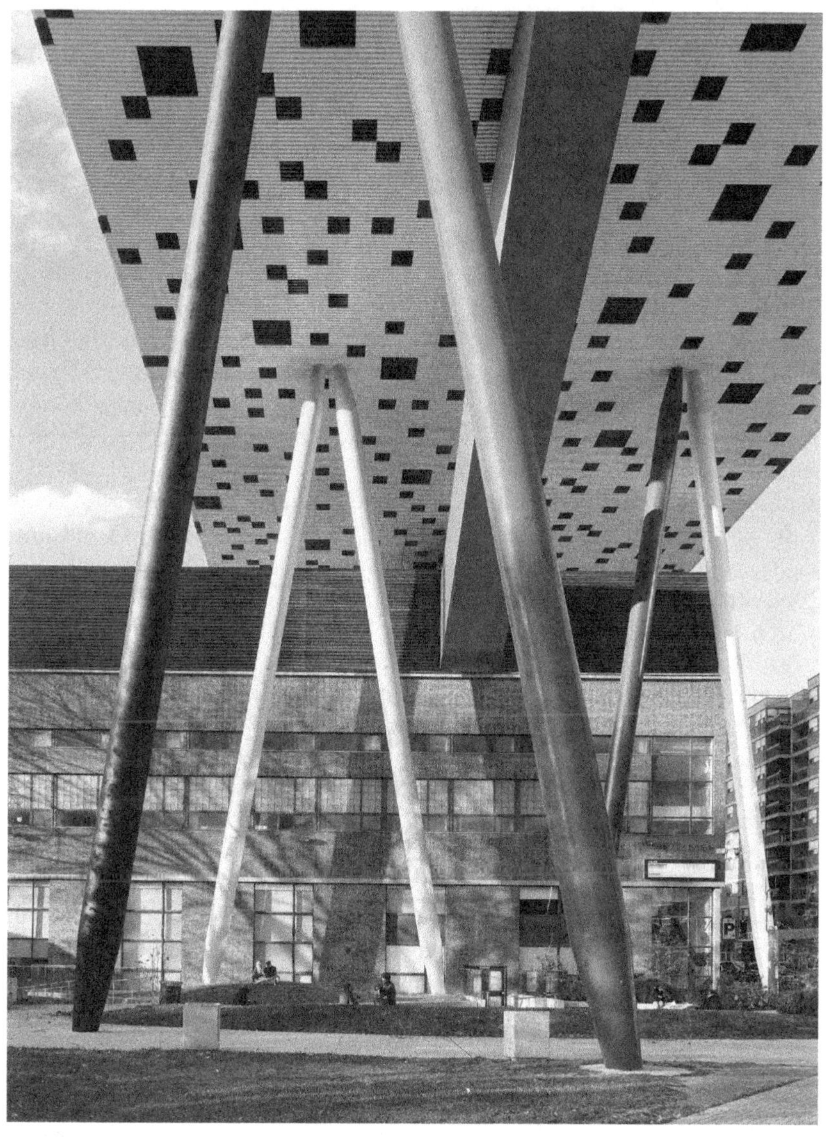

2.4   OCAD University, Rosalie Sharp Centre for Design, Toronto, ON, 2017. Photo credit: Martin Iskander/OCAD.

university by the province and began awarding BFA and BDes degrees in 2002; it did not officially change its name to OCAD University until 2010. OCAD has trained many notable alumni including Franklin Carmichael, Michael Snow, Ian Carr-Harris, Bruce Mau, Barbara Astman, and Rebecca Belmore. The university is located on the ancestral and traditional territories of many nations, including of the Mississaugas of the Credit, the Anishnaabe, the Haudenosaunee, and the Huron-Wendat.

As the largest school in this study, located in Canada's largest city, OCAD is the highest profile art and design university in Canada – a point that British architect Will Alsop's dramatic architectural addition in 2004 (Sharp Centre for Design) visually underscores.[12] The award-winning building was completed at a pivotal time for the school, representative of its push towards growth and its transition to university status. In 2007, OCAD launched its Digital Futures Initiative alongside a number of new graduate programs: Criticism and Curatorial Practice; Design; and Interdisciplinary Art, Media and Design. By 2018, it offered seventeen undergraduate and seven graduate programs, with about 250 full-time equivalent faculty.[13] The total number of full-time or full-time equivalent students enrolled in 2017–18 was 3,917, with an additional 1,927 continuing studies students (OCAD 2018b).

The twenty-first century for the school has been defined by change and expansion. It received a variety of extra government grants to support infrastructure and program development and committed to growing its fundraising efforts and public–private collaborations. For example, Imagination Catalyst was launched to support student entrepreneurs, as was the Strategic Innovation Lab (formerly the Beal Centre for Strategic Creativity) to connect design thinking to strategic foresight planning. Program initiatives include an Indigenous Visual Culture program, the opening of the Inclusive Design Institute and an Inclusive Design MA, and a digital painting and expanded animation program. Certainly, expanding degree programs and research initiatives incur new spatial needs, which have included the Sharp Centre and the acquisition of buildings at 205, 230, and 240 Richmond Street. OCAD's spotlight in *Maclean's* university ranking review – the most widely promoted annual ranking of Canadian universities – has students championing its "fertile" environment, rigorous programs, and non-stop time in the studio. That said, the much-acclaimed Sharp building was poorly designed for studio education (Ainsworth-Vincze 2011b). Consequently, since 2016, and with a promised $27-million provincial investment that was later slashed (OCAD 2019), the university has undertaken the Creative City Campus project, a major expansion and revitalization of its main campus.

OCAD is a much larger and more layered institution than the other two universities included in this study, requiring more infrastructure, administration, and staff – not to mention faculty – and it has been widely recognized for its

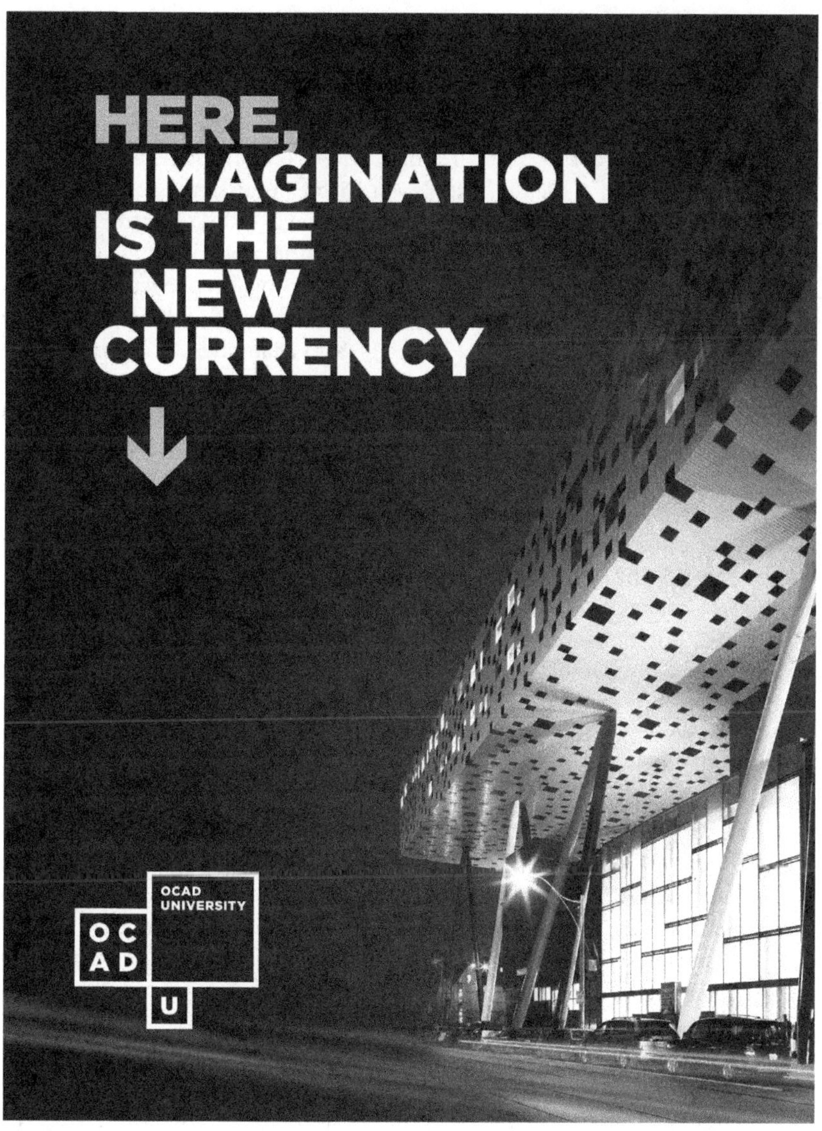

2.5 "Here, Imagination Is the New Currency." Recruitment poster, OCAD University, 2014. Photo credit: OCAD.

ambitious entry into creative economy discourses. This is in no small part due to the strategies used to grow the school – OCAD's media image is generally bolder and more entrepreneurial when compared to the other schools. Catchphrases like "creativity counts" and "imagination is the new currency" are part of OCAD's annual reports and certainly invite economic association (see fig. 2.5). In the pages of *Canadian Art*, Noah Richler praises the school's adaptability, celebrating it as the embodiment of Florida's (2004) creative city concept. As Richler explains, OCAD recognizes but does not fall prey to perceived binaries of art and commerce; OCAD is now charting "an altogether different destiny – an image and a sense of self that are a reflection of the changing city as well as very much shaped by it" (2008, 91). Sara Diamond, OCAD's president from 2005 to 2020, is widely recognized as a powerhouse behind these many changes, looking to push the school especially in terms of advanced design and media technologies; as Richler assesses, "Diamond has thrust OCAD into the vanguard" (Richler 2008, 91). Similarly, other media articles feature President Diamond as an impressive leader who is exceptionally committed to her job, from descriptions of her leaping off a burning passenger train in Argentina (during a work trip, of course) to her hosting gaggles of students for dinner at her house (Jermyn 2010). However, although not in such a high-profile fashion as NSCAD, questions around the institution's stability and organization have entered public discourse.

The expansion of its programs and initiatives has stretched resources at OCAD in many different directions. Questions of financial stability surfaced, for example, when OCAD Senate held a vote of non-confidence after the controversially expensive third-term renewal of Diamond's contract by the Board of Governors in 2014 (Chiose 2014).[14] Questions around employment equity were also raised when a contract faculty member lodged a complaint against OCAD with the Human Rights Tribunal of Ontario over racial discrimination (Kuitenbrouwer 2014; Deschamps 2014, 2015). This complaint and its negotiated settlement established a range of commitments to change, starting with a presidential task force on the underrepresentation of racialized and Indigenous faculty and staff at the university (OCAD 2017). This has led to initiatives such as a cluster hire of five Indigenous faculty members in 2018 and five Black faculty members in 2020.

Other media stories have reported that the school is still wrestling with the transition to university status, with faculty and administration disagreements exacerbated by concerns around the distribution of resources, enrolments, and provincial funding. Importantly, it has been a period of considerable growth for some, but not all, areas. As one newspaper article explains, "government largesse has sparked growth at the school that was exponential, but unequal. New departments and graduate programs sprung up while the more traditional visual arts waned in prominence" (Chiose 2015). This article cites an internal report commissioned by administration to address transition woes, which identified issues such as the high turnover in administration, shifting and over-ambitious priorities, and communication problems between administration and staff. OCAD's Board of Governors (2015) issued a formal response to faculty and staff about this article, noting that "with creativity comes dissenting points of view, and there is an abundance of creativity at OCAD University." While listing many of the school's recent accomplishments, this official response did acknowledge that OCAD "faces funding, space and sectoral change issues"; however, it went on to rebuff the news story, stating that "the article fails to acknowledge and appreciate the great strides our university has made in its development and growth." Both the initial criticism and the Board of Governors' response align with wider disagreements at the school over the key priorities and contributions of art and design higher education.

Importantly, I regard recent conflicts as just one part of a wider history of struggle at OCAD, where the tensions are more pronounced because of the school's size and location. There have been bitter struggles over contemporaneity and art education in the past. For example, in keeping with the cultural moment of the 1960s, students at OCA challenged the existing administrative structure and called for more participation in decision-making (Wolfe 2001). Further, faculty were embroiled in aesthetic debates over tradition and modernism, as well as practical issues such as job security, with, for example, mixed faculty interest in a tenure system (Lord 1970; Wolfe 2001).[15] After a number of disagreements over the direction of the school, a report was commissioned in 1968 to review governance at the school. It proposed a major update and reorganization, one that would place it more in line with other higher education institutions. Even at that point, questions were raised about how to establish quality and merit for faculty and avoid stagnation or distance from contemporary developments in art. As the report explains, "Council's greatest challenges will be the assessment of intellectual and professional quality, especially when associated with radical personalities, against the appeal of the orthodox" (Wright 1968). The ensuing OCA Act was rewritten and presented to the province for approval in 1969, allowing, importantly, for student and faculty representation on a nineteen-member council.

This spirit of change also led to the hiring of a bold new president, Roy Ascott, whose short but infamous term ultimately ended in acrimony. The controversy over Ascott's time as president in 1971–2 becomes representative of competing visions of art education. Without any administrative experience or a clear agenda – not to mention a dishonest curriculum vitae that he used to secure the job – Ascott rankled many with his wide-ranging plan to revolutionize OCA's approaches (Wolfe 2001, 67–8). His management style was provocative, to put it mildly. For example, he distributed a vinyl record of himself talking about his education philosophy to students and faculty, complete with a close-up of his smiling face on the cover (fig. 2.6), and he abolished formal classes, grades, and departments – practices that many faculty and students found hard to navigate. But he had many defenders, too, and his vinyl recording testifies to an idealist project:

> The overall philosophy of the college … is that that we are not simply throwing out art, like some sort of sausage machine, students who will simply satisfy the immediate needs of business and industry, but we are bringing students into the world who can create alternatives not just to existing jobs, but alternatives on all levels: alternative images, alternative forms, alternatives structures, alternatives systems … even alternative relationships between human beings. (Ascott 1971)

While this recording is a relic of institutional self-promotion in the past, at the same time, the language speaks to a different sort of creative ideal. Certainly, Ascott's version embraced a much more radical trajectory of total social transformation. But the impulse towards carving out a distinctive institutional identity remains constant, even if the content changes. For example, OCAD's most recent vision statement is as follows: "Transformed By Imaginations: OCAD University challenges you to audaciously and responsibly pursue the questions of our time through the powerful interplay of art, design, the social sciences, humanities, and the sciences" (OCAD n.d.a). Here, the desire to craft an identity as a comprehensive university is clear in the statement's reference to all academic disciplines and responsible knowledge production, but maintains a touch of flair through the use of words such as "audaciously" and "imaginations."

Emily Carr University of Art + Design (ECUAD)

As of 2018, the Emily Carr University of Art + Design (fig. 2.7) offers nine undergraduate and two graduate programs covering art, design, and media. The university sits on unceded Coast Salish Territories (the traditional and ancestral territories of the Musqueam, Squamish, and Tsleil-Waututh Nations). Like NSCAD, the school was offering degrees well before its transition to university designation. In 1989, Emily Carr offered degrees through the Opening Learning Agency, and by 1994 it was independently granting degrees (BFA and BDes). It launched its first graduate program in 2006, a Master's of Applied Arts (MAA) program, which sought to distinguish itself from the traditional MFA by emphasizing applied professional practice across areas of specialization – be it art, media, or design (Griffin 2006).[16] ECUAD is the second largest of the three schools covered here, with just under 2,000 full- and part-time undergraduate and graduate students enrolled in 2018 (Universities Canada 2018). ECUAD has managed to chart a pretty even course; as longtime President Ron

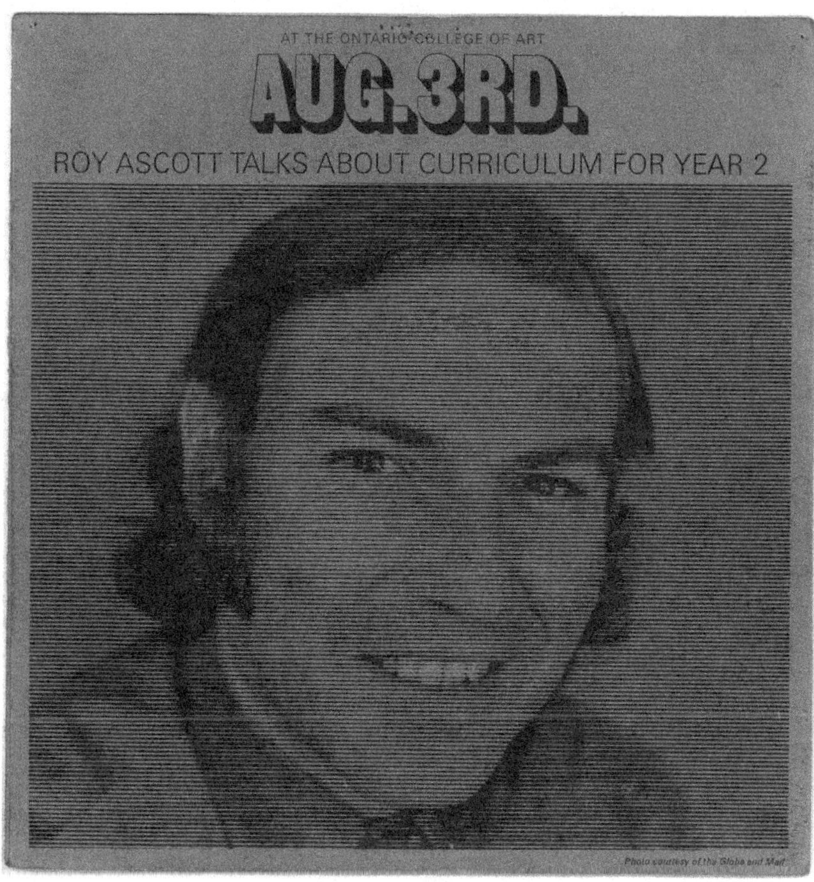

2.6 Roy Ascott, vinyl recording, OCAD University, 3 August 1971. Photo credit: OCAD University Archives/Visual Resources.

Burnett (1996–2018) explained: "It's a very lean operation … but we've learned to make it work"(as cited in Bradshaw and Moore 2011). Recent notable alumni include internationally recognized artists such as Douglas Coupland, Stan Douglas, and Brian Jungen. ECUAD has been referred to as "indisputably the best art school in Canada and a major reason why Vancouver has become such an internationally important centre for visual arts over the last few decades" (ECUAD 2013a). Recently, Emily Carr has been able to boast that it is the top-ranked Canadian art and design university internationally, and the only one from Canada to break into the top fifty according to the annual QS World University Rankings (Grauer 2021).

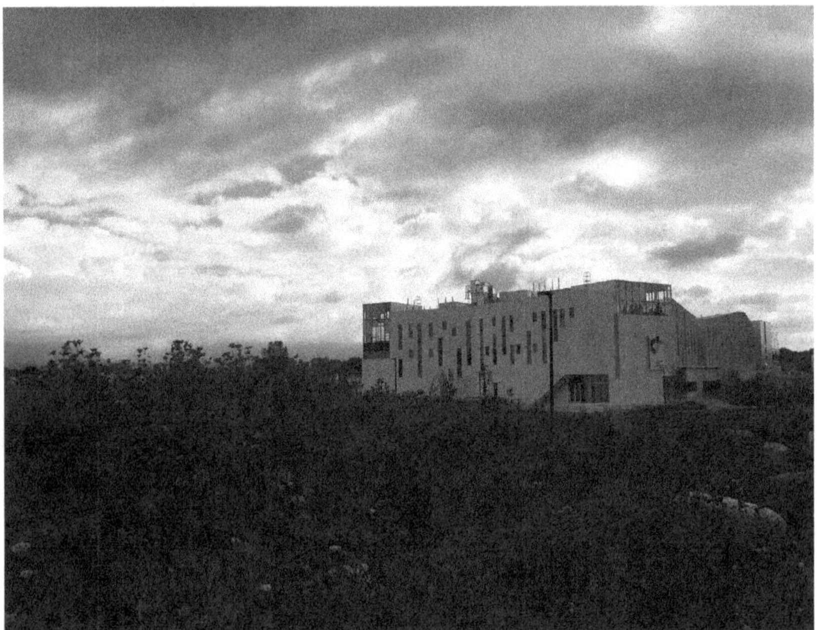

2.7 ECUAD, Great Northern Way campus, Vancouver, BC, 2018. Photo credit: Author.

Emily Carr University was founded by the British Columbia Art League in 1925, many decades later than the other two schools. Then named the Vancouver School of Decorative and Applied Arts, it offered both day and evening classes, with eighty-nine students enrolled during its first year (Henry 2001, 101). From the start, the school responded to two artistic traditions. Many of the faculty, including the second director, Charles H. Scott, were looking to models of art education from the Glasgow School of Art with a clear interest in industrial design and everyday applications for art and craft production. The other stream was more interested in the expressive qualities of art and current developments. Canonical Canadian artists Jock Macdonald and Fred Varley were among the first faculty members, but they departed the school to start the British Columbia College of Art in 1933. This separation is largely attributed to a conflict over visions of art education, as well as shrinking salaries at the school during difficult economic times (Richardson 1994, 130). The breakaway British Columbia College of Art proved not to be economically viable, but the original school survived the dispute; with a name change and a new building, the Vancouver School of Art opened in 1936.

From the start, ECUAD had a notably strong craft and design profile, which has been attributed to a number of circumstances. In addition to faculty strengths in these areas, students in the Depression era and during the Second World War were more likely to pursue practical outlets for their creativity. In the postwar period, interest in both fine and commercial art grew, and more international influences began reaching the West Coast (Henry 2001, 111). Further, the influence of art education models like the Bauhaus school cultivated attention to the social benefits of good design and the merging of art and craft. By 1952, the school moved to another, larger building. The 1960s saw the school in step with the wider cultural moment of experimentation and questioning such that "grades were all but eliminated, classes were open, and students worked on self-directed projects long into the night" (123). As a long-standing faculty member at the school recounted, "By 1964, Vancouver was witnessing a healthy atmosphere of experimentation in the arts … Life at the Vancouver School of Art … was both exciting and confusing. Traditional approaches to art making and teaching were in flux" (Hillman 1994, 143).

Compared to the other art universities, ECUAD is unique in that it was under school board authority until the 1970s. For a short period, it was part of the Vancouver Vocational Institute, only to become an independent college in 1978 under provincial mandate. At this point, the province renamed it Emily Carr College of Art and Design (fig. 2.8). This act was not without controversy, and both faculty and students protested this move to honour a historical painter as out of step with contemporary developments in art and design. Certainly, questions about the continued relevance of the Emily Carr namesake – especially in terms of her representation of West Coast First Nations – have been ongoing (Fulford 1993; Douglas 1991; Moray 2006). The 1980s and 1990s brought considerable expansions, including a move to the school's now iconic Granville Island campus (Fig 2.9). The industrial design department opened a second building, and course offerings were expanded as part of the degree programs. With these changes, the school became Emily Carr Institute of Art + Design in 1995, then, Emily Carr University of Art + Design in 2008. With this program growth, however, the spatial limitations of the campus became increasingly apparent. Accordingly, institutional resources were devoted to developing an alternative, with ECUAD relocating to a new campus, the Great Northern Way, in Fall 2017.[17] Considerable optimism exists over the role the school will play in growing the neighbourhood around the new campus (Dixon 2015; Gold 2014). In fact, there was more media speculation over what would happen to Granville Island after the move, rather than the future of the university in its new location – a compliment, of sorts, because it acknowledges how the school contributed to the vibrancy of the island. Because of the new campus, ECUAD has been the recipient of some high-profile donations, including $5 million

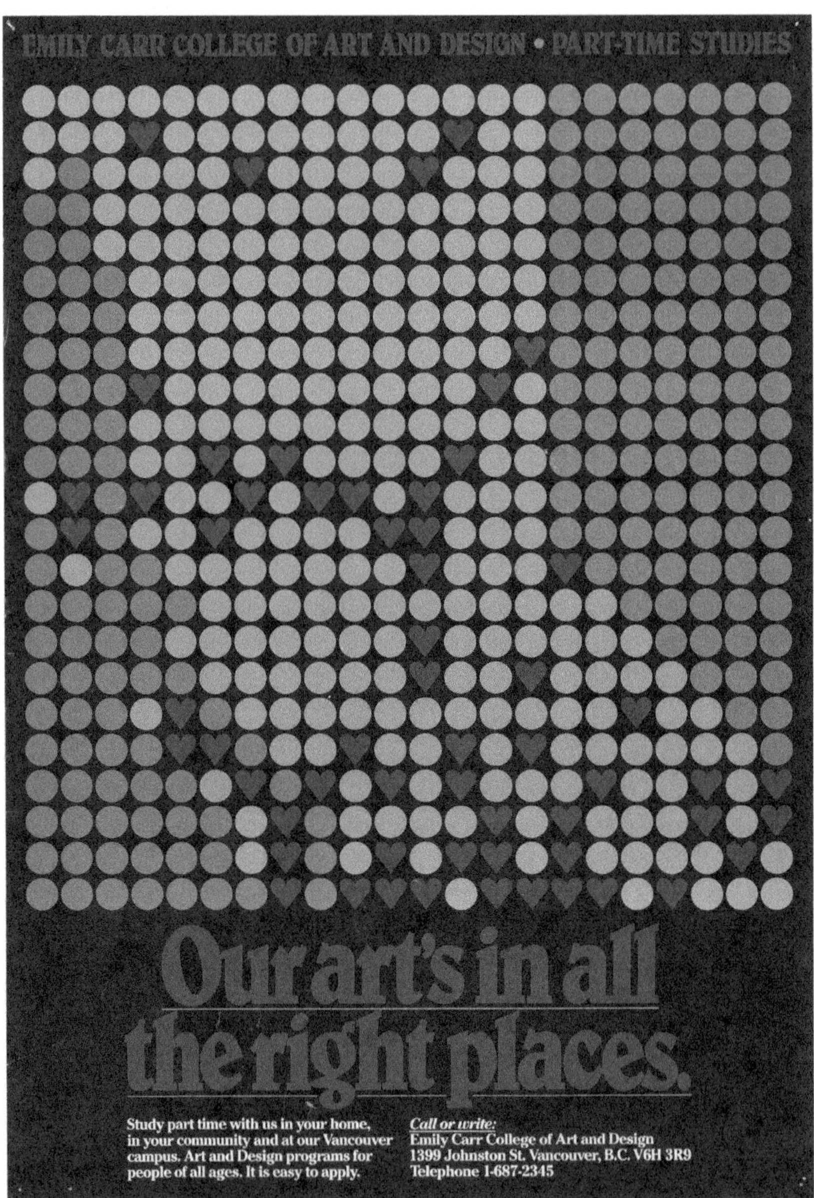

2.8   "Our art's in all the right places." Recruitment poster, Emily Carr College of Art and Design, 1982. Photo credit: ECUAD Archives.

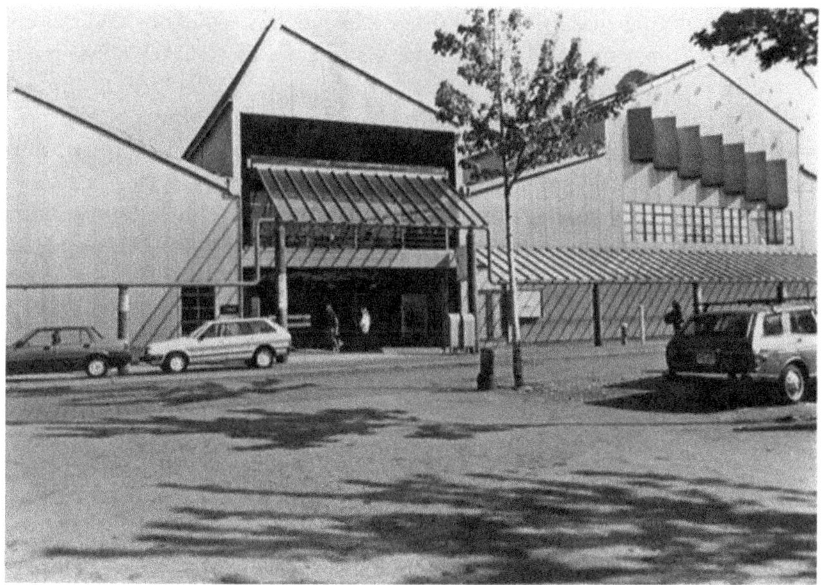

2.9 Main entrance, North Building, Emily Carr College of Art and Design, Granville Island campus, c. 1980s. Photo credit: ECUAD Archives.

from the Audain Foundation for the visual arts in 2013 and $7 million from a real estate developer – reported to be the largest gift ever given to an arts-only university in Canada (ECUAD 2014). ECUAD has also received $113 million from the BC provincial government.

In general, there is less public controversy and debate around ECUAD's operations as compared to the other two schools. There has been considerable stability in leadership, which interview participants acknowledged as a steadying influence. Ron Burnett assumed the presidency in 1996 and held this position until his retirement in 2018. Burnett described his retirement as a "positive move" for the institution that would allow the current rush of changes to be "accelerated and further developed" (as cited in Lederman 2017). Media coverage of difficult events related to the school are largely outside of the institution's control – for example, a non-fatal stabbing between "feuding art students" (Omand 2015). Generally, even the students are described as "unlike the ambivalent big-university crowd," and they speak enthusiastically about the small school and facilities (Ainsworth-Vincze 2011a). Public debate about so many recent changes (e.g., the university status, the new campus) is slim to the point that one arts blogger gave it a name: "Vancouver complaisance" (Third 2015).

It is worth noting that ECUAD did not expanded as rapidly as OCAD and has not had the same level of financial uncertainty as NSCAD. Some interview participants from other universities made offhand references to the fact that ECUAD seemed to have a better relationship with the provincial government. However, this is not a point those working at ECUAD expressed during interviews. Rather, participants insisted that the new campus was a result of tireless efforts on the part of the university's president and administration rather than an especially receptive provincial environment. ECUAD also faces more limitations in terms of provincial support for and recognition of research development.

In BC, there are two types of university – those with a research mandate, and those, like ECUAD, labelled as "special purpose teaching universities."[18] Senior administrators at the school explained to me their frustration with provincial gatekeeping in this regard, noting that that the tiered system fundamentally misunderstands the nature of art and design research and scholarship, and that the research universities in the province are too scared to see their own resources diverted to support any change in these classifications. This designation as a special purpose teaching school also impacts Emily Carr's ability to attract new faculty because the province uses the designation to limit faculty pay scales. Further, special teaching university status raises concerns over the autonomy of university governance at these schools because of the composition of the senate under the existing University Act. By the Ministry of Education's account, these institutions are designed to "focus on teaching excellence" with only a limited research mandate that focuses on "applied research and scholarly activity that supports the institution's programs" (as cited in Charbonneau 2008).

With the opening of its new, purpose-built campus in 2017, ECUAD has recently spent more time in the public spotlight, with many news stories focused on the school's impressive new building, in addition to a few questions about design choices, governance issues, and corporate donors (Sandals 2017; Lederman 2017; Wong 2018). Yet overall, the move has encouraged some positive public discourse about the contributions of art and design higher education.

Conclusion: New Challenges, Familiar Stories

In addition to providing a snapshot of the contemporary landscape for these universities, this overview also pinpoints enduring tensions that have shadowed these schools from their origins. Research too often assumes that our current moment is awash with new problems, but the above account also highlights recurring issues: tensions between applied and creative work, conflicts between market and aesthetic evaluation, and trepidation around resources and value.

First, the union between the fine and applied mandates of art higher education has never been uncomplicated. The origins of these universities stem from a mix of interest in the utilitarian and vocational features of art and design instruction, the value of art and culture for social improvement and moral elevation, and the value of fine art for enrichment and education in itself. And, from their conception, creative dispute and discussion is central to the process of institution building. As a description of student critiques at the Ontario School of Art in 1880 explains, "It is quite possible to talk too much over the work, but there is no denying the utility of mental friction. Ideas rubbed together sometimes produce a spark of truth" ("Ontario School of Art" 1880, 311). Further, adding to late-nineteenth-century emphasis on the social and cultural refinements of art, throughout the first half of the twentieth century there is steadily more emphasis on art education as self-actualization and creative expression (Pearse 2006, 23). Thus, these different narratives have also been featured within the history of art and design higher education in Canada. For example, NSCAD is acknowledged as an early "exemplar of the coexistence of industrial drawing and 'fine art'"(Pearse 2006, 9). As Pearse explains, the school met two objectives: "to sharpen the skills of industrial designers and provide instruction in the fine and decorative arts" (9). And OCAD, although founded by a fine art organization, was largely modelled on Britain's South Kensington School and its focus on industrial art and design (Stirling 2006b, 88). When, in 1912, the Ontario provincial government created two seemingly different institutions to account for technical training (Toronto Technical School) and fine art training (Ontario College of Art), in practice these streams were not so clearly divided (98).

Second, the union between art higher education and the economy has never been uncomplicated. Arguments for the economic utility of these schools have always been made to promote their development. The South Kensington model was associated with economic development and job opportunities for the working classes. Hopes were high that bringing art education to Canada would encourage industrial advancement, not to mention greater economic independence and employment prospects. As noted in the Dominion Annual Register and Review for 1880–1, "The great need of the country is the creation of skilled mechanical and artistic labour, which shall in the future make the country independent of foreign importation of manufactures"(as cited in Stirling 2006b, 88). Or as a newspaper article sketching out the philosophy of the then new Ontario art school states, "The cultivation of the aesthetical faculty is as necessary to the high type of civilization as intellectual culture, physical development, and material progress" ("Ontario School of Art" 1876, 2). That is, the multifaceted nature of the contributions of art and design is clearly linked to material *and* intellectual progress. Consider also the founding objectives of NSCAD in 1887, which were to "provide technical instruction and art culture to persons employed in various trades and manufactures" (Stacey and Wylie 1988, 14), which certainly links these skills to both employment and cultural education. Further, this mandate sought to "open up new and remunerative employment for women" as well as train teachers and "educate public taste" through exhibitions and fine arts classes (15). Thus, this history involves a constant mixing of art and economy. My study does not claim that the creative economy discourse within higher education is a uniquely contemporary invention; rather, I am elaborating upon its current shape and characteristics.

Third, discourses around art and design education have always been double-edged. On the one hand, the historical record is full of advocates who testify to the value of these schools and champion art education and research as key to society's betterment. On the other hand, the brief overview I have provided points to how these institutions are frequently dismissed and undervalued within the multifaceted landscape of higher education. There is still wider trepidation around how to measure and account for the contributions of advanced art and design teaching and research. As Pearse argues in his research on art education in Canada at the beginning of the twenty-first century, the "situations in both 1901 and 2001 are alarmingly similar" (2006, 119); meaning, the struggle for resources and recognition is characteristic across periods. In the chapters to come, I will explore the most recent iteration of this struggle.

In the next section, I examine how these tensions take shape via concrete examples, from the growth of research planning to the rise of evaluation culture to debates around tenure and precarious employment. Hereafter, I will be using the pseudonym Imagination University – except when referring to specific documents or contextual details when needed – and gathering together what are shared dilemmas around the meaning and value of creativity and art, design, and media work within a specialized university.

Everyday Work at Imagination University

Meet the Faculty

The following chapters are organized around the experiences and insights of faculty members and upper administrators. The profiles below (listed alphabetically) introduce the diverse artistic work trajectories and the art, media, or design specializations characteristic of those employed at Imagination University. These are seventeen composite portraits I have constructed from the total interview sample of fifty-four participants, so each profile combines details from usually three (at times two or four) participants' work histories and professional biographies depending on the commonalities identified across sets of transcripts as follows: career stage, training/education, area of specialization, attitudes, concerns, and social identity. All quotations included below are from interview transcripts. See the Methodological Appendix for more details on the process of creating composite portraits.

Anita

Anita is an experienced upper administrator at Imagination University. She has an MFA and a PhD in an interdisciplinary field, and she is a respected media artist and scholar with many external recognitions (grants, awards, exhibitions, and publications). She is widely regarded for setting new research agendas and expanding programs at Imagination University. As an institutional leader, she is demonstrably concerned with the university's profile and public perception, and during our conversations she spent considerable time correcting misperceptions about the institution and was proud to share its many accomplishments. She is both serious and optimistic about the importance and contributions of art and design. Anita is keen to connect issues within the institution to wider political and economic contexts; the school is but a "microcosm" and "distinctly unable to resolve the most pressing issues without wider supports and changes."

She is less interested in re-examining the institution's past and expresses some exasperation with those who are "not quite as up to date as they could or should be" with advances in teaching and/or research. Her interests are clearly future oriented. She has been at the school for over ten years.

Ayana

Ayana holds a BFA and an MFA and has been an exhibiting visual artist for over fifteen years. She previously held artist residencies and fellowships and has taught "one off" studio courses here and there, but her current position at Imagination University is her first tenure-track appointment. She does not disguise her disappointment over her experiences within the institution so far in terms of both tangible resources and supports, as well as overall attitudes and informal practices. As a racialized woman and new appointment, Ayana provides ample evidence of how she is subjected to extra scrutiny and social penalties (e.g., micro-aggressions); worse, she explains, this all happens while being celebrated under the "diversity parade." The art world within the school and elsewhere is, despite claims to the contrary, "shamelessly white supremacist." She has been at the university for just under five years, and, despite the appealing job security, she is forthright about questioning whether she will continue on this career trajectory.

Chianne

Chianne is an artist and curator with an interdisciplinary PhD, an MFA, and a BFA. She has exhibited works and organized shows across Canada, and she recently held a prestigious curatorial fellowship and grant. Chianne readily discusses how her Indigenous identity has shaped her work experience at the university. She has been an active contributor to dialogues around indigenization and decolonization, and she has been involved in developing new courses on contemporary Indigenous art and curating. She notes she must spend a lot of her personal and professional time "educating others on Indigenous issues," which can be "like its own full-time job – but with no extra salary," and this is in addition to usual early career pressures around teaching and career development. Chianne characterizes Imagination University as genuinely "interested" in changing its relationship to Indigenous art, artists, and curriculum, but how it plays out is still "very uneven at best … sometimes deeply problematic." Overall, she describes her time at the university so far as "pretty good" and "not bad." She plans to submit her application for tenure soon.

Claire

Claire is an art historian who describes herself as "a pretty straightforward academic scholar." She has done some curatorial work as well. She holds a PhD in art history and claims a "decent" history of publication, but she says that these publications "don't really matter all that much" in the art school context. She describes herself as a bit "at odds" with many other faculty members, even the university as a whole, because she is not "an artist, creative practitioner, or whatever you want to call it." She expresses some fatigue and impatience with the "eccentricities" of the school and is evidently disgruntled by a perceived lack of recognition for art historical scholarship. Further, her work experience has been impacted by a chronic disability that is largely invisible and thus something for which she has not been well accommodated. She includes substantial service work as a central part of her work history at the school. With over twenty years of work experience at Imagination University, Claire has a long institutional memory that she draws on regularly to make sense of changes.

Darryl

Darryl is a current vice-president and former dean. He is a designer who had substantial industry experience before he moved into academia. He came to Imagination University from a comprehensive university. Darryl holds a practice-based PhD and collaborates regularly on academic publications and projects, and he has received a number of grants and awards for his design work. He prides himself on his academic management expertise and skills, especially given the many challenges the university faces. He is a dedicated and straightforward administrator who voices some exasperation with a few of the "more original types and personalities" who seem keen to "make things longer and harder." He is not overly sympathetic when faculty come to him with lists of problems and excuses. He is a genuine advocate for design's potential to transform social environments and relationships, but in his accounts of everyday operations, Darryl does not easily identify with those who struggle to meet career objectives. As he says, "Sometimes, you just have to do the job. The expectations are not unreasonable."

Dominic

Dominic is a full professor and well-respected conceptual artist and writer. His work has been exhibited and published internationally. He holds an MFA and a research-based PhD, and he has received external awards, arts council grants, and research grants. He is well respected in the university and wider Canadian art world. He is an active department member who has taken on many service roles and who demonstrates a very strong commitment to graduate student development. He plans to retire soon and is among the longest-serving faculty members at Imagination University. He is thoughtful and a bit perplexed about how to interpret the mix of very positive and very negative developments at the university in the recent past: "[I] can't complain … I continue to have a very rich career, a gift, really … but I also don't know what to make of things now."

Heath

Heath is an upper administrator who has led the development of research at Imagination University. He has been essential to establishing research planning documents and agendas, though not without some difficulties due to "strong resistance by some." He firmly believes in the value of research and the need to enhance research agendas and activities at the school. He has a humanities PhD with a conventional academic research background, but Heath speaks of how he has developed an immense appreciation and understanding of artistic research practices and knowledge. He moved to the school from a comprehensive university to take up his current administrative position. He is a bit weary of the demands of academic work, and he thought the school would be a better alternative to the "publish or perish" intensity of his previous university. The stresses at Imagination University, he explains, are rather different. There are some "organizational anomalies" and established practices that he has struggled to make sense of, let alone change. According to Heath, the school has "an artistic way ... that has its advantages," but it is also "way more chaotic" than other universities.

Jack

Jack is a visual artist and assistant professor who has been at Imagination University for almost ten years on a recurring contract, which means he cannot apply for a promotion. He has gallery representation and some dedicated collectors, and he has an active exhibition history with some notable solo and groups shows. He holds an MFA from a Canadian program and locates himself as both inside and outside of the "artist and academic hybrid" culture that is so unique to the school. While there are many things he admires about the overall creativity of the environment, especially mentoring students, he is also fairly disillusioned about changing tides of "heavy handed" administrative directives always searching for "Fame? Popularity? The new new?" During our interviews, he discussed at length the fragility of artistic currency, something related to his professional experiences inside and outside of the university.

Kat

Kat is an assistant professor and craft specialist in a newer program with growing demand. She has extensive experience as a community-based artist and working with at-risk youth. She sells a bit of her work "here and there" and gets the occasional commission, but this is not a substantial portion of her income. She describes her art as "non-commercial ... not really orienting to a market – whatever that is!" She regularly participates in and helps to organize community art events. She has an MFA and is a graduate of Imagination University, but she feels "definitively ambivalent" about her own degree process and the "real need" for credentials to get a job within the school. As a new faculty member, she has struggled with how to navigate the various arms of the school and the often unclear, if not "totally contradictory," advice she has been given about how to deal with different administrative components. She has been at the university for less than five years.

Len

Len is a full professor and craft specialist, a self-described "artist and artisan" who trained in both Europe and the US. He advocates for quality fabrication that "is about time and patience," something that he feels risks being lost if students and even professionals do not spend enough time crafting by hand. He enjoys teaching and is not "too bothered by internal politics and all that," but he does actively dislike the "arrogance" of the wider art world and status games. At the same time, he remains committed to developing new directions within his practice and challenging himself. He has been blending craft, art, and technology with considerable success over the past few years and has won several grants and external awards as a result. He has taught at Imagination University for over twenty years.

Maretta

Maretta is an illustrator and graphic designer with a BDes, an MA, and an MDes who moved to Canada to take her position at Imagination University, leaving her employment at another university overseas. She somewhat sheepishly admits that her move was less motivated by "a passion" for Canada than it was by exhaustion and frustration with her previous university position. Although she has been a collaborator on several grants and funded projects, she does not think of herself as an "artist-academic or researcher" but as a more general "creative practitioner." She has worked at the university for over ten years. She has done a stint as department chair but notes that service demands are becoming so unmanageable for everyone, and that the responsibility of being chair is "very, very undesirable." Yet she also notes, drawing on her experience within another national context, that "it's much worse elsewhere!" She finds some reason to be optimistic about a number of new initiatives, especially around diversity and new courses, but she does not hide her concern about workplace stresses and many organizational constraints.

Marnie

Marnie fell into an upper administrative role at Imagination University largely "by accident." And, true to most accidents, the experience has been a mix of "chance and disaster." She has been dean for three years, even though being an academic administrator was never a career goal or even an interest for her. But the school's need was high, and she had a "sense of obligation – no one wanted the role." She thought the position might mix up the routine of teaching and offer more challenges, but she has never thought of herself as a manager. She dislikes the "many unpopular tasks" she has to navigate, and she is stuck at the "front line" in terms of both faculty and student discontent. Marnie has an MFA in the visual arts from a well-respected Canadian school and has been "slowly" working on a PhD. She has been working at the university for almost fifteen years; before that, she held contract positions at different universities. In the past five years, her work patterns have noticeably shifted. She "occasionally" still exhibits her work and spends some time on her artistic practices but finds that more and more of her time is consumed by teaching or administrative work.

Mel

Mel is an associate professor who specializes in design and new technology, with a mix of commercial and "more arty" work experience before she settled into her university position. She has a BDes and an MA. She was hired as part of a new design program and she maintains a small lab, a "student lab, really," as part of that initiative. There was no one with her type of expertise when she started at Imagination University. She had worked with "predominantly male creatives" in the industry, and she locates the university environment as one that is "generally better … more open overall." She notes that she enjoys the creative autonomy she has experienced at the school and when navigating potential partnerships. She feels comfortable turning down partnerships that are "aesthetically or ethically questionable." But she does feel pressure from the upper administration to pursue "any [and] all" types of funding and partnership opportunities because her area of specialty is in demand. This was especially hard for Mel to navigate before she had tenure. She has worked at the school for almost ten years.

Nate

Nate is an art historian, critic, and curator with a career trajectory that sways towards the academic side. He completed his PhD in Art History in a well-known program outside of Canada. He is an active faculty union member and expresses more than a touch of cynicism about day-to-day operations. He is quick to point out the limitations of the neo-liberal framework dominating higher education and does not reasonably expect to see a sudden change in course. Despite his generally dismal pronouncements on the university's prospects, his commitment to the distinctiveness of the school is clear. He genuinely positions the university as more creative and critical than others and believes in the "moments of heightened humanity and solidarity" that are often part of artistic communities. His involvement with the faculty union adds to his overall workload, but he feels that commitments to labour and activism are also an obligation in this line of work, where he readily describes himself as "pretty privileged."

Patrick

Patrick is a full professor and designer specializing in user-centred, inclusive product design. He advocates for the importance of design to wellness, accessibility, and inclusion, and he genuinely believes in "dignity via design." He has an MDes that he pursued many years after he started his faculty position. He has been very successful with different types of funding, participating in a number of research projects and collaborations with private and government funders. He is a long-serving faculty member who has worked for over twenty years at the school. He has witnessed many changes and attempts to "reorganize [and] rethink" art and design education. He is a bit ambivalent about the trend to make the school "more academic" and links "invention and originality" to the study of real-world, hands-on learning.

Saeed

Saeed is a full professor and experimental film-maker and photographer with a BFA completed "so very, very long ago." His works have been very well received because of their provocative explorations of identity and culture. He was hired at the school almost thirty years ago "as an artist, to be an artist." His body of work has been included in exhibitions on contemporary Canadian art, and he is often mentioned in publications on art history and criticism for his contributions to the Canadian art scene. Saeed openly discusses his struggle to balance his artistic career with teaching, supervision, and administrative duties, especially as one of the "few visible minorities around decades ago." He feels deeply ambivalent about many recent changes and misses the less academic and "more art focused" feel of the past. He is concerned that the critical potential of art is becoming eroded in the current environment, especially with so much effort directed towards both regulation and entrepreneurialism.

Shaina

Shaina was hired four years ago at Imagination University and holds a BArch and an MFA. She situates her work at the intersections of art, media, and design and hesitates to make distinctions between art and design or to have to "choose between the label: am I an artist? A designer?" She has a dedicated "maker studio hub" on campus and has organized a series of community and student maker events to promote a more "collaborative and experimental mood here. We need to keep the energy up." Shaina sometimes feels a bit self-conscious as a newly appointed faculty member; she is the youngest and latest hire in her department, and because she was hired in design, she has not been able to build connections to the studio arts in the ways she would like. She is frustrated by how program streams prevent her from being able to mentor and teach students from all areas, and she feels the university "misrepresents its openness" to change and working across areas.

This brief introduction to the study's participants touches on questions of professional identity, institutional processes, and creative value and evaluation that are central to the analysis developed within each chapter. Brought together, these profiles and perspectives set the stage for the themes and tensions that surface within the specific examples of change I discuss in the coming chapters: the growth of artistic research culture; the rise of audit culture; new demands placed on creative identity at the service of the institution; changing perceptions of employment security and creative currency; and multiplying institutional uncertainties.

Welcome to the Department of Non-applied Creativity: Strategic Planning, Defining Value, and Talk of Research

Research has become a status issue, as much as a conceptual or even practical one.

– Frayling, "Research in Art and Design" (1993), 5

Hence, the question is not "What is artistic research?" but "What is academia?"

– Borgdorff, *The Conflict of the Faculties* (2012), 72

It's possible to become a very, very important artist without having a degree, without having any kind of attachment to academia whatsoever.

– Dominic, study participant

A simple, typewritten sign taped to an office door reads "Department of Non-Applied Creativity." At a guess, this sign is intended to be a cheeky rebuttal to the frenzy around the creative economy, and the labs and research groups that have sprung up in its wake at Imagination University. While plainly stated, the concern behind this sign is clear: it makes a claim for resources devoted to open creative exploration not tied to commercialization and measurable outcomes. This sign is representative of a number of debates concerning the art and design university as a research institution and how the growth of research has impacted institutional culture and practices. A heightened emphasis on research is widely cited as one of the biggest recent changes at Imagination University. From Dominic's perspective, it is the most significant change: "In terms of research, the transition is quite remarkable." Heath has been central to strategic planning and research development at the school, and he describes this transition as follows: "Research was present as kernels and seeds ... less explicitly referenced or defined or captured ... Now it's a full-blown pillar."

Universities have an increasingly important and contested role within artistic training and the professionalization of art, with many debates existing around both the practical and aesthetic consequences of university-housed artistic training and practice (Singerman 1999). Research in art and design is representative of competing versions of managing and applying creativity in the present. To speak of research at an art and design university carries a contour of debate very specific to the fine arts. The first part of this chapter reviews some of the debates on artistic research: is research just another way of framing artistic practices and processes? Is it a term to be viewed with suspicion – a means of neo-liberal territorializing of arts higher education? Is it the outcome of key social and conceptual currents in contemporary art and design experimentation? Then, I review the ways recent strategic plans try to reconcile the tensions and bridge different versions and values. Finally, I turn to everyday talk about research to examine how faculty and administrators navigate and understand these issues. Institutional actors made sense of this transition to research, its impact on their own work, and contestations over value in different ways. Research in these accounts is linked to both positive changes (more expansive and inclusive concepts of art and design) as well as new inequities (those deemed "unfundable" or less valuable within the culture of research). Thus, research is rightly understood in contradictory ways within the institution.

Accordingly, this chapter develops a nuanced portrait of the recent life of research at Imagination University. While many faculty demonstrate genuine commitments to artistic research practices and articulate well its varied contributions, research is also an indicator of institutional reorganization under the new spirit of creativity and its tensions with artistic creativity. The institutional-artistic critique in this chapter capably identifies a number of concerns and constraints accompanied by this rise of research, but where the compromises required between the orders of creativity move between the three forms identified in the introduction. This chapter demonstrates how the emergence of niche bureaucracy and multiplying specializations represents one of the new spirit's many reordering effects.

The Dilemmas of Research at the Art and Design University

One of the most vigorous contemporary debates within art and design hinges on questions of research.[1] As Belcher sums up, "In an increasingly market and research-led university education sector, the status and validity of artistic research has never been more crucial and yet also, it seems, never more contested" (2014, 235). This section explores how the art and design university defines and values artistic research contributions within policy and planning documents. Through the analysis of research planning documents, I position the art and design university as a mediator of conflicting perspectives on the value of art and design research. Institutional texts play a key role in establishing and mediating norms and practices. As Chapman and Sawchuk remind us in their study of the emergence of "research-creation" categories within academic policy, "universities and other degree granting institutions have firmly established protocols and practices for what constitutes valid scholarship that act as normative frameworks for modes of presentation" (2012, 6). My analysis demonstrates how this collection of plans assembles different versions of the cultural, social, and economic value of artistic research that are, at times, incompatible. Here, I argue that it is not the definition itself that is the most contentious feature of university research planning; rather, it is defining the value of artistic research that invites conflict.

The literature on arts-based research has grown steadily over the past decade, with scholarship tackling the issue from a wide palette of perspectives – be it individual, psychological, educational, social, or philosophical (Biggs and Karlsson 2010; Douglas and Carless 2018; Elkins 2009; Hannula, Suoranta, and Vadén 2005; Jagodzinski and Wallin 2013; Leavy 2009, 2018; McNiff 2013; Rodgers and Yee 2015; Sullivan 2010). Here, I am gathering views on the "uneasy, but challenging" (Borgdorff 2010, 44) relationship between artistic research and academia at the thoroughfare of higher education. To be clear, much of this literature is advocating for how arts-based methods of inquiry can challenge and expand social science research methodologies; for example, as part of participant action research or ethnographic work (e.g., Barone and Eisner 2012; Cahnmann-Taylor and Siegesmund 2008; Knowles and Cole 2008). While not a clear-cut division, I am addressing debates specific to artistic research (also known as art, media, and design research; practice-based or arts-based research; creative research; and research-creation) and academic knowledge within the dedicated art university rather than the wider world of the humanities and social sciences.

It is not controversial in itself to declare that some art does, and some art does not, count as research (Frayling 1993, 4). Frayling's three modes of artistic research – research *into* art and design; research *through* art and design; and research *for* art and design – are often cited to help clarify distinctions. The first of Frayling's types, research into art and design, is "by far the most common" (4). This is the stuff of theses and dissertations that examine the history, theory, and aesthetic developments of the arts. The next type, research through art and design, recognizes how the process of making art produces material, technical, and aesthetic insights. Finally, research for art and design refers to the many ways that artists and designers might gather information and sources – that is, the various themes and topics necessary to provide depth to creative production. Research for art and design generates directions for aesthetic exploration and interpretation of the world – "research where the end product is an artefact – where the thinking is, so to speak, *embodied in the artefact*" (5). Borgdorff

(2012) seeks to further clarify this last category.[2] Here, he takes his cue from Frayling's definition but pushes its implications such that artistic practice is both part of the research process as well as the result (38). Taken together, Borgdorff identifies the distinguishing features of artistic research as "*in and through the acts of creating and performing*" (147).

While there is general consensus that these definitions remain open to adaptation and reconsideration (Belcher 2014; Chapman and Sawchuk 2012; Grennan 2015), the ongoing question of "where, precisely, the distinction lies between *art practice in itself* and *art practice as research*" remains (Borgdorff 2012, 144). There is perceptible unease from many artists and designers about what the term *research* signifies and requires, and the fine arts doctorate, much supported and maligned, becomes emblematic of this quest to appropriately mix academic and artistic research perspectives in universities (Buckley and Conomos 2009; Butt 2017; Elkins 2009; Macleod and Holdridge 2004). As a response to the rigidity of categorization that tends to accompany academic research principles, artistic research discussions often trade in grey zones of concepts, trying hard not to reinstate binary oppositions between, for example, art versus design, art versus craft, art versus science, or craft versus industry. Yet these efforts invariably make the work of definition less – not more – clear. In this sense, the difficulty of characterizing what constitutes artistic research is a fairly predictable outcome of the mixed inheritance of art and design education – one that includes everything from technical training to avant-garde experimentation.

An abiding concern in the literature is how to ensure that the less tangible features of aesthetic knowledge – the deep conceptual and embodied qualities of artistic research or design thinking – are not dismissed or forced into more standardized methods, models of success, or applied outcomes. There is marked interest in critically examining the practices of evaluation and legitimation of this research in higher education (Adams 2014; Baxter et al. 2008; Mason 2008; Matcham 2014), yet how the university can accommodate and validate important features such as "unfinished thinking" (Borgdorff 2012, 181) and failure (Barber 2009, 55–9) as research principles and outcomes is not easily answered. For example, Jagodzinski and Wallin turn to Deleuze and Guattari, Heidegger, Nietzsche, and other philosophers of rupture to argue that most arts-based research within the academy upholds the interests of the institution, and "at the expense of repeating a subjectivity that serves current neo-liberal and capitalist ends" (2013, 3). As they maintain, even some of the most promising emergent practices are not "radical enough for the posthuman condition we find ourselves in" (3). Similarly, Nelson offers an exuberant and ambitious proposal for artistic research that contests how it is "methodologically sanitized" (2009, 25) in academic contexts. But on the other end of the spectrum, we have empirically driven research directed towards better understanding fine arts research practices within universities (Macleod and Chapman, 2014; Macleod and Holdridge 2004; Paltridge et al. 2011). Although less provocatively stated than the former examples, they voice similar concerns that the possibility of sustaining a critical artistic agenda is compromised when it is only understood as another category of academic research. As Candlin explains, the "practice-based PhD, which emerged from a predominantly left-wing tradition, may also be closely linked with conservative education policies" (2001, 303).

Ultimately, the stronger validation of these research practices within the art and design university comes with a double edge; this validation also invites forms of justification and evaluation that artists and designers find concerning. Taken together, the trepidation voiced within recent debates indicates how developing research plans within a dedicated institution is a demanding task.

Strategic Versions and Visions of Research

The twofold mandate of universities as centres of research and learning has its origins in nineteenth-century German models of higher education. This seemingly natural union between teaching and research has not always been the case but emerged out of changing ideas about economics and education (Graham and Diamond 1997; Rüegg 2004). Even in Canada's extensive, publicly funded system that promises a largely consistent quality of education, research within universities is a way to make distinctions between the calibre and status of institutions and individuals that are inseparable from wider social inequalities (Robbins 2012; Side and Robbins 2007). Research is a central feature of discourses of academic freedom, even if definitions of academic freedom and the line between ethics and expression are also under scrutiny (Woodhouse 2017; Turk 2014, 2017). Yet under tightening government budgets for higher education and slow economic growth, pure research – especially in the arts and humanities – feels the squeeze (Belfiore 2014; Donoghue 2008). Shifts in the political climate reverberate across higher education, and research funding and agendas are notably vulnerable.

The growth of the art and design university as a research institution is an important development to concepts of advanced research within higher education. I am interested in research planning documents for a number of inter-related reasons. First, they represent ideal positions and involve a process of institutional self-representation that must appeal to diverse expectations and criteria. Second, the development of these plans requires input (variously practiced) from the university community. Third, research plans need to pull central concepts in several different directions to satisfy diverse audiences while aligning with wider strategic plans. Finally, dedicated research plans are a requirement for many external funding opportunities. My interest here is not to assess the veracity of these plans or to analyse the specifics of each institution's method of creating these plans, but to acknowledge their place in constructing and representing narratives around the objectives and values of art and design research. Borgdorff astutely observes that "the entanglement of artistic research with art practice and with artistic development is so close that a conceptual distinction often appears contrived" (2010, 45). With this in mind, research planning documents charged with making distinctions easily veer into the terrain of "contrived." But even while we can accept the artificial dimensions of these documents, their implications are far from trivial (Smith 2005). As one plan curtly states, "this plan will guide policy, infrastructure, and resource allocation" (ECUAD 2013b, 1).

The awkward union between artifice, duty, and impact in research plans does not go unnoticed. As an experienced administrator, Darryl readily identified the pragmatic requirements: "We could not afford to omit it [research] as a growing thing ... and there are only so many objectives and so many goals that you can express in plans. You wouldn't say that we're so distinctive that our goal is to produce the least well-equipped and adept artists – that would make us really different. Who's gonna say that in a strategic plan?" In practice, as Claire explained of managing the process while department chair, the "division of labour" required to make plans establishes the conditions necessary for reaching agreement by allowing everyone "to input their bullet points," but with so much editing and multiple revisions it also leaves the origins of some key points "unknown or forced through" by certain individuals. The process is described as both "haphazard" and under the control of "one headmaster." Claire summed it up as follows: "General buy in is pretty low in an everyday sense," but a few "well positioned players" manage to realize and manage their interpretations, nonetheless. Maretta also shared a story about an embarrassing mishap with cutting and pasting from previous documents; in practice, there are considerable time pressures around producing what are "purportedly finely crafted documents," and the documents often end up "feeling pretty imperfect."

An art and design university has to establish research goals and priorities, but with faculty that might wholly or partially reject the characterization of their professional activities as research – certainly an unusual scenario given that the contemporary university model generally presupposes that faculty are teachers and researchers, even if how this is expressed varies considerably. Further, the technical and applied inheritance of these schools intersects with their status as interlocutors within theoretical and aesthetic developments in contemporary art and design; this mixed legacy sets the stage, I argue, for necessary eclecticism in research planning that must capture the multiple areas that fall under the domain of art, design, and media research. At the same time, it is this heterogeneity that is always at risk of being minimized when it is pressed into the conventions of institutional planning that are not widely regarded for their creativity.

Negotiating a "Radically Ambiguous Future"

In my initial survey of fifteen years (1999–2014) of material (strategic plans, strategic research plans, annual reports, and advertising and recruitment material in print and online), I located many descriptions of art and design research (see also Liinamaa 2018). In the earliest research plan available, artistic research is characterized by its "primary emphasis … on innovative intellectual investigations into visual meaning, expression, and communication" (NSCAD 1999, 1). This indicates a strong focus on visual culture aligned with academic rigour. Other early research plans (e.g., NSCAD 2003, 2006) stress the need for infrastructure and institutional support with a desire to "make research a major emphasis in the university" (2003, 2). They identify the need to grow the school's research culture, which by implication acknowledges its currently weak presence. Yet as research planning develops, research becomes cast more and more in terms of innovation and the creativity economy (ECUAD 2010; NSCAD 2009a, 2009b; OCAD 2012a, 2012b). The initial attention devoted to the intellectual and aesthetic specificity of this research no longer surfaces as a defining feature. Instead, these plans develop more expansive definitions that recognize the distinct "research ecology" (ECUAD 2013b, 1) of art and design institutions; we are frequently reminded that there are many "appropriate methodologies" (ECUAD 2013b, 4) and "many approaches to research" (NSCAD 2013a). In fact, one key strategy for supporting such diversity is to avoid presenting a guiding definition. Instead, this planning discourse articulates different concepts and characteristics at different moments; for example, there is a veritable buffet of associated terms that might be used, such as "knowledge, experience, originality, reflection, risk, experimentation, innovation, invention, flexibility and adaptability" (NSCAD 2013a, 1). Or, as another plan similarly puts it, "boldness, courage, risk, vision and innovation" (OCAD 2006, 47).

In keeping with trends in academic literature, practice-based research surfaces as a comfortable catchall term. For example, one 2012 plan covers all of its bases by placing its preferred gathering term of "art, design and media research" under the umbrella of "practice-based research" (OCAD 2012a, 1). Another explanation distinguishes between applied versus practice-based research, defining practice-based pursuits as those that integrate "the professional practice of an artist or designer with specific research questions, methods and outcomes" (ECUAD n.d.). The description continues to characterize practice-based research in a manner reminiscent of Frayling's (1993) explanation discussed above. Another research plan foregrounds an even more general common ground term, *making*:

Art and Design institutions focus on practices and processes of *making*, and on a reflexive orientation to making and material culture. Praxis, or critical making, the joining of making and theory, forms the basis of our research and educational practice. (ECUAD 2013b, 1)

While extremely general, this version allows for an understanding of research premised on praxis – where reflection and criticality are defining features of research. In this example, we have a very general definition (*making*), but one that casts artistic research as not neutral but critical in orientation. However, if not everyone identifies with such a critical project, it seems yet another way to avoid potential controversy is to present a definition of research that is so neutral that it is not specifically tailored to art and design practices at all. For example:

> Successful research practices find common themes: the identification of significant questions, issues and/or interests for inquiry; the development of a body of knowledge and understandings of the contexts in which questions, issues, interests are positioned; the employment of a relevant method of inquiry toward an outcome; and the communication of the outcome of the inquiry to the communities which have an interest in the research, including the public. (NSCAD 2013a, 1)

In similarly general terms, another document characterizes art and design research as a "deep, complex thinking process" that can actively contribute to both "cultural ecology" and "creative economy" (OCAD 2006). Here, research is succinctly positioned to capture the interests of any potential stakeholder.

Taken together, we can discern efforts to maintain an inclusive definition. An amount of consensus exists around the significance of a big tent approach within research mandates, but this is not to say that these documents can avoid debate or disagreement altogether. While not absolute oppositions, they argue for art and design's social and cultural contributions, and, at the same time, the economic value of these practices; but pursuing the potentially incompatible dimensions of these alignments is beyond the conventions of planning. However, the turn to economic justification is representative of the heightened pressure on universities to adhere to a stronger business model, further complicated by greater financial precarity after the reverberations of the global economic upheavals in 2008.

In more recent plans (see NSCAD 2013a; ECUAD 2013b; OCAD 2012a), the expansion of research values and goals becomes clearer. By analysing the central concepts used to describe artistic research in these documents, I have gathered the range of terms used to describe the cultural, socio-political, and economic contributions of advanced art and design research: cultural values (aesthetics, expression, experience, critical thinking, cosmopolitanism, history, recognition of diversity); socio-political values (health and well-being; environmental health and sustainability; inclusion and participation; ethics; equality and change); and economic values (industry, commerce, product development, creative industry growth). In one regard, an ideal version of art and design research emerges in these characterizations; this ideal version is methodologically open and connects aesthetics to collective responsibility. This perspective on research aligns cultural production with criticality (NSCAD 2013a), regards the imagination as an agent for social and political change (OCAD 2012a), and places community and sustainability at its centre (ECUAD 2013b). These plans stress that art and design research should be distinguished for its cultural contributions, the circulation of ideas and artefacts that expand our repertoires of expression, perspective, and knowledge – all of which help nurture respect and diversity.

Yet these research ideals exist alongside attention to art and design research's "seminal role in today's economy" (OCAD 2012a, 1) and the championing of economic values across these plans, such as entrepreneurship, industry, private partnerships, product development, and technological innovation – essentially, all of the components of a flourishing creative economy. The growing emphasis on economic benefits and the triad of economy–innovation–technology is not just a matter of perception by faculty; the priority placed on economic benefits and applied innovations is enshrined in the language of the plans themselves.

While tensions between the aesthetic and the economic are traceable throughout the plans, they sit alongside a strong dose of future uncertainty; plans, to be sure, are always projections that must assess present practices in terms of future predictions. Consequently, while the concept of the future occasionally features in these plans, *how* it features is worthy of note. While these plans make reference to the future significance of artistic research in terms of technology, sustainability, and the need to "educate ethical leaders for a viable future" (ECUAD 2013b, 5), I would like to draw attention to the uncertain future that also surfaces. As one plan puts it, transformative research will help to nurture "students that are ethically autonomous, able to think critically, and courageously step into a radically ambiguous world" (ECUAD 2013b, 4). Another argues that art and design research can help us respond to the "indeterminate, chaotic and undemocratic characteristics to our everyday lives" (NSCAD 2013a, 5). Terms such as "radically ambiguous," "indeterminate," and "chaotic" are not generally featured descriptions in university plans; "undemocratic" is even more acute as a future spectre. These abrupt but powerful references both reinforce the potential contributions of research and cast a shadow on the future of higher education in light of drastic and changing circumstances, both local and global.

In contrast to the planning genre that strives to smooth over contradictions, the next section turns to faculty experiences and interpretations of the growth of research, and in a tone quite distinct from planning discourses. These characterizations demonstrate how researchers and administrators grapple with the new armatures of creative research specialization.

Talk of Research

The title of this section is a nod to cultural sociologist Ann Swidler's *Talk of Love* (2003), a book that carefully demonstrates the value of analysing the cultural repertoires that inform how social actors assemble and mobilize meaning in given scenarios, drawing on multiple, often contradictory frames of reference. These repertoires become especially strong during transitional periods as individuals seek to locate meaning against wider uncertainties. And, as other cultural sociologists have carefully documented, talk is increasingly central to both artistic practice and navigating art worlds (Gerber 2017; Fine 2018). Here, I argue that "talk of research" is a way to understand institutional changes that hinge on the growth of research culture at these schools, and how actors position themselves vis-à-vis this shift. Studying artistic research through talk about research is twofold. First, it requires being attuned to how people describe their experiences and the values and frames of references they draw on to explain and account for actions. These accounts are connected to but not reducible to institutional constraints and possibilities. Participants offer many compelling accounts of the value of research: creative innovation, artistic satisfaction, career security, institutional sustainability. Second, it requires studying what is not mentioned: What frames are rejected to the point that they are not talked about at all? Thus, positioning absence or subtlety, especially in terms of how critique functions, is "more ambiguous and difficult to interpret" (Swidler 2003, 16). In the following discussion, the intricacy of artistic critique becomes clear as the growth of research is simultaneously valued and treated with scepticism. There are many ways institutional actors demonstrate a genuine commitment to quality research practices and relay the distinctiveness of artistic research and its importance to the specialized culture of the art and design university. At the same time, critiques emerge around how research is put to use; principles of artistic creativity are employed to reject the disruptive and divisive features accompanying the rise of research within institutional life.

"Passion and Pleasure": The Sincerity of Distinction

Participants offered many descriptions of art and design research. Mel explained the nature of this research as follows: "It has, you know, depth and breadth, some kind of theoretical, historical [context], and involves engaged attachment to a question, a question that has many, many features and that may be compounded by what has already been researched, published, and produced." She went on to say that it must balance an "interest in originality" with "modesty" and "careful execution." Faculty referred to the following characteristics as essential to university-level research in art and design: rigorous development of themes across time and projects; critical attention to process and ongoing reflection; conceptual thinking; dedication to experimentation; driven by curiosity rather than client demands;[3] engagement with social context and, when possible, social change; a commitment to advanced research ethics; reframing the contemporary organization of knowledge; and a capacity for public significance. Often those who at other points in our conversation were deeply suspicious of the "research turn" provided thoughtful responses to the wider question of what constitutes artistic research. Thus, at some level, talk of research tries to genuinely make sense of the place of artistic research within university culture and provide accounts that clarify the relationship of research to pre-existing practices.

In this vein, participants offered a number of reflective and process-oriented accounts that made sense of artistic research by emphasizing its distinctiveness when compared to conventional academic definitions. When I meet Shaina in her spacious on-campus studio, she is reviewing plans with a graduate student for a large-scale commissioned project. There is another student working at a small computer station in the corner. The scene is genuinely a mix of artist studio and classroom, and Shaina immediately declares her interest in centring the research dialogue on what is specific to art and design. She shares with me a number of insights into artistic research that move away from the "problem finding" approach[4]: "It grows out of passion and pleasure, something that is often totally dismissed but crucial to aesthetic exploration." Importantly, "being in love" with your topic or process can be a part of the conversation in a way that it cannot in conventional academic research.[5] Of note here, Shaina explains, is the importance of "freedom within methodology" that traditional academics either poorly grasp or understand as "intellectual weakness." No one during any interview argued that artistic research can or should be evaluated according to the same criteria as existing models in the humanities, social sciences, or natural sciences. Rather, the overriding message is that a new paradigm is needed. But as Mel notes, "We just aren't there yet in terms of total legitimacy." Regularly, faculty made a case for the need to value the specialized knowledge of art and design, while also respecting its interdisciplinary scope and diverse methodological overlaps with other disciplines. While the emphasis on difference generally follows Bourdieu's (1984) theory of distinction in that leveraging distinctiveness provides legitimacy to cultural value and status,[6] in the case of artistic research, the artists and designers I interviewed also created distinctions to make sense of uncertainties within the research process and reorder value associations of research. The definitional talk of research indicates how it can meaningfully inform creative practices.

During an almost two-hour long interview with Dominic in his comfortable and eclectically decorated living room, we speak extensively about this question of artistic research. Dominic, with his interdisciplinary PhD and lengthy history of practice, is widely regarded as a model artist-researcher – so much so that two other participants referred to him as an example of sustained and conscientious practice. "What does it mean to be regarded as a model?" I ask. He pauses to gather his thoughts and then says, "It's not forced … it means both artists and academics respect your work." He goes on to say that research is "conceptually embedded, already necessary to the creative process," and that attempts to insert research into a project just for the sake of it, such as for funding, is "to the detriment of research and art." Next, Dominic provided me with two different parallels for describing the artistic research process. First, shelving books as a metaphor for the creative research process.[7] Though the tedious labour of returning books to the stacks, you slowly start to build a sense of the networks and connections between ideas, but you have to physically move, circulate, push, pull, and constantly return used or abandoned books home. This process is ongoing, embodied, and demanding. The other metaphor for the research process he offered was the mathematical Fibonacci series, where every number is the sum of the preceding two numbers. Thinking of the Fibonacci numbers as "kind of the golden meme," this captures well the necessarily generative, additive, and unfinished nature of the research process.

Dominic's descriptions of artistic research are thoughtful and sincere, and this remains pertinent, even though as a "model artist-researcher" he has an investment in the status of research at the university. He views the more recent institutional changes to better accommodate research with some optimism; research, he tells me, has elevated the overall quality of work produced within the school. But he also recognizes and readily discusses a number of limitations, such as the stress on entrepreneurialism and the unequal distribution of resources, especially through competitive funding exercises. He sees evidence of progressive changes alongside what he termed the "research rhetoric." For example, he explained how the MFA graduate program has become more diverse because artistic research fosters more expansive practices and identifications with art. He provided two examples of graduate students, both women from "atypical creative backgrounds" engaging in work that "might have found less of a home not too long ago." Further, he also noted examples of how faculty appointments were becoming more diverse as artistic research is valued because "many artists from under-represented backgrounds are leading the way." Specifically, he provided the example of recent Indigenous artists hired at Imagination University and other schools and noted that women are gaining prominence in "guy heavy" design areas. These changes, he reasons, are related to the growth of artistic research culture, something that is not sufficiently acknowledged by those who hold an "anti-research sentiment."

Strategy from Above? Deciphering Institutional Agency

During interviews, upper administrators eagerly itemized research funding successes at Imagination University. In general, the higher ranking the administrator, the more positive and consistent were his or her accounts about the state of research at the university. I do not think that this desire to summarize grant successes was mere boosterism on their part, but it does signal the significance of research funding to this tier of university management. The need to cite and display numbers to me during interviews, to supply concrete evidence of research activity, was proactively responding to charges that research was *just talk* at the school and not a substantial activity. When I met with Anita, the bulk of our conversation focused on research and her ambitious vision of how to expand research funding opportunities and enhance graduate programs. We sat in her office, drinking mint tea, while she provided a well-plotted itinerary of existing research programs and opportunities at the school. When I asked how she would describe the research culture at the school, she hesitated before she answered. She started her sentence with "Well, um …" and then replied with funding statistics. Numbers were substituted in place of an answer about collective characteristics or shared values. For vice-presidents and presidents especially, funding achievements served as proof of a strong research culture, not specific qualities. This slip between research culture and research funding suggests an underlying uncertainty around exactly how to make sense of this research culture. Anita continued to discuss circumstances outside of the school as "a menace" to this research culture that she struggled to define: "There are many, many external constraints, barriers to growing that here. This can't be stated enough."

While upper administrators use external forms of recognition and impediments to discuss research, participants not currently in administrative roles readily offer some sort of critique of how administration handles the issue of research. Faculty frequently objected to their perceived inability or disinterest in protecting the unique qualities of art and design higher research and instead just wanted "any, I mean *any*, sort of research" (Shaina). Practically, individuals noted the many challenges of growing administrative and organizational research infrastructure and expressed uncertainty around responsibilities: "It's in a bit of a state of wax. It's not as clear as it should be and as it is at other universities" (Kat). Chianne, who holds a prestigious research grant, discussed how she had to regularly seek out advice from colleagues and the research office at a nearby research university because Imagination University had no experience managing such a large-scale grant. She was somewhat wistful in this account, where she described she felt more "in step" at this other university; she noted endless minor conflicts (e.g., how to pay assistants; organizing collaborative projects) impeding her research program because "there is a huge emphasis on research" yet "everything" is really oriented towards teaching.

Three key explanations emerged within everyday talk around research development – each conceiving of and responding to questions of institutional agency differently, and each moving between accepting and questioning the alignments of research with the new spirit of creativity.

(1) *The entrepreneurial university and creative economy.* The first explanation argued that the institutional mobilization of art and design research is where the new entrepreneurial university model and creative economy meet; at its worst, it is a symptom of capitalism's grip over higher education. This approach is best captured in a conversation with Nate, who was keen to distance himself from what he termed "the ideology that clusters around the term *research*." He was very critical of how research was being used to invite more and more private enterprises into the university and to reinforce the "student–consumer" model that impacts freedom of inquiry. His response, it seems, was to claim, "I would never describe anything that I do as research." And this is despite the fact that such a statement stands in contradiction to his professional self-description: "I'm foremost an art historian and curator. I write art historical essays." Nate embraced ambiguity as a counterstrategy – a way to critique the university's move towards research specialization and elaboration. The desire to invite contradiction (How, exactly, does an academic write art historical essays or curate art exhibitions without doing research?) instead of clarity around research is representative of how some faculty navigate their discomfort with how research is mobilized for non-academic gains. Participants expressed their discomfort with the topic of research within the university in a number of gestural ways too. For example, the use of body language that expressed disinterest, like sighing or eye rolling. Another type of response was to not meaningfully respond to questions about research at all, as Patrick ("There isn't much to say … they are keen to build more research") and Jack ("It's been overdone here") did.

(2) *Surviving austerity.* The second explanation stressed that research is a necessary part of surviving as an art school under austerity in higher education. Darryl summed up the stakes of research from his perspective quite clearly: "With research, there is no question now … It's what you have to do as an art university. People think it's somehow a debate, or some sort of consultation, like, maybe something to consider at some point. Nope. It is *survival*." Compared to the first account, where the university is cast as an entrepreneurial agent, this image of survival reorganizes how the agency of the institution is characterized. In this version, the stress is on changing contexts of higher education and hard-to-navigate scenarios, such as government and inter-university competition for resources. This response focused most on external pressures – the higher-ups point to the higher-ups, if you will. Individual administrators expressed their commitment to promoting the distinctiveness of art and design research, but how this could or should happen was invariably directed by wider constraints; external limitations are front and centre in these explanations. As Anita complained, it is impossible to grow a "truly international"

research profile because "we're a poor institution and we don't have that kind of money." And Heath emphasized that administrators are often "cast as the villains," when the "perpetrator" is the provincial government's funding formula; the numbers "speak for themselves with declining support and demands for other sources of funding and partnerships." Without the resources to better support faculty research, the institution struggles when compared to a comprehensive university's ability to communicate results and be in line with "how output gets measured" (Anita). External valuation is a pressing issue in this regard: "I have huge concerns around the criteria for outcomes-based assessments of universities. I think the art and design schools are in that context. There is still a lag around how to adequately measure cultural outputs" (Marnie). With research, as Marnie goes on to explain, the university must constantly negotiate a bind: "It's essential and essentially misunderstood … so, like, good luck." Upper administrators noted the many barriers in place to establishing a research profile including the measurement of outputs and qualifications; competition from other universities over resources; misunderstanding around the nature of art and design research; and the limited number of grants for specialized art and design research. Taken together, there are tangible reasons that the art and design university faces a strong comparative disadvantage.

(3) *Confessions of a strategist.* The third approach positioned research as a way to realize strategic benefits – be it for one's own practice or for the institution – and in ways that could impact "a little or a lot of what you actually do" (Mel) depending on your own needs. One recurring response under this category was that, as Kat said, the research turn "kind of didn't matter *that* much"; she went on to elaborate and say that research growth means you can do whatever you want, whatever you still do – "just call it research, sometimes." So, in this version, employing research is regarded as a surface transformation, a shift in discourse, but one that only impacts individual creative practices if you want to deploy the discourse to your advantage. For example, Shaina recounted that she was able to use research strategically to get some financial support for an interdisciplinary media workshop she was organizing – but she would have planned the workshop regardless. She said it was useful to use the research frame, but she could have continued on without it ("without the coffee and muffins").

The self-identified strategists are the institutionally savvy individuals who know how to navigate the changing landscape, and with considerable reflexivity around their manoeuvres. They speak openly about how to navigate this contradictory sea of demands. I sat with Len in the middle of a studio crowded with recent works. With great agility, he manoeuvered around a number of breakable sculptures, pointing out to me stages of his work and design components. He carefully explained how he had achieved a measure of success with different funding bodies, including the Social Sciences and Humanities Research Council (SSHRC) – the "holy grail of funders." Granting bodies have, he recounted, an "endless appetite" for new technology, so he incorporated this into his craft practice and labelled it a research trajectory. He claimed that he really "knew next to nothing" about the technology side and hired students to help with "most of the computer stuff." He made it clear that his ability to respond to changing social contexts and interests was crucial to his success and research profile. But he located this as a way to confront the "arbitrariness of the popular" in art and design. He spoke at length to me about the absurdity of recognition and success in the field, noting everything from the role of curators to the place of private galleries and collectors. Accordingly, he saw exploiting an "appetite for the new" as a way not to minimize but rather maintain the creative integrity of his work. Thus, what some might label as opportunism was quite the opposite by his assessment: you "play the game" for creative protection, not exploitation.

Len's characterization of being strategic as a way to protect his artistic practice finds resonance with how administration at times framed the issue as well. Administrators voiced a desire for a more strategically minded faculty who "understood the benefits of working within research planning discourse" (Anita). An ability to capitalize on the rising current of research is always a "win-win scenario" (Darryl) for the institution and individual. Heath described his job to me as one that centred on cultivating stronger "strategists"; he would work individually with people in order to help them "suss out options [and] opportunities" and overcome the "serious difficulties" of not having research profiles and previous grant success; "They [funders] always reward previous success. So, it's about success. We need success." But he further qualified that funding success was not about "heroism" – it was about "creative security ... [faculty] don't seem to get that well." However, this view of research as a win-win way to reinforce your creative practice also leaves opens the spectre of a lose-lose dynamic, especially for those who do not feel they easily fit into the art and design research mandate.

"That's Not Research": Territory and Austerity

Research was not always a welcomed topic of discussion during interviews. I had a quarrelsome but not unfriendly interview with Claire. She energetically voiced her disagreement with all things to do with research at the school and noted her irritation with a follow-up question on research culture at Imagination University: "what research culture?" She corrected me – "It's artistic practice. There is a difference." As a more conventional academic researcher who does not locate her historical or curatorial work as "creative or artistic," she was adamant about the fact that, whatever the name or official status of the school, this was "not a university." She described how she felt embarrassed using the title when dealing with colleagues from other institutions. "Why?" I inquired. She replied that it "diminished respect" for "serious" academic research. And it was clear, based on other information she provided to me about her career trajectory and interests, that by "serious" she meant her own type of art historical research. The more we talked, the more she stressed that, from her perspective, artistic practice was claiming the title of "research" in order to make a claim on resources and expand limited funding possibilities. She noted it was itself a "creative response" to austerity, but it meant further institutional resources were being diverted from "complex academic research."

For those who identified most as academics and not also creative practitioners, the growth of research at the university comes with some irony: it seemed to intensify their outsider status within the creative hierarchy. Based on his experiences with research planning, Heath admitted that there was often a "notable antipathy" towards the art historians and other more traditional academics. He explained this simply: they receive "way less recognition" for what is "slow and complicated work." Claire also described how her research and that of her colleagues was less valued, and how, over time, this had significantly impacted her ability to have a positive relationship to her work: "You soldier on … and on … and on." Curiously, research talk at the school for the relatively small group of "pure" academics can have an exclusionary dimension. Claire described her frustration as follows: "Regular research is not enough" – you have to be "more and more. It's an acceptable cliché that academics are too boring, boring. The artist is invited to do research, but it doesn't go both ways." As Heath similarly elaborated, the tension between art versus design is "more trumped up compared to day-to-day things … but everyone feels free to dump on art history." Curiously, the new spirit of creativity's expansive impulses even impact areas more removed from artistic creative practices because now everyone feels the pressure to be creative.

Although one conventional research group feels excluded, others from non-traditional research areas finally feel included and recognized both by the university and other granting bodies. For example, Mel spoke highly of the number of opportunities afforded by growing research at the school and viewed it as productively pushing back against "the unfair exclusion, especially of design, from ideas of what is higher education research." She explained how the shifting climate had made her skill set highly valued as there were not enough qualified individuals to fill university positions. When describing her early work experiences, she characterized her work as "totally unnoticed, even derided," but now she has a permanent faculty position, a small lab, and numerous collaborative projects with private and public funders. In between showing me details from a current project, Mel argued that this current scenario would have been "absolutely unthinkable" not so long ago. Shaina also noted that while people "wrangled" over some of the definitions and boundaries of practice, "this new openness to design, art, aesthetics, research" had made her own interdisciplinary career trajectory viable: "I never thought doing this meant you could even be a professor in a university!"

The "Unfundables"

During a coffee shop interview with Chianne, when discussing how to navigate her recent grant within the school, she explained that it was not research itself that was the source of conflict, but rather how it becomes framed as competitive: "Those kinds of things that actually perpetuate a sort of competitive culture and that's really no fault of the university or your dean or, you know, the public relations person." Specifically, she identified a number of day-to-day things that facilitated a sense of competition or division, such as featuring only researchers with external grants in university campaigns and on the website, the constant references to the achievements of a relatively small number of people, and the use of limited models of successful practices or projects. In sum, this heightened anxiety around the need to be competitive also dramatized gaps in how research is viewed and valued – that is, there are orders of "fundable or unfundable projects." But this unfortunately translated into, as Chianne described it, a sort of "fundable or unfundable person."

Chianne's comments centre on the inclusions and exclusions accompanying the rising status of research. She rightly identifies that there is something about research talk that facilitates divisions. One version of "unfundable" that surfaced in adthministrative talk are the individuals who have not kept pace professionally; here, talk of research can involve demarcating boundaries between young and old, current and dated, and productive and unproductive. Such individuals are deemed out of step with the new spirit's valorization of novelty. As Darryl explained to me, a faculty member's role is "to inform and to lead the discovery process," and the most "honourable way" to achieve this is by "practicing what you preach." Here, a moral order is clearly drawn upon to describe productivity. Thus, research surfaces as a way to demarcate administrators' fear of unproductive, if not outright unruly or disobedient, faculty. That is, faculty who are not supporting the research agenda merge into the category of "troublesome individuals" (Anita). Anita attributed the following characteristics to this sort of disruptive employee: they do not demonstrate their commitment to the viability of the institution; they work less than they should; and they don't fulfil all of their duties. Heath painted these individuals as key roadblocks to growing research:

> They don't develop and they're very frustrated people. They're people who create the most amount of challenge for administration because they're, at the root,

unhappy with themselves, you know, they haven't progressed, and most of the battles they wage are battles of entrenchment to keep the new ideas and new avenues of discovery out there rather than in here.

These individuals are characterized as a scourge on the institution, and the root cause is explained foremost by personal failing, not a response to or product of institutional culture. The faculty who disregard these research initiatives are working "to their own liking, but not mine" (Heath). As Marnie explained, "even people who have PhDs here don't publish as much … There is somehow less commitment." Accordingly, the suspicion that the institution mobilizes research to undergird hierarchies of value holds some truth. At times, administrators do use research to distinguish between productive and unproductive employees with recourse to individual fault. While this may be said of any university, what is specific to this case is that a research framework for valuing and ordering research practices is still relatively new at Imagination University and intersects with many of the new spirit of creativity's key principles; for example, heightened interest in creative entrepreneurialism; instrumental approaches to funding and collaboration; professionalization via advanced degrees and research labs; the championing of technology; and applied problem solving. With artistic research already hotly debated within the wider field, these shifts at Imagination University further open up uncertainties around the value of one's own creative work.

The Rise of Niche Bureaucracy

The message, if it was ambiguous before, is now squarely stated: research is a key requirement within the university life of art and design. Its rise at Imagination University, while part of its move to university status, also coincides with the pressure to expand and commercialize creativity, demonstrate applicable knowledge, and become savvy creative leaders and experts. The task of research planning is to demonstrate in legible terms the diverse characteristics of art and design exploration, and to attempt to bridge conflicts between artistic creative values and the new spirit. But the challenges are numerous. As one academic plan promises, the university will build researchers who are "creative innovators who problem solve within profound constraint" (NSCAD 2016a, 3); thus, alongside the future uncertainty identified earlier in this chapter, "profound constraint" now has a role in the discourse of planning. That said, many of the sentiments voiced in this chapter will ring true with fewer and fewer faculty in the years to come. As long-term artistic research institutionalization sets in, crafting plans and agendas become normalized. More recent research plans are less discursive and more streamlined (ECUAD 2018; NSCAD 2016b, 2019; OCAD 2018a). As Marnie put it, "this [research] isn't even a question now, with new hires. They know the scene. They know how to say they *do* research."

Together, the analysis in this chapter demonstrates the everyday operations of the new spirit of creativity as defined in chapter 1, especially in terms of entrepreneurialism, professionalization, and tangible applications and outcomes. The research planning documents offer insights into the process of articulating and mediating changing perspectives on research, while talk of research is a way to scrutinize how this shift is understood by institutional actors. First, the new spirit of creativity is double-edged. It invites disagreements over the meaning and value of artistic creativity as a specialized pursuit. The embrace of research is critiqued by many for its capacity to mobilize new as well as existing inequities, but also identified as an urgent need and remedy for previous exclusions. Research is a way to capture both the future as a form of survival (a way to survive austerity) and the future in terms of the new and yet to be discovered (a pathway to progressive change). Faculty expressly identified the distinct textures and pleasures of art and design research, yet also recognized that it exacerbated workplace stress and expectations.

Second, the new spirit of creativity institutes more distinctions and categorizations around creative activities. Of the wide-ranging changes required to support research, "there's a whole level of administration that didn't even exist" (Patrick). As Mel similarly explained, the ratio of administrative roles to students is likely higher than that of many research-focused universities. Nate referred to this expansion and intensification of research and research-related administration as something "that has required a whole new kind of niche in bureaucracy, which also has an effect on faculty members." Niche bureaucracy is a concept that well captures the need to make more distinctions around artistic creativity. Certainly, specialization, hierarchy, and the division of labour are central features of bureaucracy (Weber 1978). With the new spirit, research is added as another feature to be carefully managed under the domain of bureaucratic specialization, creating new demands on both faculty and administration.

Third, this chapter identifies a number of strategies employees use to critique and defuse potentially damaging implications; for example, rejecting the term *research* altogether (Nate) or, alternatively, vigorously embracing it (Len). Even the unnamed mass of Anita's "troublesome individuals" may well be engaging in forms of work resistance to co-opted creativity. Together, preserving artistic creativity, including its alliances with many forms of artistic research, grounds the institutional-artistic critique in this chapter. Participants named many concerns and consequences of artistic research's intersections with the new spirit of creativity.

This chapter establishes how there are multiple compromises made between artistic creativity and the new spirit of creativity including more diverse types of creative research activity, funding possibilities, and possibilities for inclusion. For example, recombination allows for interesting hybrid arrangements between research and artistic practice and more diverse definitions and approaches. This form of compromise relation can positively contribute to the overall research culture at Imagination University. Mutual concession in this case identifies the compromise arrangements that grow out of the wider recognition and inclusion of art and design as research into academic discourse and funding streams. This loosening of academic definitions – the recognition of artistic credentials and more funding sources – is a type of concession on the part of academia and government support. However, this shift also requires adaptations on the part of faculty and administrators in order to fit into and access these new avenues of recognition and funding. Yet vulnerability features in this example when the compromises required are too imbalanced, foremost serving institutional interests and gains at the expense of diversity and belonging. The new spirit of creativity can be used to dismiss certain artistic practices and disrespect individuals; its central principles can be mobilized to justify divisions, competition, and exclusion at Imagination University.

Chapter Four

Audit Culture: The Ambiguities of Creative Excellence

Ayana, a pre-tenure, racialized faculty member, described to me the degree to which her job performance at Imagination University is more heavily scrutinized than that of others, often with no clear process or justification for why she has to regularly deal with unwanted "special attention" from her chair and even the dean. She traced the origins of this behaviour to a student complaint she received during her first semester at the university – something that "could happen to even the best prof," but which unfortunately happened to her just at the onset of her position. The conflict emerged over what was a challenging creative exercise in her classroom; a student, "at a guess, misinterpreted" the exercise, but as Ayana defends, it "is my job to push creative boundaries … I didn't even think about it." For her, what made this situation especially troubling was that when she asked, for example, why the chair was now dropping in unannounced to her class, her question and related concerns were dismissed by using the language of professional development opportunity; as Ayana characterized it, the "scrutiny" she experienced was passed off as "a professional development opportunity" for her. This institutional surveillance was framed in terms of support, even though a number of the interactions violated the school's collective agreement, but as Ayana said, "What do you even do?" Not without irony, she noted that this so called "support" was markedly absent when the student first lodged the complaint; few readily expressed solidarity with her around the unpredictability of students and classroom activities. While relaying the toll of this experience on both her health and professional life, the objective of her story was clear: the language of professional development was deployed to obscure an underlying problem – discrimination shadowing everyday operations. Ayana was certain that this experience was connected to her status as an untenured, racialized female faculty member. The scenario described here is a troubling account of how evaluation can be put to use at Imagination University, and one that resonates with current research on especially racialized women's experiences in academia (Ahmed 2012; Henry and Kobayashi 2017).

While Ayana described how she was evaluated and penalized for being out of step with white institutional culture – the university as "white space" (Anderson 2015) – this was also a conflict over creative pedagogy. She developed a provocative classroom exercise, which, it appears, was deemed *too* creative by the institution.

While the previous chapter explored the growth of research as a key transition at Imagination University, this chapter examines another related change: the increased formalization of day-to-day procedures and mechanisms of evaluation and accountability. There is considerable academic research on expanding practices of evaluation and measurement within universities; this research examines the wide-ranging effects of new assessment and management techniques, especially in terms of ever multiplying demands and expectations placed on employees (Brenneis, Shore, and Wright 2005; Deem and Brehony 2005; Hedgecoe 2016; Shore 2008; Strathern 2000a). This is no different at an art and design university; faculty regularly produce documents that explain and account for their personal and departmental activities and achievements. What is different, however, is the premium placed on creative excellence and accomplishments at these institutions. If "academic excellence is produced and defined in a multitude of sites and by an array of actors" (Lamont 2009, 3), this chapter demonstrates how creative excellence within academic institutions is hard to characterize, especially because it is defined by a wider array of actors outside of academia. As Gerber frankly captures it, "defining 'quality,' like 'value,' is a real problem in the arts" (2017, 7). What happens when creative practices and audit culture meet within Imagination University?

This chapter examines how the new spirit of creativity develops frameworks for the evaluation and accountability of artistic activity. It elaborates on what sort of criteria are mobilized within the university to measure quality and productivity. In art, design, craft, and media, peer-review processes are often less formalized compared to the gold standard of double-blind peer reviews for academic publishing that features so strongly in academic research career trajectories. In the arts, a community of peers recognizes the quality and contribution of a work when, for example, it is included in a major exhibition or film festival, but the process of inclusion by a curator or the infrastructure of decision-making in a gallery or organization is much more diversely realized compared to that of an academic journal article or government funding agency. Moreover, the impact of an artist's or designer's work to those without specialized training can be extremely important to discussions of quality; being positively embraced by a community or general audience is a sign of achievement. Further, unlike academic journal articles or books, which are not remunerated, potential outlets for peer recognition in the arts include a much wider range of unpaid and paid scenarios as key markers of professional recognition. For example, commercial success in terms of art sales or gallery representation can be highly regarded because it is so difficult to achieve.

Consequently, this chapter focuses on how institutional actors navigate and understand conflicts around artistic quality and creative outputs; it identifies informal and formal mechanisms at key moments of institutional judgment: hiring, the curriculum vitae, and performance review/promotion. The examples discussed in this chapter highlight the role of informal mechanisms to the culture of evaluation at the university. As Ayana described above, her identity and creative practice fell under scrutiny, but this sort of pressure and surveillance was not counted by the institution *as* evaluation. The new spirit ushers in new ways to judge creative practices, yet an enduring feature of the artistic critique, as sketched out in chapter 1, is a resistance to standardization and rejection of the regulation and evaluation of creativity. When applied to university evaluation culture, the artistic critique rejects many features of the quantification of ideas and the implementation of metrics that institutions rely on to organize and prioritize ideas of value and professional contributions. However, as this chapter also documents, compromise arrangements develop as the merging between metrics and creative criteria occurs nonetheless.

Designating and Measuring Creative Value

The union between institutional evaluation and art and design practices is especially fraught. Universities are tasked with the production and, increasingly, measurement of knowledge, while artistic practices are often limit cases that dramatize the social production of designations of value; thus, they are more likely to produce debate or uncertainty. This curious marriage creates a distinct culture of producing and questioning evaluation and accountability mechanisms at Imagination University.

The sociology of valuation and evaluation stresses the role of collectively generated, socially produced commitments to ideas of quality and how different modes of legitimation and boundary making attribute meaning and value (Boltanski and Thévenot 2006; Hutter and Throsby 2008; Lamont and Thévenot 2000; Zelizer 1985). As Lamont argues, the sociology of evaluation and valuation is "useful for understanding the cultural or organizational dimensions of all forms of sorting processes and for connecting microdynamics of exclusion to macrodefinitions of symbolic community and patterns of boundary work" (2012, 202). There is currently a heightened interest in these processes because measurements and determinations of value have myriad implications for how hierarchies are maintained, or, conversely, how heterarchies might flourish (Lamont 2012). The critical study of evaluation provides another perspective on the social production of inequality and meritocracy, where the stakes, put simply, are quite high. As Shore and Wright argue, the "glass cage of coercive transparency" capably invents new mechanisms to authorize exclusions (2015, 422). Yet at the same time, the dilemmas of evaluation are such that collective commitments to quality work and excellence are not empty. For example, while all universities pursue discourses of excellence in teaching and research as part of their public responsibilities, these claims are not pure artifice. Generally, faculty do not in private confess a true commitment to mediocrity. Rather, when individuals do not feel fairly assessed, there is a readiness to identify a flaw within the criteria for excellence, not a flaw in the aspiration for quality. As Lamont's study of peer review argues, more often than not there is a genuine commitment to the production of quality research in disciplines. Most academics, even while acknowledging that objectivity is not a stable category, "still care deeply about 'excellence' and remain strongly committed to identifying and rewarding it, though they may not define it in the same way" (Lamont 2009, 11). Imagination University is no different, but it must deploy both artistic and academic criteria to measure quality within art and design practices, and this, not surprisingly, invites uncertainty and contestation.

It's All in the Form

It was an exercise in failed experimentation. No matter how expansive my ideas, there was just no, like, actual form available.

– Mel, study participant

In the above quotation, Mel is not talking about the inability of her creativity to find material expression. Instead, she is talking about a piece of paper – that is, her need for a form that she could fill out that would justify and explain the research, material, and budgetary needs of an especially prolonged teaching and research project. When trying to inventively harness resources, a recurring stumbling block is that there is simply no existing administrative route to recognize a project's needs and approach; the trenches of administrative paperwork are such that few interconnections are easily dug. But what Mel found so remarkable and baffling was that "so many, many documents" seem to inspire "such reverence" – people obey the available form. Mel recounted that the people she was consulting for help were not making up excuses – they genuinely wanted to help – but the absence of correct paperwork was deemed an insurmountable barrier. Others explained this power of forms in terms of budget lines that determined how things could and could not happen, especially, it was noted, in terms of collaborative possibilities across areas: "We don't have a budget line for that," mimicked Shaina, when she was talking about trying to develop a seminar for art and design students from different areas. While these examples are symptomatic of a need to guard resources during times of scarcity (and adhere to established accounting practices), there are limited options within everyday operations for supporting a range of creative, collaborative opportunities. There is an absence of institutional documents to account for work in different combinations or unexpected ways. The domain of institutional accountability constructs limits to creative practices.

There is a substantial body of scholarship concerned with the rise of audit culture in universities and its emphasis on elaborate measurements of quality and productivity. Here, the term *audit* is used to capture the extension of the logic of accounting to institutional life. Audit culture includes the many types of performance measures and quality assurance protocols embedded within institutional practices. Parker and Jary predicted the impacts of audit culture's institutionalization as follows: "[F]orms of scrutiny will hence be translated into committee structures and audit technologies to ensure that goals are being met. 'Quality' research, like 'quality' teaching and administration, will require bureaucratized regimes of surveillance to ensure that it is achieved, labelled and rewarded" (1995, 328). Or as Shore and Wright explain, "audit has been released from its traditional moorings, inflated in importance, and now, like a free-floating signifier, hovers over virtually every field of modern working life, and has now become widely applied to realms with no previous association" (2000, 59). Audit culture within Canadian universities is aligned with new public management trends in general and the valorization of transparency and efficiency within public service provision (Griffith and Smith 2014). For example, some disciplines are more vulnerable than others; the humanities are regularly identified as out of step with the new stress on measurable outputs. Its time-intensive research processes and less immediate or applied results, not to mention less direct employment pathways for graduates, places it more at odds with new public management principles. So while hostility towards the academy historically has been preoccupied with humanities disciplines (Belfiore 2014; Donoghue 2008, 1–23), audit culture gives this animosity contemporary ammunition and a wider target as the fine and applied arts gain profile as university degree programs.

Strathern explains the importance of understanding the impact of audit culture as follows: "Procedures for assessment have social consequences, locking up time, personnel and resources, as well as locking into the moralities of public management" (2000a, 2). Ongoing assessment exercises subtly erode the quality of institutional relationships and experiences in a number of ways, with pronounced consequences for universities and academic workers. First, evaluation metrics set the stage for easily dividing up academia into winners and losers – or, rather, low and high performers. Resources and esteem are attributed accordingly, and the workplace veers towards greater stratification along the lines of not only hierarchies of temporary and permanent employment (chapter 6) but also productive and unproductive researchers (chapter 3). This facilitates a climate of competition that serves to reward individual pursuit at the expense of collegiality and support (Sparkes 2007, 532). Too much stress on profile and research prestige can cultivate a workplace culture of self-interest.

Second, it establishes a dynamic of surveillance and mistrust between employer and employee. There is an animating presumption that workers, when left to their own devices, will not be sufficiently productive. Employees' professional autonomy gradually diminishes when day-to-day operations start to unfold from this underlying suspicion (Lorenz 2012, 607). This climate extends to the use of language itself, where audit culture enables a distortion of terms like transparency, efficiency, and accountability. As Strathern argues, an emphasis on transparency and appearance always means that another "kind of reality is *knowingly* eclipsed … As the term accountability implies, people want to know how to trust one another, to make their trust visible, while (knowing that) the very desire to do so points to the absence of trust" (2000b, 309–10).

Third, when universities place so much stress on measurements of value, performance, and efficiency, it starts to negatively interfere with a university's commitment to the advancement of knowledge (Collini 2012). Audit culture starts to foreclose, not invite, innovation and risk because outputs and time management are less predictable when research or teaching becomes more experimental. Yet, as Parker and Jary argue, it is not just a matter of designating changes in higher education as "simply good or bad" (1995, 319); rather, scholars need to carefully examine how shifting university management rationales and practices often mix positive and negative effects together. We need to understand these combinations to effectively mitigate the negative consequences.

Within this wider context, the arts have been especially suspicious of the rise of audit culture in universities, in no small part because these areas produce work that does not generally do well under standardized metrics. It does not sit well with the principles of artistic creativity. Further, there is a tradition of heavy resistance to the academicization of art and formalization of curriculum specific to art schools (Adler 1979; Tickner 2008). The academicization of art and its accompanying apparatus of determining quality are often criticized for constricting creative practices and possibilities, and even artistic identities (Suchin 2011a, 2011b). Canada, however, has not yet been pushing through standardized research or teaching assessment with the same vigour as other countries. Compared to, for example, the UK or Australia, Canada represents an enviably less pronounced metrics-driven university environment. As Maretta noted, compared to her previous position at a university outside of Canada, "here, it is still manageable … there, it is impossible to manage all of the expectations … the hours a day on admin stuff and nothing else."

There are a number of external ways that creative practices are evaluated at Canadian art and design universities, such as via arm's length public funding bodies such as SSHRC,[1] the Natural Sciences and Engineering Research

Council (NSERC), and the Canada Council for the Arts. But there is an array of other forms of recognition as well, such as juried awards, exhibitions and festivals, and corporate partnerships that are not necessarily directed by a formal submission process or awards committee. Here, peer recognition can have many informal dimensions that are not readily captured. For example, inclusion in a prestigious exhibition or festival program can depend as much on art world networks and the predilections of the curatorial team as it can on systematic evaluation and decision-making processes. But even within government funding bodies, peer juries are used to account for quality and expertise, yet often without directly spelling out what this means except in very general terms (such as saying the work in question "makes a contribution to the field" or "shows evidence of creativity and originality"). SSHRC describes its review process as follows: "Grants and fellowships are awarded through an independent merit review process designed to ensure the highest standards of excellence and impartiality. Merit review is a transparent, in-depth and effective way to allocate public research funds" (2021b, para. 1). As the definition suggests, it is the transparency of the review process that ensures effective, merit-based peer review; this is a way to leave open questions of interpretation and quality to the individual review committee.

In addition to these external examples, collective agreements are also a resource for understanding institution-specific internal evaluation procedures. Marnie discussed the example of an outraged faculty member who contested the appointment of tenure to another individual: "I got cornered in the hallway, 'Why did that person get tenure?' ... All I can say is, 'This is your collective agreement.'" One collective agreement used the language of peer review dozens of times and in a way that seemed to both justify the performance evaluation process and place responsibility squarely on peers, rather than the institution itself (OCAD Faculty Association 2016). Generally, these agreements refer to achievements in teaching, professional practice, or scholarship, leaving considerable flexibility around how professional performance is to be assessed (e.g., ECUAD Faculty Association 2014; Faculty Union of NSCAD 2016; OCAD Faculty Association 2016). While discretion cannot be dismissed simply as resolutely positive or negative (Satzewich 2014), it does invite the potential for unevenness in interpretation.

Institutional actors regularly perceive missteps in how evaluations are enacted. Both institutional and informal processes meaningfully impact careers and employees' relationships to these careers – just ask any faculty member who feels that they have been unfairly judged. These policies and procedures have clear consequences for employees. The next section examines experiences of evaluation, both in terms of performing evaluation and being evaluated. A number of questions and conflicts arise in practice, especially when the peer reviewers are your colleagues and (at times) friends. The terms of reference become wider – both inside and outside the institution – and more open to interpretation when creative practice is under scrutiny.

Judging Others and the Boundaries of Creative Practices

The following section explores how artists and designers describe processes and conflicts that emerge over the assessment of creative practices at Imagination University. Conflicts are telling examples of boundary making within professional practice. As Gerber argues, "conflicts take the form of distinct routes to valuation; they do not pit value against values but aim to include some bases of value while excluding others, and in doing so, they shape the boundaries of artistic practice" (2017, 29). These accounts reveal how employees determine and navigate boundaries according to the demands of institutional and personal contexts. When participants identified uncertainty, conflict, or critique, the examples regularly concentrated on the following: hiring, performance reviews, tenure and promotion, and the curriculum vitae. Taken together, the analysis demonstrates how disputes often emerge at the intersection of informal and formal cultures of evaluation and where tensions exist between artistic creativity and the new spirit of creativity.

The Hire

The hiring process was one of the most frequently identified sources of disagreement over evaluation. Hiring lays bare questions of how to evaluate credentials – a process that was regularly identified by committee members as "beyond just a list of items to check" (Nate), necessitating more than simply following the description of requirements in the advertisement. As Mel explained, the required qualifications can be clear (e.g., an MFA, a PhD, a record of publication and/or exhibition history) but individuals are prone to value some features more than others. Descriptions of these included, for example, specialist knowledge that makes a certain publication, exhibition, or collaboration come to be disproportionately weighted. Individuals may be equally qualified, but their creative products are not equally valued. Mel provided the example of a candidate who had been included in a group show at a prestigious museum. She described a heated dispute in the ranking of the short list because of interpretations over the value of this particular achievement, of whether to measure it as "more than a *just* a show – is that possible? What does that even mean?"

When participants provided examples of hiring disputes, the bulk of the cases centred on questions of quality of the so labelled "creative outputs" and the value of graduate degrees. In both art and design, small-scale independent publications and even self-published books are an important part of demonstrating currency, but they may have little name recognition and do not follow standard peer-review processes. Thus, how to assess questions like relevance and impact often becomes harder to ascertain. As Dominic commented, "What does audience or relevance mean when you do small, experimental work? … What if not having an audience is a good thing? … We just aren't always sure." Saeed similarly explained how the process too often works to the detriment of artistic creativity: "It so often flourishes in diverse and marginal places, and this is very hard to measure in formal procedures." There is necessarily a problem of future tense within the hiring process. Shaina talked about how difficult she found sitting on a hiring committee for the first time because of the tensions around quality and qualifications. She described the pressure to "see the future" during the hiring process, because creativity in art and design is something that you "can't totally measure in the now" because it is often only "recognizable later." This, in turn, relates to questions of how to assess credentials that invariably trip over the complicated status of advanced research and degrees in the arts (chapter 3). This issue of graduate degrees was presented as a "loaded question" (Maretta) for many reasons. It created awkwardness (best-case scenario) or professional disrespect (worst-case scenario) within committees because people may or may not possess the credential under discussion: "What you are saying about a hire applies to someone in the room, but um, people forget." In this sense, comments that one candidate is less qualified because they do not have a PhD can sting a colleague unintentionally.

Underlying these conversations is how to evaluate professional experience versus education within a context where an increasingly higher premium is placed on academic achievement within the university. As Claire noted, when her department was having a debate over the value of terminal degrees, two members had complained that the artists with PhDs were "'too academic' – they didn't say quite that, but that's what they mean." She explained to me the connotative meaning in more detail: these candidates do not bring the same level of artistic practice to the job because too much of their time has been devoted to academic inquiry. This is a recurring concern voiced by participants. For example, Patrick, who does not identify as "you know, a PhD artist … but as an applied artist and designer," worries that these very academic art practices are "too cerebral" and "less useful" for students and teaching. So in one context an artist or designer with a PhD is highly valued, but other times, depending on the area and the constitution of the committee, there can be clear "hostility … or antipathy" (Claire) towards graduate credentials.

However, advanced degrees were not always pitted as a have or have not scenario within the university. In other cases, hiring committees were more concerned about external perceptions and potential conflicts. With these examples, committees struggled with whether academic funding bodies would accept terminal MFA or MDes degrees. The committees were comfortable with valuing professional and applied expertise sometimes above advanced degree attainment, but would the external funders agree? Marnie described a specific case where she was on a search committee for a prestigious research chair, one in a new design and technology area where the committee was concerned about what the applicant pool would look like. In this case, the committee was not split over the PhD as a requirement or not – they thought the best candidate may or may not have a PhD. The concern was "whether or not the funding body would expect a PhD." The committee had a lengthy discussion when designing the advertisement about whether or not to require it. Members of the committee were worried that if they did not, this might discredit their hard-fought status as an emerging research institution. Conversely, if they did require it, this might invalidate the specificity of art contexts and credentials. In the end, the position did go to an individual without a PhD, and with relative ease. In terms of how to manage anxieties over external expectations, Heath reflected, "Maybe it never mattered? Things are changing so what to expect is a moving target at all points."

When the topic of hiring did emerge, if participants did not pinpoint moments of conflict over credentials or priorities, they identified conflicts over austerity – the infrequency of being able to hire despite ongoing needs. Sometimes this meant that faculty simply could not recall being part of a recent hiring committee for a permanent position, but when they could, the reduction in job opportunities created its own set of problems over assessment. Specifically, when a tenure-track hire search is launched, there are usually many, many qualified applicants. Saeed describes this as "above and beyond … what you might expect, or what previous searches had produced." Claire threw up her hands, a sort of gesture of defeat, when she described the last hire in the department because there were so many roundly qualified applicants: "We almost didn't know what to do … It was overwhelming, so many people." When there are so many applicants, the issue becomes one of "micro attention"; this is how Claire described the act of looking hard to find ways to exclude people, especially because so many meet the desired qualifications. The concern here is that points of exclusion start to seem more and more trivial, and more and more open to individual biases and wider norms. So, as Chianne characterized it, people start to look for more random points to highlight – one publication or conference, or the location of a residency. And, these might, she tentatively suggested, be "more about your own biography." She used the example of herself wanting to do a residency at a celebrated arts centre. When she reads an application, does someone who has been awarded such a prestigious residency stand out more to her, because of this desire? It is both about personal biography but also the affirmations of dominant culture. So, in various examples cited across interviews, participants noticed that high prestige associations are more likely to be used as a heavy-handed metric to separate a large group of equally qualified individuals.

Following this line of reasoning, in a tight job market, you might create a stronger web of exclusion, not a more robust realization of excellence. The limits of meritocracy and its ushering in of many assumptions about talent and value (Littler 2017) become clear as faculty reflect upon and analyse the hiring process. Many participants' descriptions of the hiring process counter the predominant idea that intense competition creates stronger procedures and stronger applicants. These accounts suggested an alternate reading. As Dominic argued, the weak labour market strains existing issues in the hiring process – often, no one "wants to take chances" – and by chances, he means "going off the script" of standard qualifications. Instead, "flashy" things, which are impressive points of distinction, can be lodged in ways that create easy tiers that do not allow for more time and reflection around accomplishment as a process. It can miss the "complex process that is part of artistic work." Instead, the current climate requires "sweeping points for judgment," one that also has serious consequences for artistic diversity; namely, it is most likely to align with dominant genres and creative identity norms. Generally, this dynamic will favour those who already fit the "ideal type" or the "current fashion"; in this regard, Dominic is pinpointing how assessments of artistic practice are also about hitting the mark of creative currency, which is subject to change and more likely to reproduce itself under conditions of economic constriction.

The Creative Self and the CV

A centrepiece in the above conversations around credentials is, of course, the curriculum vitae (CV). Sparkes (2007) portrays the complicated relationship to the CV that university culture produces through the perspective of Jim, a professor and director of research in the UK. Jim is preparing with a sense of disquiet for the upcoming Research Assessment Exercise:

> But here, in this arena, he feels obliged to play a game in which the *curriculum vitae* as a central feature of academic life and an autobiographical practice becomes a call to account for the self that one is. When the panel members read the *CV* and the publications as performance outcomes, they are reading the self-story of the person. As part of this routine, they are encouraged to read the gaps and listen to the silences in the *CV* in terms of what it tells them about the person – about the self. This self is then judged accordingly and consequences follow. The *CV* as an autobiographical practice and presentation of self is a risky business. (2007, 535)

Drawing on Sparkes' perspective on the CV as an "autobiographical practice" and "risky business," this section identifies different ways participants struggled with how to represent their artistic identities on paper through this defining form of institutional testimony. The CV for many artists and designers stands in distinct contrast to the portfolio, which is generally regarded as a more accurate and telling account of one's work. As Patrick says, "In design, it's portfolio or bust." This stress on the portfolio instead of the CV as the better representation of not only one's work but also one's self appears at other points in the institution as well. For example, at OCAD, a portfolio is described to students for admissions purposes as "a collection of work that represents your individual creative and technical experiences and accomplishments and should be a visual representation of who you are" (OCAD n.d.b). Or, as Kat explains, the "the best picture of my work is my portfolio … but a university is somehow more about everything else." She continues to describe how "everyone judges your professional practice, but actually spends very little time carefully looking at what you do … What if my work is just really terrible? They don't catch that. Supposedly it's everything … but no one really *sees* it."

When it surfaced in conversations around qualifications and evaluation, the CV was regarded as an institutional document that is "tedious" and "formulaic" (Jack) – an "exercise in paperwork" (Ayana) for all types of review. The CV is an imperfect capture of aesthetic practices. Yet when participants spoke of career documentation in forms like the CV and review reports, one of the strengths of the art and design school is that individuals take these things, as Mel puts it, "with a grain of salt." The CV may well be the default standard for academic evaluation in universities, but in this context, faculty readily recognized its limits. This is best represented by the way people distinguished between the CV and the self by stressing that it is just a "piece of paper" (Jack), "a form letter" (Nate), or a "pile of stuff" (Kat); these phrases make clear it is inanimate and distant from artistic identity. This is a way to make sure it is not mistaken for the creative self. So, apart from required reviews, in practice there is also the sense (outside the hiring process) that "no one cares as much about stuff like CVs here … because it is about the work itself" (Ayana). In an environment that specializes in questions of representation, scepticism around the capacity of a CV to represent one's achievements is easily grasped. The CV is made to matter, so it does "have weight – grants, funding, you know" (Shaina) – weight that employees linked to perception and profile. But the CV was also described as flawed, literally. As Shaina confessed, it is "so hard to keep track of dates … titles … everything. I don't always get it 100 per cent." She admitted to errors in her own self-accounting of her timelines and activities. But this was not distortion, she explained, because she had completed everything she said she had, but she might forget to add things, or maybe gets a few dates wrong. In essence, not aiming to be "100 per cent" was also a resistance to this format for presenting career information. In a similar spirit, Chianne spoke of trying not to put too many details about her career on the university website for public consumption; this was a way to "avoid categorization" as well as the sort of "comparisons" on which so many institutional representations thrive.

This was a common thread – an objection to institutional modes of presenting achievements – for both aesthetic (poorly designed, unattractive) and informational (the need to demonstrate achievements) reasons. The portfolio is a point of contrast to the limits of the CV and is considered a more reliable portrait of one's achievements and skills: this is where the quality of your creative practice is more evident. Drawing attention to the value of the portfolio is a way for faculty to disarm some of the more deleterious impacts of the merging of the CV and self that university evaluation culture cultivates. While the premium placed on the portfolio can be challenging within the wider gig economy of cultural work (Ashton 2015), within the context of the art and design institution, and where job security and social networking is not on the line in the same way, it becomes used as a measure of contrast. The portfolio is better able to capture quality creative work that the CV is more likely to diminish. The CV, in this context, is aesthetically inattentive, and this rankles employees when their expertise hinges on aesthetic knowledge. There is a clear critique of the aesthetic limitations of the institutional format and its embrace of the new spirit's quantifying impulse – and this critique (at times) creates a helpful separation from a demanding contemporary university climate that too often reduces an individual to a CV. But this raises another dimension to the issue: how exactly are CVs put to use?

Review and Promotion

While performance reviews and the procedures for tenure and promotion are set by established criteria in a collective agreement at Imagination University, these criteria always require interpretation. To be sure, the stakes are high when not only job security is on the line but also professional reputation for those involved, and there are many aspects to interpretation.

Faculty did not hesitate to identify, as Chianne put it, "really amazing work" produced by their colleagues. It seems no one struggled to identify excellent work from their own perspective, and with little talk about the need for transparency and process. This is not how it is cast. So, "What is amazing work?" I inquire. Well, according to Len, it is something that you immediately "get or recognize." Heath concurs: "You know it." According to Ayana, it is something that "is time and complexity" and "sustained process." As Mel says, it is "not the same year after year … this is growth, adaptations," so evidence of change becomes a point for consideration in terms of quality. Accomplishments identified as impressive included the following: exhibitions, solo or small group, especially in major public galleries or internationally recognized venues; grants of all types; awards – someone noted a jury prize at a film festival and another person an award from a professional association; a large-scale collaborative project with other major institutions; a book being published, which could be a conventional academic one, a popular book for a general audience, or a trade art or design book; and a community project that benefits a wider group. People generally did not mention peer-reviewed journal articles or conference presentations in the accounts of what stood out as evidence of notable achievements – tasks that are considered a staple of academic achievement. If publications were mentioned, it was books and generally not peer-reviewed journal articles, and when individuals specified types of books, the examples used were art books and independent press books.[2] The most stellar accomplishments are those that "stand out" (Patrick). Yet this order of quality was noted widely as the hardest to find – relatively infrequent, but easiest to spot – and few were troubled around the social or institutional contexts that shaped perceptions of quality (except, as noted above, during aspects of the hiring process). While no one used the term *genius*, these descriptions are the closest moments throughout this entire study to reinforce creativity[3] as some sort of elusive, individual talent.

While faculty regard their own perceptions of excellence as trustworthy, when they recounted personal experiences of being evaluated, the conversations most often turned to discouraging moments when accomplishments were not fully recognized during the evaluation process. These events are always characterized as notably upsetting both personally and professionally and usually hinged on disagreements around quality and productivity. High-quality work is overlooked because of slower productivity, or the calibre of achievement remains under recognized. For example, Jack recounts a conversation with his dean about an instance of the latter. He wanted to know what had happened during his review; in his words, "[he] had just worked [his] ass off" and felt this was not accurately reflected in the review. He recalled what the dean told him: "Oh, you did great, but your show wasn't really important enough to get an exceptional review." Jack cried foul at this elusive criteria of "important"; his work was included in an exhibition at a major Canadian public gallery, but, to his mind, the reviewers were applying criteria appropriate for promotion to full professor, not yearly review. Reading between the lines of the dean's comments, Jack deduced that an international venue, apparently, was what one needed to be regarded as "spectacular." But as Jack groused, "Who does that, especially at an early career stage?" And, as he continued to explain, he really had little recourse to challenge this assessment, especially given his rank and status as a full-time but contractually limited term employee.[4] Further, his query had been posed during an informal conversation with the dean. If anything, he felt that there was an unofficial component of "wait your turn" in terms of recognition, where the school did not want to reward him too much, too early, because this disrupts ideas around the "endurance test of art" as well as institutional investment. While Jack deftly identified different components that contributed to the review, including wider ideas about the relationship between time, quality art, and employment status, he was also quite clear that this experience had been very disheartening. And he definitely felt that there was a high level of off-the-record associations around artistic career development impacting the formal process.

Chianne described a similar situation while preparing for a yearly review. During a conversation with her chair, she recalled being told that earning her PhD did not really count as creative or scholarly activity; instead, her chair said it looked like she had a considerable gap for the first two years of her position. In this case, Chianne explained that the implication was "you should have finished your degree before you were hired." But as she pointed out, she was hired without the degree: "They knew!" She noted the deep irony: earning the highest degree credential was somehow a strike against her since it was seen as an impediment to her productivity and not an essential component of her profile and expertise as an artist-researcher. Further, she was hired to anchor the university's new commitment to Indigenous art and culture, yet in practice, her own qualifications were hesitantly recognized instead of celebrated. This is a telling example of the sort of micro-aggressions Indigenous scholars experience at Canadian universities (Bailey 2016; Canel-Çınarbaş and Yohani 2019).

Kat voiced her general frustrations with the review process as follows: "You have all the right things, but then don't have the right things, but when you are worried about something, it will turn out fine. Instead, it will be something else that's not fine or misinterpreted." For Chianne, this "something else" was being penalized for earning a PhD, but for Kat it centred on an independently published book that was "a grassroots manual for creative change, really well received though." Kat was advised by a dean during a tenure and promotion discussion that favourable recognition of this popular audience book "couldn't be guaranteed" – something she felt was deeply insulting to her time, labour, and creativity. In sum, there is an uncertainty around what to expect or predict of the professional evaluation process that is specific to art and design because of the heightened uncertainty around creative recognition and qualifications.

Collegial silence is another, perhaps less recognized, feature of this process. This is a strategy people spoke of when not being sure about how to evaluate someone in a given scenario, like tenure and promotion, but it came up in terms of grant and jury competitions as well. When there is no "Aha!" moment of excellence, faculty expressed some doubt about whether or not they were being "fair" in their evaluation – what are the valid points to bring up? Importantly, the examples participants provided about this dilemma focused more on issues of productivity than quality. As Patrick put it, "I might not, you know, get someone else's thing, but I don't say … 'that's not good work.'" He continued to explain how he must respect "creative differences" and assume that it is quality work. However, what did raise questions about quality for him were gaps in activity or not a lot of production of any sort – things that suggested "low commitment." But there was a qualifier offered here as well: "If it's very slow to do and make, like a feature length film or an insane installation work, but you can tell when it's a slow practice instead of a no practice issue." This was referred to elsewhere as "no follow through … or incompleteness" (Anita), "stunted activity" (Len), and "unclear direction" (Heath). These characteristics were most concerning when in the context of hiring or promotion. Thus, evidence of commitment and perseverance are more important to these assessments than aesthetic judgment. There is considerable room to respect another's themes, style, or medium; however, ample evidence of professional activity is required to pass the test of commitment to practice. And, in participants' responses, the need for a tenure and promotion committee to see this evidence is tied to the difficulties of making a career in art and design overall. As Shaina made clear, "growing a career … it's hard. It's exhausting, so easy to not do. It is the true test, the marathon you don't run." The difficulty of surviving in the arts is cited as why activity level is so decisive when files are being reviewed, especially early career; "If you are not active now, early on, you are done" (Ayana). So, evidence of ongoing creation is way to establish accomplishment, while at the same time it avoids what could be much thornier questions of aesthetics and quality.

When output stands in for professional commitment, however, there are consequences for individuals who are perceived to have a weak commitment to their creative practice and/or job. This is another version, as discussed in the previous chapter, too, of how in practice Imagination University seems to divide its workforce up between those who are deemed creatively productive and those deemed creatively unproductive. As Marnie explained when speaking about her early career and performance reviews, "I was not taken as seriously when my children were young." Likewise, Claire noted, "I have a number of chronic health issues, so I think my patchwork of activity raised questions." In instances concerning health or caretaking responsibilities that had impacted career development timelines, the outcomes were positive in the end – they were all promoted – but the perception was that these matters persist, and often because of informal practices. That is, subtle slights or micro-aggressions that "suggest you aren't really it [an artist]" (Marnie). In these cases, it was this everyday dimension that was the real issue. As Claire explained, she felt as if she were being judged regardless of what her actual performance review said, and this created stress and strain; she could not just "blurt out medical complexity" to account for her absence during a meeting or in the hallway. But further, it is the uncertainty around what does and does not matter that has such a powerful, everyday workplace effect. As Shaina explained, "I don't think my kids are a liability to my career, but then I doubt myself. Like, colleagues ask me about my kids, which is good, but not about my work … like they wonder if I am doing anything and think it will be embarrassing if they ask. It's just a sense that might be happening." During interviews, only women noted struggling with how health or caretaking responsibilities were impacting everyday perceptions of their creative practices and job performance (see chapter 5).

While the general tendency was to respect creative diversity, ideological concerns did surface in the context of tenure and promotion, where participants noted feeling at odds with some of the themes or assumptions being made within a creative practice. Sometimes this was described as feeling like someone's output was not socially relevant enough: "Like, what's this even, er, for? Or, who?" (Nate). Kat, for example, explained how she had trouble with art practices that seemed "too indulgent" and "purely self-referential … not in the world." Being too commercial could also be a problem, but only when a practice was seen to be "purely commercial," meaning it was boring and pandering to the patron: "You can be commercial … it's allowed … being dull, that's another issue" (Len). This is something faculty wanted to be able to address during reviews but found they could not. As Saeed summed it up, "Can boring bar you from promotion? … It can't" – but as he went on to suggest, maybe it should, because it is one of the only things that distinguishes the art and design university from other universities.

Dominic was more philosophical about this point, where boring was an informal criterion widely used, but not without some irony. He drew on the example of John Baldesarri's *I Will Not Make Any More Boring Art* (1971). The double bind is written into the artistic project itself: repetitive, tedious lines of text asking you to avoid the very thing it is doing (making boring art).[5] Thus, this work is an appropriate parallel for the complications of mobilizing evaluation criteria within an institution. It uses the evaluation category of "boring," while simultaneously critiquing and producing it. In a very different type of example, Marnie focused on a particular example on a colleague's tenure file for promotion to full professor. She discussed feeling uncertain about how to review a history of professional activity that seemed to consistently imagine social identities in a very conservative way: "It was concerning but not so explicitly that I could exactly say, ah, 'this is racist.' What do you do in this sort of scenario? You cannot ask or object." Nate later explained that, frankly, even if an artwork was explicitly racist, the professor would probably somehow, "distortedly," be covered by academic freedom. Dryly, Maretta noted that "social change, even with the idealism of art school … aren't part of tenure and promotion"; intellectual disputes are part of the experience of committee reviews, but "can't be mentioned." Yet, significantly, these disputes have the ability to intrude in indirect ways. As Marnie concluded, since her experience she has always carried doubts about this person, and this "probably might" influence future work relations.

This brings up another dimension to the way formal evaluation intrudes into everyday work life. Faculty often made distinctions around their approach and responses when it was their own department or faculty, and when it was another professional context of peer review, such as a grant or jury committee. Some mentioned that they felt the need to keep quiet about question marks they had about an individual's professional record more so when it was a colleague within their own institution, and not an anonymous external reviewer. This is captured by what Patrick called "good or very good means mediocre" during performance reviews. He explained that in the context of the university, it is his job as a good colleague to augment what everyone does – and, secretly, "hope it's not as weak as I think it might be." Because, as Nate put it, "Am I just being a jerk anyway?" In terms of collegiality, individuals recognized it is probably best to remain quiet within their immediate context, something that is not required in more anonymous review scenarios like a grant adjudication committee or blind peer-review context that can protect you from "any personal implications of your professional opinion" (Marnie). The size of the university is crucial here. Imagination University is small, so this makes it hard, even behind closed committee doors, to feel like any conversation is strictly confidential: "You need to act like nothing is in confidence … this you learn along the way" (Jack). In this regard, anonymous review is regarded as the ability to be franker in your assessment. But at the same time, blind review allows people to be "as a matter of course … too harsh, unrealistic. *Too* harsh" (Claire). Individuals identified the two-sidedness of the scenario of internal versus external peer review, where as a colleague, silence is a way to provide more support and openness to your co-workers' practices, yet in a way that means peer review may not be as rigorously applied as within blind review contexts. But the upswing is that it will not be unnecessarily harsh either. Context and existing relationships shape the process in important ways that are more resilient to formalization yet also harder to pin down.

The Openness and Uncertainty of Interpretation

This chapter identifies a number of insights around the growth of evaluation culture as one key consequence of the new spirit of creativity. Senior administrators regularly acknowledged that what constitutes an art and design practice is more open to interpretation, and this is an opportunity and a trial: how does the institution settle on processes of organization and evaluation? At the same time, the artists and designers in this chapter expressed deep commitments to quality and integrity in artistic work. Faculty discussed excellence in terms of immediate recognition that is hard to account for – you always "know" or "get" the really brilliant work or profile. But most, it seems, do not fit in that category. Faculty voiced clear scepticism around the appropriateness of many types of evaluation and in a manner that is in line with the strongest features of artistic creativity and the artistic critique. The artistic critique has been especially critical of attempts to reduce creative work to standardized outputs and economic values, and this concern surfaces throughout this chapter. There is widespread unease at Imagination University that conventional university evaluation approaches can jeopardize creative diversity. Yet institutional-artistic critiques of standardized measurements are also not so straightforward. In keeping with insights from the wider literature on informality and cultural work (Gill 2002; McRobbie 2015; Wreyford 2015), this chapter has demonstrated that informal or less clear processes for measuring value and quality persist within institutions too. Individuals are keenly aware of the wide discretionary and interpretive components that determine so much of what happens, yet these are often hard to point to or name and can swing either way. They recognize that it can be used to protect or support colleagues and to push back against the formality of documents such as the CV, yet the limitations and oversights in the process are keenly felt when you have been subjected to an unfair evaluation. The sense that you are being judged or watched, but with no way to verify it formally, is unnerving. Likewise, faculty recognize that sometimes ideological disagreements are hard to shake. Thus, despite a tendency to reject standardized metrics, at times the openness of interpretation becomes a source of disagreement between institutional actors and anxiety for individuals. With institutional evaluations of creativity, compromise comes via formal types of mutual agreement, as with collective agreements that set out terms around hiring, review, and promotion (mutual concession), but also in day-to-day arrangements that forge hybrid forms of artistic and academic judgment to make sense of the need for artistic-academic specificity (recombination). These evaluation processes, however, can also exact compromises that institute new forms of precariousness within Imagination University (vulnerability).

At its worst, evaluation culture under the new spirit of creativity can cover up and justify discrimination and risks violating the labour and equity policies in place, as was the case with Ayana at the start of this chapter. Evaluation that is not even recognized as such can be even more threatening than formal frameworks. Or it can constrain creative practices and collaboration, as was the case with Mel's quest for a "form" that could account for her activities. Similarly, when twinned with austerity (e.g., fewer hires), evaluation is not a catalyst for meritocracy; instead, judgment seems more arbitrary. You need to find more and more ways to dismiss the achievements of others and make abrupt decisions around what constitutes excellence. It validates more prestigious and elite forms of creative value. Consequently, the new spirit of creativity and its emphasis on tangible outcomes, expansiveness, and instrumental vision can blur boundaries between formal and informal assessment, disguising some of the more detrimental dimensions of audit culture.

Chapter Five

Performing at the "Shit Show": The Conscripted Performers of Institutional Identity

The term "shit show" surfaced during my first interview with Kat, a more recently appointed tenure-track faculty member at Imagination University. She referred to her day-to-day work life as a routine act of "performing" at a regularly playing "shit show." These two key themes – performance and institutional disorganization – guided our entire conversation. The first theme (performance) started with the demands made on Kat's identity as an artist, demands that she found very unexpected. It seemed to her that without adequate resources (e.g., studio space, equipment, advising staff) to support students, a key pillar of the institution's recruitment and training strategy was to rely on the personality and draw of the artist-professor. Her identity, she explained, was at the service of the institution, but at considerable cost to her own sense of self and capacity to fulfil all the requirements of the job. The pressure to perform her role as an artist for the institution, and to have the success of the performance measured in terms of student numbers and forms of public visibility, made for a burdensome work environment. The second theme from this interview hinged on the organization of the institution itself, which other faculty members variously described as "fragmented" (Nate); "maddening, full of changes" (Saeed); "unstructured" (Maretta); "maze-like" (Len); and "scattered" (Ayana). This is the "shit show" – all the things that linked back to administrative processes that people spoke of with caution and uncertainty. This chapter examines another key transition under the new spirit of creativity's shift towards entrepreneurialism and instrumentalism at Imagination University: how institutional identity and image interferes with employees' creative identities.

The first section of this chapter advances a multidimensional understanding of performativity (Alexander 2011; Butler 1988, 2015; Callon 1998; Mackenzie 2008), stressing the relevance of both the economic and cultural facets of the concept to the organization of work at an art and design university. Performativity is also relevant to understanding shifts towards performance-based assessments and the commodification of knowledge in higher education

(Kenny 2017; Roberts 2013). In this case, I use institutional performativity to discern the new spirit's repositioning of cultural labour at Imagination University. Identity conscription, when the institution draws on the creative identities of its employees to rebrand and assert creative success, is one main feature of the new spirit's institutional performativity. In the second section, this chapter explores how faculty at Imagination University demonstrate keen awareness of how creative identity and institutional identity entwine. To understand the textures of performativity within the logic of institutional organization, I identify three strategies that faculty use (identity-recognition, identity-disguise, and identity-protection) to critique and disarm institutional co-optation and its blurring of work and non-work time and professional identity. In the third section, I elaborate on how evoking "shit" – what I term in this chapter *institutional abjection* – is a way to critique the heightened vulnerability experienced by some workers, especially untenured women and racialized faculty. The conclusion of this chapter makes a case for the many reasons why scatology (from Bataille 1985 to Freud [1940] 2010 to Kristeva 1982) is an apt description of the performative character of cultural work in a public university under the new spirit of creativity.

Compared to other universities,[1] as well as to the creative and cultural industries, the art and design university is a relatively progressive workplace from a gender equity perspective. It has been widely noted, however, that the creative and cultural industries "are better at recruiting women than at keeping them" (Conor, Gill, and Taylor 2015, 12). This is especially salient because, while feminist critics of the cultural economy have carefully dismantled its "cool, hip and egalitarian" image (Gill 2002), current research continues to demonstrate the successful maintenance of gendered creative hierarchies and the consequences for women-identified workers, especially racialized women, in these fields. In this light, Imagination University represents a sort of "best-case scenario" for women in these fields. However, this chapter tempers any easy celebration of the university as a progressive workplace by examining the costs of institutional performativity on employees' identities. Thus, while institutional-artistic critique informs a range of critical responses and tactics, the compromises between artistic creativity and the new spirit veer most towards vulnerability in this chapter.

Institutional Performativity and Cultural Work

Kat was not the only participant to draw on the language of performance when describing the many ways she had to execute her artistic identity for the institution. Shaina similarly described how she felt like the lead character in a "puppet show," especially during her first few years at Imagination University; she was expected to nimbly respond to any number of directives from above, such as the request to develop a new and innovative program, to secure external research grants, and to pursue private–public partnerships. To be a puppet in the performance places even more emphasis on constraint and raises a central issue when evaluating the confluence between cultural labour and performativity: assessing the role of coercion.

Women-identified faculty members, most often pre-tenure, referred repeatedly to their experiences at work as "performing a part," "playing a role," or "acting." However, in the context of our conversations, these phrases were not expressions of uncertainty around how to inhabit their new positions (i.e., not evidence of impostor syndrome). Instead, when participants referred to their work as a demanding sort of performance, they were critiquing a range of procedures and techniques that solicited and legitimated the staging of such roles. For example, student recruitment activities were identified as one way Imagination University wanted to have distinctive artistic personalities on display. As Shaina explained, "You can't link the success of this program to my personality. It's not just me. I've seen it happen to a lot of other people. It's just like a trend that happens." Further, this "trend" – to rely on the dynamic personality of an artist – seems to operate in lieu of other forms of support. Shaina continued:

> They expect students to be like, "Ooh I want to work with this professor, I really like them," and then they're gonna take their classes and come to this school, rather than giving the appropriate support in the studio or making sure that the program is sufficiently funded so that students can experience success.

Kat provided further insight when describing how she was pressured to become a "cheerleader" for the university:

> They're like, "Every one of our new programs needs a champion." And I'm like, "No, you mean that you want a cheerleader." Champions are like … they are successful. Cheerleaders just talk really nice – really well … I'm the program cheerleader and I'm supposed to do all the recruiting. I teach most of the courses.

Cheerleading, in this sense, is another form of puppetry. You are not a full participant in the game, but it is your duty to support the outcome, nonetheless. Cheerleaders are usually relegated to the sidelines, and Kat accurately uses this comparison to convey her sense of constriction. Her recourse is to draw attention to the strategic distortion of the meaning of *cheerleader* on the part of the school. Taking my cue from how participants drew on the language of performance to describe difficult aspects of their work, I use performativity as a critical concept that can help to disentangle the larger stakes of these descriptions; performativity can capture the everyday procedures of an institutional and economic context that asserts both growth and austerity.

Economic sociology and cultural sociology recognize performativity as a concept attentive to the social constitution of meaning and the temporality of social practices and identities. Within the context of Imagination University, assembling an understanding of both economic and cultural dimensions of performativity is a way to assess how often vaguely identified experiences of neo-liberalism are constituted and practiced. Critical social science challenges the claims of dominant economic models and their purportedly transparent representation of the world. As Mitchell identifies, economics realizes its importance, "not just for what it says but for what it does" (2005, 298). These models are "world-making," but as Christophers argues, "the performativity of economics can end up being a rather empty truism unless the wider social and political materiality of such economics is explored and conceptualized" (2014, 83). The implications of this are striking: a model starts to create the world in its image, not the actual circumstances purportedly directing the model. Callon's assertion that "economics, in the broad sense of the term, performs, shapes and formats the economy, rather than observing how it functions" (1998, 2) opens the dialogue between economic and cultural performativity.

Callon's actor-network theory approach has been an influential framework for rethinking the study of economics. For Callon, performativity is a "convincing" approach to understanding a central contemporary paradox: "How can a discourse be outside the reality that it describes and simultaneously participate in the construction of that reality as an object by acting on it?" (2007, 316). By developing the concept of socio-technical *agencements*[2] – basically, "professionals and observation tools required to carry out the calculation" (321) – Callon demonstrates the ongoing construction of textual and material complexes that constitute economic performativity (assemblages, as actor–network theory would have it). This approach stresses how techniques and tools shape and circulate economic discourses across an institution and does not confine analysis to specific actions or decisions by administrators. Thus, in the context of this discussion, it recognizes the economic logic of institutional austerity as produced and explained by webs of action, interaction, and effect.

Similarly, MacKenzie (2008) identifies three levels of the performativity of economics, from weaker to stronger versions. The first is the "generic performativity" of everyday ways that sees economic concepts put to work by market participants, policymakers, and regulators; so, while economics is performed in a way that is not external to everyday processes, this generic level is not using concepts to actively shape or impact these economic activities (16). Conversely, the second level, effective performativity, refers to actions that make a difference: "the use of a theory, a model, a concept, a procedure, a data set, or some other aspect of economic process to count as effective performativity, the use must make a difference" (18). The third level, what MacKenzie terms "Barnesian performativity," is where economic processes or outcomes are altered in order to better conform to the model, which creates "self-validating feedback loops" (19). For example, a university declares a new austerity model for organizing operating budgets. To meet these objectives, an art program must prove its economic worth to maintain its funding, but this model does not recognize the higher costs or specificity of delivering studio courses; in turn, enrolment drops because of lack of learning and recruitment resources, which then validates the initial claim that the program is not economically viable. However, this mismatch between economic theory and practice opens up space for "counter-performativity" – best captured as the unintended consequences of this economic ordering. So, while the administration further streamlines resource distribution to paper over the disjuncture between everyday practices and formal economic objectives, counter-performativity diminishes institutional sustainability, creates uncertainty, enables work distance, and even voices criticism (Cushen 2013). These are the disorienting organizational components observed by faculty that I cited in the introduction. Hence, if we bring the uncertainties of economic world-making to social and cultural identity, the relevance of performativity to Imagination University becomes clearer.

Beyond economics, performativity is also a key concept in cultural sociology and the study of everyday life. The performance of everyday life is inseparable from questions of power and social identities (Alexander 2004, 2011; Butler 1988, 2006, 2015; Goffman 1990). Alexander's scholarship on performance and power, in keeping with his wider work on the autonomy of culture, theorizes a meaning-centred cultural pragmatics between social ritual and strategy: "All ritual has at its core a performative act" (2004, 534). The success of a social performance depends on the seamless interconnection of the various parts, while a failed performance conveys artifice and contrivance (529). In this regard, cultural pragmatics effectively centre the performative grammar of power, bridging macro and micro lineages. This approach stresses the importance of context and multiple components such as audience, actors, staging, scripts, and mise en scène that are all part of who has access to the means of symbolic production. These components dramatize what authorizing perspectives are on display and what practices of authenticity are required to legitimate the performance. Alexander describes how securing a successful performance is more challenging in the contemporary moment given the "ambiguous and slippery contexts for performative action in which we find ourselves today" (529), where disillusionment and scepticism of authenticity become more pronounced as a feature of social openness. As he explains, "creative efforts to mount counter performances" (568) are necessarily part of the dynamics of social performance. In this context, faculty compile the small-scale failures of institutional performance (for example, the failure to convincingly justify budget allocations) and create forms of counter-performance that critique and expose the character of institutional performativity (to be discussed in the next section).

Butler also excavates a theory of performativity rooted in both social constraint and possibility. Her theory of gender identity uses performativity to account for the instability of identities amidst relations of inequality: "Gender is in no way a stable identity or locus of agency from which various acts proceed, rather, it is an identity tenuously constituted in time – an identity instituted through a *stylized repetition of acts*" (1988, 519). The processes of instituting and constituting are significant here – both are required, mutually informing performative iterations, but repetition betrays an underlying instability that can also open up possibilities for resignification. With performativity, there exists critical possibilities for the "the cultural transformation of gender through such acts" (521). Placed in the wider context of her oeuvre, the double-edged nature of performativity grows into a theory of precarious living (2006), as well as collective action and embodied solidarity (2015). As another facet of social identities, Butler uses precarity to explain lives defined by insecurity, unpredictability, and differential exposures to risk and violence. Butler accents how the embodied nature of performativity comes, at times, with personal costs. In the context of Imagination University, this surfaces, for example, within participants' accounts of the physical and psychological stress of trying to keep programs afloat without the required resources. Kat summed this up succinctly as follows: "I didn't anticipate how/what a toll it would take on me and the rest of my life … for that to be formally in place as a strategy from the university."

Together, these theoretical perspectives on performativity ground the relevance of the concept to organizational practices. Performativity aligns with economic and social power, and in ways that shift how institutional actors define, reward, and accomplish tasks (Kenny 2017). In this case, the concept of institutional performativity disentangles diverse declarations and interpretation of the neo-liberalization of higher education and its impacts on everyday work life (e.g. Brownlee 2015a; Giroux 2014; Taylor and Lahad 2018; Tuchman 2011; Whelan, Walker, and Moore 2013; Simpson 2014). Employees used the term *neo-liberalization* to describe current challenges at Imagination University in three main ways.[3] The first interpretation referred to conflicts over scarce resources. Common examples cited for this were unmet requirements for studio space or materials, non-existent department budgets, the disregard of student needs, and the refusal to provide new hires despite demonstrated need. The second interpretation emphasized the displacement or outright refusal of responsibility; this referred to moments when the institution would use economic reasons to minimize or deny their responsibility to respond to an issue or problem. Common examples cited for this meaning were blaming external circumstances when topics of labour security or equity emerged. The third version underscored the way individual-level approaches were expected to explain or solve collective problems. This championing of individual responsibility means individuals have to navigate institutional problems on their own – it becomes an individual burden to deal with insufficient studio space or student complaints about reduced course offerings. Other examples participants cited were when individual decision-making or choice was expected to solve wider organizational issues; for example, administration suggests that faculty use their time more efficiently rather than address increasing teaching and service workloads.

I offer these examples and associations with neo-liberalization to describe how this much-used term is understood in practice. It is a term that has currency as a catchall, but I want to make clear that it is most meaningful when tied to the study of specific experiences and formations. Employees capture and characterize these conditions in ways that indicate the dilemma of repetition and effect that concepts of economic and cultural performativity always pose in the above theoretical accounts – be it Callon's socio-technical *agencements*, Mackenzie's feedback loop of economics, Alexander's aesthetics of performance and power, or Butler's socio-cultural theory of identity performativity. The relationship between repetition and effect remains central: the repetition legitimates the effect – it justifies the conditions that then validate the initial intervention. Accordingly, the discussion in the next section illustrates how these features of institutional performativity impact work identities under the new spirit of creativity. Yet, also in line with the above literature, these dynamics simultaneously invite counter-performances of artistic critique that can destabilize and reassemble meaning and protect artistic creativity and identity.

Creative Identities at Work

There is considerable interest in the construction of creative identity as part of occupational identity in cultural work (Fine 2018, Morgan and Nelligan 2015; Taylor and Littleton 2012, 2013). A defining feature of cultural work has been its heightened emphasis on identity and image as part of the worker's toolkit for success, and this emphasis is representative of wider shifts in labour and economy. It is a familiar line – that the move to a knowledge and service-based economy has dissolved many of the presumed divisions between work and life, work and identity, and produced more hybrid work-based subjects. With changes in work and labour becoming harder to predict, the relationship between work identity (paid work) and personal identity (sense of self) has been a central theme in contemporary critical perspectives on work and employment (Beck 2000; Du Gay 1996; Ross 2004, 2009; Sennett 2007). In an offhand comment towards the end of our conversation, Len described his gay identity as "an advantage" in the specific art and design environment (in contrast to a comprehensive university). Being gay, he explained, was a type of "cultural capital" because art schools view mainstream identities with suspicion. The tone of this comment was both serious and in jest, but the truth to the point is cutting. The "joke" is that he knows that his sexuality is being used to uphold the institution's image as progressive and tolerant. Against a wider contemporary landscape of work–life hybridity, this sort of personal–professional identity bleed for artists and designers assumes distinct features within a university context, especially for historically marginalized identities.

Gender, as a socially ascribed identity, becomes important to discussions of professional creative identities in a number of ways, where dominant concepts of creativity continue to disadvantage women in the acquisition of top-tier creative roles (Gill 2014b; Jones and Pringle 2015; McRobbie 1998; Stokes 2015; Wreyford 2015). Yet masculinities are also subject to this creative hierarchy where, for example, working-class young men similarly struggle to inhabit the role required for success (Morgan and Nelligan 2015). Taylor (2011) argues that women's identifications as creative workers draw on conflicting articulations of creativity and norms of feminine subjectivity. Social expectations of women's "other directedness" conflict with the idea of self-actualization through creative work. This conflict between creativity and sense of responsibility to others is something that can be drawn on to the benefit of Imagination University. Yet meeting this dual demand comes with a cost at the level of identity. As Shaina explained, she was surprised by "how much the university's expectation of you is strongly linked to your identity and your personality, and I found that's the transition I found the most difficult. I didn't expect to have it precipitate an existential crisis."

What Shaina described is both the emotional labour and work devotion required to be an artist for the institution. Creative identity in this context is strongly tied to both of these concepts. Blair-Loy's (2003) "work devotion schema" provides a cultural account of how employers and employees justify and maintain an allegiance to work. The schema requires the following: allegiance, provision of rewards (not only financial but also social), intensity, and single mindedness. For example, allegiance is secured with the promise of rewards such as "upward mobility, financial security, a positive sense of identity and recognition from peers, challenging and autonomous work, collegiality, and even transcendence" (22). Increasing rewards, however, also bring increasing demands, and "her work may take on a single-minded, emotional intensity that fuses personal and professional goals and inspires her to meet these goals" (22). While Blair-Loy's research on work devotion and successful professional women is not widely cited in the cultural work literature, it captures many important features of the gendered characteristics of work commitment and its conflicts. The culture of many professional workplaces now orients around work devotion and the ongoing demonstration of an employee's worth; identity performance becomes proof of dedication to work. In many cases, the importance of the work devotion schema becomes clear only when it is transgressed. These are the moments that people are most likely to draw attention to during conversations and most often use to judge the missteps of others – for example, the complaints expressed in chapter 3 by upper administrators that faculty are not producing tangible research outcomes at the same pace as other institutions. In part, the moral undertone that comes with the presentation of this scenario is one of disappointment that some faculty lack a commitment to advancing the institution. And, similarly, in chapter 4, the perception that uneven productivity might indicate a low commitment to one's creative practice surfaces during performance assessments.

At the same time, even if a breach has happened, this does not necessarily mean that there is agreement around how the demonstration of devotion has been fractured. For example, active participation in the faculty union was a divisive issue in terms of work commitment. For some, contributing to the union was an "obligation" (Nate) or "responsibility" (Mel) to the need for ongoing dialogue around working conditions and practices. However, others expressed disagreement with the strategies and approaches of the union; it was "time wasting" (Patrick) or cast as "tedious complaining" (Darryl). In essence, one view sees the faculty association as a violation of work devotion – nothing is more condemning than to be a waste of time – while another view sees it as an expression of dedication to the job and all its responsibilities. Importantly, work devotion always exists alongside critique (Blair-Loy 2003, 24–6). Imagination University requires higher levels of work devotion as creative identity expression, even as awareness of this requirement and the ability to critique it coexist, but this comes with affective repercussions.

As Hochschild's [1983] (2012) classic study of the centrality of emotional regulation within employment demonstrates, there is no one type of emotion at the core of emotional labour. Instead, emotional labour can require the careful refinement or solicitation of any range of positive or negative affective responses within paid employment. Thus, it is the equality of distribution of requirements and impacts that becomes a key question for the critical study of labour and employment. As Hochschild explains, "In any system, exploitation depends on the actual distribution of many kinds of profits – money, authority, status, honor, well-being. It is not emotional labor itself, therefore, but the underlying system of recompense that raises the question of what the cost of it is" (12). During times when employees must do more with less because of budget constraints or calls for greater efficiencies, the demand for emotional labour is even higher; yet alongside this, management and policy create conditions that inhibit its supply (125).

Emotional labour is more expected and desired with the consolidation of economic performativity outlined above; it is part of the rise of the "service oriented" university.[4] Within higher education, emotional labour assumes many forms (Constanti and Gibbs 2004; Meanwell and Kleiner 2014; Postareff and

Lindblom-Ylänne 2011; Woods 2010), including tools such as the Higher Education Emotional Labour (HEEL) scale (Berry and Cassidy 2013). Teaching difficult topics relies on an unacknowledged and invisible emotional labour for instructors, but especially because it is not evaluated as work within the increasingly complicated metrics for productivity advanced by contemporary universities (Koster 2011, 62). Even just the everyday management of extension requests is a delicate balance of student and instructor well-being (Abery and Gunson 2016). Academics continue to value the amount of autonomy they have with decision-making and variation at work, and yet how much this will change as more and more accountability measures are implemented (as is the trend) remains key to current research (Hemer 2014, 493). It is increasingly difficult to deal with the encroachment of other work on existing work, where work intensity and load are the most commonly cited sources of stress (Anderson 2006, 580). However, there are ways that academics develop strategies to resist and maintain academic research identities, even as this often increases the life–work overlaps. As Anderson explains of her research results, "[A]cademics had radically different notions about what constitutes 'their own' time … [and] several academics referred to research as their 'own work.' They thus clearly delineated their 'real work' – research – from their administrative responsibilities" (585).

Within the creative and cultural industries, emotional labour is part of the intensity of creative production in the industry (Hesmondhalgh and Baker 2008); specifically, emotional competency becomes a way for especially women to secure or maintain work (Kerr and Kelleher 2015). Gill (2014a) explicitly connects the emotional labour of academic work and cultural work, noting how both types of worker struggle to meet the often-unreasonable employment expectations that extend beyond the geography of the workplace. She locates commonalities between the two domains and their models of identity and success, such as DIY-biography, reputation-based opportunities, and network sociality. Like the cultural industry, Gill notes that university cultures of surveillance, uncertainty, and time pressure produce detrimental effects, including socio-psychological injuries that are now incorporated into everyday worker identities. Consequently, a key challenge is how to better understand the "psychic life of academic and creative labouring" (25). There is perhaps no better place to start than to consider the hybrid case of artist-academics within higher education.

One Position and Many Jobs

Maretta explained that she had not one job but many to fulfil, both part of and distinct from her university employment. She emphasized her endless multi-tasking during our interview, when we chatted in her office/studio space as she moved student projects around and took random bites of a chicken wrap. She explained how she imagined the distinctions and overlaps:

> That's more my, like, general professional identity rather than me as a kind of [employee] … But at the same time that identity is evaluated as part of this thing … yeah, you have to be really good at this job, but you also have to be doing all this other stuff. Yeah, it's like ten jobs in one.

Given this complexity, in this section I locate a number of strategies faculty members, especially women, employ to resist institutional co-optation: identity-recognition, identity-disguise, and identity-protection. The example of Kat at the start of this chapter represents identity-recognition. This is when an employee is aware of and able to critique the demands of institutional performativity. This is captured by the different ways participants deployed the language of performance and talked about feeling pressured to script their creative identities in ways aligned with institutional identity and strategy. Other examples included the need, as Shaina dryly noted, "to always be your best self" at school events, and the "hunger," as Ayana described it, for you to have a "bigger, better, bolder" social media profile that, conveniently, references the school frequently.

The next term, identity-disguise, is when employees intentionally mask the desired solicitation of characteristics. This surfaced in chapter 3 as a critique of the commercialization of research – the different ways people would deny or displace their knowledge or skillset (e.g., Nate) – but it is especially relevant here. Importantly, this strategy demonstrates both awareness of the identity demands of work and also finds a solution to identity bleed via heightened ambiguity. Disguise is a way to foil expectations and demands placed on your creative identity. Other examples include reworking labels and boundaries of practices. Chianne explained: "My interdisciplinarity is hard to characterize … this is, like, a good thing … less pressure actually. It's a bit hard to tell what's going on. I like that." Or, as Mel commented, "When people here say, 'You're a new tech designer,' I just say, 'Well, not really.' This way, they can't figure out what to expect when they are trying to force an idea or creative label on me." Likewise, limiting the amount of information about your creative practice on your university profile, as Mel discussed in chapter 4, is also part of this approach. This is a strategy that makes the terms of reference harder to stabilize: you are less likely to be asked to perform if the university does not like or understand your act.

The final strategy, identity-protection, is when faculty develop ways to distance their professional identity from the institution. During interviews, it became clear that creative identity from the perspective of some faculty is something that must be protected to survive; it seems survival as a professional artist or designer requires separation, otherwise the university "owns" (Kat) too much of your time. Sometimes, this separation takes the form of little things, such as not revealing you teach at a university "unless asked" (Shaina), or not mentioning your university position on your personal website (Jack). In fact, faculty identified many little ways that they manage to carve out time and maintain their creative activities. For example, Kat found a way to continue producing her smaller-scale handcrafted items because she could complete one in a short block of time and then build towards a large-scale installation. She distinctly made a point of considering this activity as "outside" of her institutional profile. However, identity-protection can also assume an urgent dimension when cast alongside racialization. In Ayana's case (see chapter 4), she felt she had "no choice" but to consider leaving her position. The "emotional and psychological toll [is] too much. Unbearable." This is the price of not fitting the institutional expectations placed upon one's identity and creative practice. In this version, the ultimate form of identity-protection is exiting the university altogether. But, in another example, it can also speak to protection from misrepresentation, as Chianne carefully explained of her uneasiness as one of the few Indigenous faculty members:

> I will never, ever let myself be used as the "face" of the organization – you know, on websites and recruitment things … I say this explicitly, and yet it keeps coming up, being rephrased, as if I won't notice it this time … The real, real issue, though, is that they want my "look" so *they* can look more progressive.

In this instance, Chianne is talking about the university's efforts to recognize diversity as an important creative value. The institution wants to employ her identity so that it can appear more current and inclusive, but they are unwilling to listen to her concerns about this approach or what it suggests about the genuineness of their commitment to belonging and equity. And this leaves her subjected to endless repetitions. This is a drain for her, but she has drawn a clear line: she will not be the face of the institution and allow her identity to be mobilized this way.

The serious stakes at the core of identity-protection bring questions of gender and racialization into focus. Only one male faculty member, also racialized, recognized the bleed between his creative identity and institutional image as a pressing issue with the potential to erode artistic creativity. Saeed's approach to identity-protection was, when required, to reduce his teaching load (and pay) in order to have more time to produce his artwork, despite the financial hit (because he generally worked on collaborative and non-commercial projects). He had made a conscious decision that, rather than do a "bad job" and still try to collect his full salary, he felt more comfortable stepping away and making space for his practice outside of the university. However, it is hard to separate his concern for institutional encroachment with his status as a racialized faculty member. In the same conversation, he also expressed both fatigue and disappointment around how under-represented social identities were responsible for advancing equity at Imagination University. In this sense, he said "representing the role of marginalized other" was a job requirement in order for the university to reconsider their practices and responsibilities. And usually, he continued, to a fruitless end. The university, he explained, is "disproportionately white" and "out of step with the diversity of the city it calls home." However, "too many pockets" of the university are resistant to considering the university's obligation to this wider social context. This was an added burden to his work duties, and he noted the absurdity that the load should fall on those already disadvantaged. All the while, Saeed noted, the university eagerly used his artistic successes to augment its profile.

Similarly, Chianne explained that as a recent appointment and an Indigenous woman, "identity work, equity work, decolonizing, indigenizing ... is all on my shoulders ... and it's not possible. There is no conversation we can really have" – except, as noted just above, when it involves promotional material. Chianne struggled with the inability to have meaningful dialogue around (never mind to dismantle) the status quo of naturalized white privilege within the institution. As she wryly observed, "after hundreds of years of colonialism" she should be "able to get a grant or two" without other, largely white faculty getting jealous, but this was not the case; she described having to tip-toe around her success. This was made all the harder because, much like Saeed, she also found herself fielding requests to place her at the centre of university campaigns: "The school is actively promoting this success." As Ayana thoughtfully put it, at issue is how the institution fundamentally conceives of racialization, ethnicization, or indigeneity itself, where instead of fruitfully "re-imagining this knowledge space ... the discussions kind of amplify binaries around race." Despite ongoing conversations, substantial changes are stalled because whiteness and privilege cannot be discussed: "The majority of the faculty present as white and the majority of the management present as white, the support staff present as white, it is predominately white." These comments echo recent work on diversity, racialization, and belonging in the academy (Ahmed 2012), including work specific to Canadian universities (Henry et al. 2017; Henry and Tator 2009; Stewart 2009; Whittaker 2015),[5] while also demonstrating how these features play out within art and design through intersecting requirements of artistic identity. The conversations cited here acknowledge and critiqued what was a double-pronged move within organizational practices. First, the university highlights the identities of racialized faculty to update its self-image as progressive and diverse. Then, it displaces much of the responsibility for equity and diversity onto racialized employees, forcing the burden for change to rest most heavily on their shoulders. In this scenario, identity-protection becomes a necessity.

Taken together, this chapter so far has illustrated the multifold intersections of performativity, creative identity, and cultural work. But, to return to my query at the start, what makes these intersections so "shitty"?

The Institution and the Abject

Much to my surprise, "shit" surfaced as a multidimensional concept during interviews. In this section, I recognize that swearing is a colloquial way to add emphasis in everyday conversation. Certainly, this is how it featured in interviews: to stress the significance of a point, not as insult or offence. But as a researcher, I felt obliged to take such emphasis seriously. Thus, I treat these regular references in my interviews as an easy to trivialize but nonetheless important way to articulate critiques of organizational practices and issues of work–life balance. And, to be sure, the effectiveness of this dynamic thrives on the resourceful nature of waste itself. So, on the one hand, as Patrick exclaimed in reference to some of the up-and-coming projects at the school, "That's creative shit." Or, in another variation, "shit-acular" (Len) was used to express positive outputs. "Shit," here, emerges as a valuable type of creative output, but this was not how the term commonly surfaced. Rather, we instead have "that's shit" (Nate) and "shit show" (Kat) in reference to impenetrable bureaucracy, and "totally shitty" (Jack) practices of everyday organization, where things "are going to shit" (Claire).[6] This usage takes the conversation in another direction, one that underscores the presence of difficult workplace priorities and expectations. Certainly, other accounts of the shifting climate in academia identify how to "feel like shit" has become a regular occurrence at work (Sparkes 2007, 524). So, what do we make of these appeals to the abject?

The etymology of the term abjection refers to a state of being cast off or separated from the whole (Kristeva 1982). Most simply, the abject is an object of disgust, and excrement widely falls under this classification. In terms of social theory, abjection is a term that accounts for how society discards that which threatens stability and order, but which can never be fully excluded: society depends on these boundaries as part of its very constitution. As Stallybrass and White put it, "The Low-Other is despised and denied at the level of political organisation and social being whilst it is instrumentally constitutive of the shared imaginary repertoires of the dominant culture" (1986, 5–6). Mary Douglas's classic text, *Purity and Danger*, deftly sums it up: to be defined as dirt in society is to be "matter out of place" ([1966] 2002, 44). Or, as Ahmed (2004) explains, through the repetition and performativity of disgust, the object becomes repulsive. Abjection adeptly accounts for how a hierarchy of human worth is a tolerated feature of contemporary global order, where great swaths of the population are deemed surplus or waste (Bauman 2011). Research on the social and political construction of abjection has been useful for understanding the rise of new forms of xenophobia in Europe, positioning nationalism as an exclusionary construct, and accounting for unresolved impacts of colonial violence (Ahmed 2004; Kristeva 1991, 1993; Stoler 2010; Tyler 2013). Compared to these high-stakes consequences of condemnation, connecting abjection to a staid institution of higher education might seem out of place. But even abjection has an institutional life, especially when placed alongside the success of neo-liberal performativity.

Certainly, the political Right has used the abject to assert their virtuousness and dispel that of others (Ngai 2009). McClintock (1995) demonstrates that abjection, as a psychoanalytic concept embedded in colonial ideologies, demarcates wretched zones and border spaces of state and economic power. Or, as Hancock argues in *The Politics of Disgust* (2004), the African-American single mother becomes constructed in media and politics as an emblematic figure of public repulsion and, thus, deserving of punitive social and economic policies. And, more recently, Tyler's (2013) empirically grounded case studies demonstrate the fabrication of abject subjects within British national politics under neo-liberalism. The comments in this chapter glance to the knowledge that there is something deeply compatible between neo-liberalism and abjection, where "shit" becomes the placeholder. As Kristeva describes, "Abjection is above all ambiguity" (1982, 11). This ambiguity resides in the inability to "radically cut off the subject from what threatens it – on the contrary, abjection acknowledges it to be in perpetual danger" (11). The abject object is the scapegoat for the fear of the unknown, which is much harder to name or to place. Accordingly, the abject is embedded in our social order, including institutions.

The abject intersects with neo-liberal institutional logics as some employees, identities, and types of work are more vulnerable, but in often ambiguous and indirect ways. Vulnerability in this case stems from the added pressure to play particular creative roles to serve the institution, and which also functions as a form of identity regulation. These performative iterations then become evidence to justify the practices themselves – everyone is playing their part! However, when employees are noting the many deleterious impacts of these arrangements and calling them out as "shitty," they are redeploying the abject in the spirit of critique. In cultural theory and practice, abjection has also been reclaimed as a category for identifying ambivalence in cultural formations and mobilizing resistance to political and cultural hegemony (Arya and Chare 2016; Berry 2016; Foster 1996). Thus, this meaning of abjection can draw on the celebration of transgression or a consolidation of critique.[7] From this perspective, there is considerable weight behind these descriptions of institutional shortcomings. These phrases are an example of the social dimension to practices of institutional-artistic critique. As Kramer argues, "scatology limits the idealization of particular narratives … the new detour to the symbolic is through the abject" (1997, 187). The case I am making here is that scatology assumes a similar function within the university. It offers an inroad to reworking institutional narratives that make inseparable the creative institution and the creative self. All of the pronouncements that rally around the sentiment "this is shit" (Mel) are ways to acknowledge how the abject is threaded through institutional life and practices and point to the seriousness underlying these offhand remarks: there are multifold costs for individuals, and for some more than others.

The Cost of Remedy

When Dominic spoke of the early years of his employment at the institution several decades ago, he referred to a moment at a faculty event: "We have a photograph of our son as a baby next to other newborns among the faculty and staff … and we were all wearing our [school] t-shirts." This was, he explained, a much earlier example of the school's "branding exercises," but quite unlike the tone of those today. So, while the identity-work blend is already apparent, it kept on the right side of collegial and collective by acknowledging and including one's life outside of work. Dominic noted the curious gender dynamics of this scene as well: the number of women faculty members was very low. If it had been higher, he suspected the embrace of faculty's progeny might not have been so enthusiastic. More recently, this chapter has demonstrated how the repetitions of institutional performativity and its mixing of creativity with austerity commands employees' creative identities for institutional gain. Driven by the new spirit of creativity's emphasis on entrepreneurialism and expansiveness, this blurring of professional and institutional identity is yet another way the new spirit has shifted the culture of work at Imagination University. But this dynamic is felt more powerfully by those who generally occupy less structurally secure positions. This chapter foregrounded performativity as a critical concept that helps us to disentangle the effects of higher education austerity measures and identity reshaping under the new spirit of creativity. Institutional pressures and reorganization under the name of a more expansive, entrepreneurial, yet underfunded, creative agenda impact employees' capacities to develop and sustain self-crafted creative identities.

As a case study, this chapter explored the gendered nature of these dynamics and examined how untenured women faculty are most subjected to institutional identity conscription, with racialization adding extra identity burdens and expectations. This chapter identified a number of strategies employees used to critique and alleviate this co-optation, mixing both social and artistic concerns within their voicing of the institutional-artistic critique and validation of principles of artistic creativity: identity-recognition, identity-disguise, and identity-protection. Together, these strategies intersect with the arrangements of creativity and compromise in telling ways. For compromise as recombination, identity-recognition and identity-disguise indicate the ways that participants use hybrid definitions and descriptions to recognize and account for their multiple roles and identities. This form of compromise identifies and reflects on the demands of one's circumstances, even if it unable to change such circumstances in any significant way. At its best, as with identity-disguise, faculty members subvert expectations – they will not provide the picture of creative identity so desired by Imagination University. In terms of compromise as mutual concession, there is little mutuality glimpsed in this chapter because of the existing context of less security within the organization for this group of faculty members; however, there are some indications of how this can change. Shaina discussed towards the end of our conversation that her sense of playing a predetermined part or role – being the "puppet" – was lessened once her activities were better supported and funded through a number of university channels:

> So yeah, since my lab has gotten a lot of love and, you know, it's started just within the last, like, year or two, it's started to feel like it has its own identity. Yeah, and with more support and students, they have started to understand and also helped to define the identity of the lab, so that's been huge.

This type of a remedy was the exception in participants' accounts, but Shaina's point is clear: with more support, her identity is no longer the cornerstone. Instead, creative identity can be more open and collaborative because, importantly, the lab now "has its own identity." This example suggests the benefits of mutuality within compromise to sustaining artistic creativity. Overall, this chapter demonstrates that creative identity compromises are more substantial for employees who must already struggle more for creative recognition – early career, gendered, and racialized employees. This is an example of compromise as vulnerability. In self-descriptions, faculty usually stressed their artistic identity over their institutional position (see introduction), but this is not entirely reducible to artistic norms of anti-institutionalism. In this example, it is a strategy for distancing oneself from workplace demands and the constraints of the school's approaches to the organization and promotion of art and design practices. Racialized faculty members' approaches to identity-protection illustrated well Imagination University's attempts to use their identities as signposts for institutional progressiveness. However, the most exacting compromise between work and creativity is having to leave your position because of this vulnerability. Ayana spoke in detail about how the personal toll and its impacts on her overall health and wellness was becoming too much to remain at the university.

She was uncertain if she would stay in her position, despite its many career and financial advantages.

When gathered together, the examples in this chapter draw attention to the "shit show" of institutional life, a position that easily finds a home in the institutional-artistic critique. This appeal to abjection is yet another way that artists and designers at Imagination University push back against the pressures of inhabiting their creative identities and offer a critique of the new spirit of creativity's institutional identity conscriptions.

Chapter Six

Navigating the Permanent–Temporary Divide: Insecurity, Flexibility, and Nostalgia

During the first two minutes of my interview with Jack, a well-established visual artist with an impressive exhibition record, he tells me that he is about to lose his job: "I have not been renewed." Pause. This was not the response I had expected. Based on my interview preparation, I was under the (mistaken) impression that Jack had a tenure-track position because he had worked at Imagination University for many years. I should have been more sensitive to the prospect of job insecurity. But here we are. I am asking him about his experiences at a university where he will soon no longer work. He is reflective and adroitly recognizes how this might impact his responses to questions about working at the university – he makes a point to say some good things about his experiences, and notes that he already has some teaching lined up elsewhere. He mentions a number of aspects he has found rewarding such as being a part of the "artistic-academic" community and having the opportunity to act as a mentor for students. Fortunately, he explains, he does have gallery representation and some dedicated collectors, which is not the case for many of his colleagues. But, after close to a decade of employment at the institution, he feels discarded: "So, at one point you know you're in. The institution likes you, you're hired, they give you responsibility, classes, awards, and then the next minute they're like, 'well, we have no use for you anymore' because of a new prerogative."

This account stuck with me, and not just because the sting of job loss hung heavy in the air. Jack's experience displayed the consequences of shifting interests that impact creative employability, even when Jack's profile conformed to an ideal type of visual arts faculty member: an active exhibition history, including success with arts council grants; a graduate degree; and strong reviews in the classroom. While he identified tangible barriers to employment stability at the institution – like a collective agreement designed to protect tenure-track faculty and the university's willingness to accept insecure contract work as necessary – he also suspected that something else was at work. He had the sense

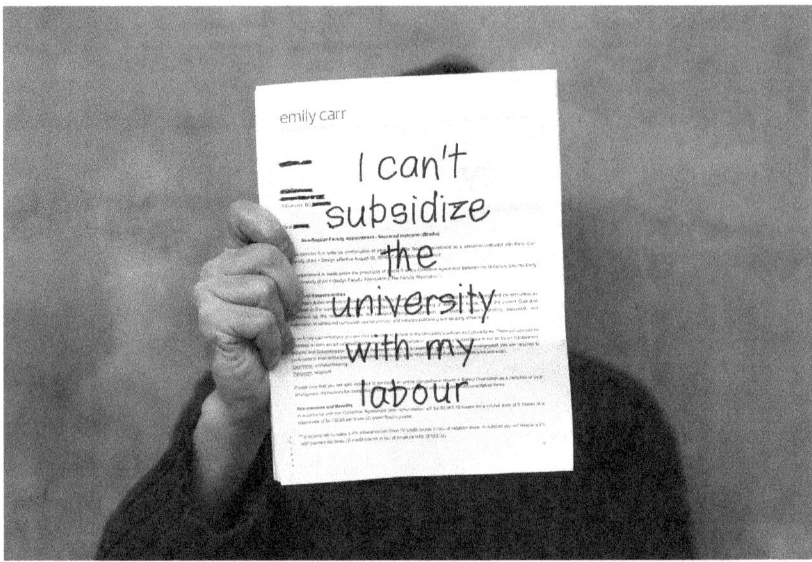

6.1 "I can't subsidize the university with my labour," 2018. From the book and art project by Terra Poirier, *Non-Regular: Precarious Academic Labour at Emily Carr University of Art + Design*. Photo credit: Ernesto (pseudonym for an ECUAD contract instructor) and Terra Poirier.

that his artistic identity was somehow out of fashion: "*You* get deemed redundant at some point."

This chapter focuses on a pressing and seemingly intractable issue at Imagination University: the permanent–temporary divide within the workforce. Sessional, contingent, irregular, part-time, casual, adjunct, per course, contract – there are many ways that these positions are referred to and described.[1] There is a substantial body of research on the rise of contingent work in academia generally; one of the most dispiriting dimensions to these conversations is that there is little evidence that this situation will substantially improve for faculty on temporary contracts. By all accounts, reliance on insecure labour in universities is only growing; it is as representative of university work arrangements in Canada as the tenure system with which the system has been traditional and widely associated. In response, this chapter makes the case that we need to better attend to the different meanings attached to contract work within the organization of the university itself. Employment security and tenure for faculty comes with a history of distrust at Imagination University, where tenure can have associations with being "stale" or "out of touch" and even "not very successful" (Nate); there is a lineage of resistance to the concept specific to art schools. While tenure is a landmark within most academic careers, in the fine arts it can be associated with a less successful, even stunted, creative career. In many respects, per course work or temporary but full-time contractually limited appointments have long been the norm at Imagination University. Accordingly, insecure work cannot be read only in terms of the recent, neo-liberal reorganization of the university; it is also an employment status long embedded in the culture of art schools (Adler 1979). There are various trajectories for how creative practitioners find themselves within academia, and how they position this teaching work as inside or outside their professional practice (Ashton 2013a). While recognizing diverse pathways into the institution, this chapter explores how the prevalence of insecure work in the cultural industries overall is used to justify its place within the university. While insecure work has always been part of the art school, the new spirit of creativity's celebration of flexibility intensifies this insecurity and its organizational justifications.

The first part of this chapter explores the existing research on contract academic work within universities in Canada. This work centres on critiques of the contemporary university as scholars grapple with both labour issues and shifting institutional values and organization. In light of the limited data on specifically art and design universities, the second section considers what, if anything, is distinct about contingent work at an art school. There is something in Jack's account, and in the accounts of others I spoke with in similar situations, that stresses the specificity of the art and design context. There is a pronounced sense that decisions are more influenced by artistic currency and style, and that insecurity is more widely accepted as innate to artistic work. It is easier to explain and accept. The third section examines how faculty and administrators understand the place of contract work at Imagination University and elaborates on everyday accounts of contingent work. I am expressly interested in how permanent employees understand the place of insecure work. Here, I examine various distancing strategies that serve to diminish the centrality of labour insecurity at the school. For example, administrators mobilize images of creative workers who demand job flexibility, or they explain a contract worker's discontent as a by-product of unrealistic expectations. And, many permanent faculty members recall their own experiences of contingent work with a nostalgic lens that celebrates the freedom from bureaucracy that this time on contract provided. Consequently, in this chapter I illustrate how artistic creativity and the artistic critique become displaced under the new spirit of creativity; what could be an opportunity for critical reflection on insecure work within the institution instead becomes a critique of bureaucracy and overwork. This case is an example of how the compromises of creative work can draw on unevenly distributed vulnerabilities.

Academic Work and Labour in Transition

The contemporary university's dependence on insecure academic workers is a regular topic of conversation within higher education circles. In addition to the substantial amount of scholarship trying to make sense of this transition, it comes up in faculty association journals, mainstream media coverage of higher education, and social media commentary as academic workers share stories about the experiences and impacts of labour insecurity within the profession and institutions. Donoghue's examination of the professor as an occupation in the US reminds present-day readers that the tenured professor who is able to research and write with considerable autonomy is a relatively new development; while "universities are timeless" (2008, xi), professors are not, and this occupational category is facing substantial challenges. Research must be careful not to assume an ahistorical understanding of university occupations, especially when considering the role of contract workers and the heterogeneous makeup of this employment group. As Kezar and Sam (2010) explain, we need to better attend to different dimensions and contexts of employment security–insecurity. They identify five main reasons why studying contingent faculty is especially complex: ideology, theory, data, heterogeneity, and historical context (8–12). Further, tenure processes are not the same across nations (Afonso 2016; Henningsson, Jörnesten, and Geschwind 2018; Herbert and Tienari 2013), and there are distinctions to be made between employment security within higher education generally, and tenure processes specifically. Certainly, the bulk of research on changes in academic work focuses on other national contexts, like the US (Baldwin and Chronister 2001; Chait 2002; Donoghue 2008; Kezar and Sam 2010; Nelson 1997; Rhoades 1998; Slaughter and Rhoades 2004; Youn and Price 2009). This research has identified many directions for analysis, such as mechanisms for job security, administrative decision-making, university funding, wider labour and employment contexts, and possible remedies. While tenure-track position ratios have diminished, in comparison to many other nations the tenure system it does have offers considerable job security (Jones et al. 2012). Yet at the same time, recent research reports intensifying precarity across higher education, and understanding disciplinary, institutional, and provincial differences remains challenging (Field and Jones 2016; Foster 2016; Foster and Birdsell Bauer 2018; Shaker and Shaban 2018).

The art and design university adds more layers to this already thorny issue by virtue of both disciplinary specialization and the history of antipathy to tenure specific to art schools. Employment security is a much-debated value in the history of the art school. As Adler's (1979) ethnography of CalArts in the 1970s recounts, the administration rejected the idea of tenure and justified this to protect the school's contemporaneity. This was "enthusiastically welcomed" (84), especially by younger faculty – a guarantee that the school would be "pruned of 'dead wood'" (85). While many faculty later lamented their job insecurity and its implications for the exercise of administrative power, CalArts is a good example of how different interpretations of the principle of secure employment for artists have taken shape in higher education.

Recent labour scholarship emphasizes how the impacts of insecure work have many dimensions beyond that of income. Vosko succinctly defines precarity as "remuneration characterized by uncertainty, low income, and limited social benefits and statutory entitlements" (2011, 2). But this assumes different contours according to occupational categories. If applied to academic work, this definition reminds us of its mixed character compared to lower wage examples of precarious work; academic contract workers must navigate considerable work uncertainty and invisibility within the university, but they also have social status affirming post-secondary education and credentials, a solid hourly wage, and often (in Canada) union representation. Yet the precariousness of this work cannot be fully understood without contrasting it with the wages and employment conditions for similarly credentialled tenured faculty. As Standing (2014) emphasizes, labour insecurity refers to more than a shortage of income earning opportunities; it also hinges on questions of working conditions and safety, job protection, income stability, and employment equity and access. To be sure, there are many varieties of impermanence, from teaching assistants to per course instructors to adjunct professors to contractually limited term appointments. The common theme is that institutions save on full-time salary costs – the largest expense in their budgets – by paying contract workers only for teaching time. Instructors are paid per course, or, for limited term appointments (LTAs), a prorated annual salary (which may involve service or research duties); per course positions outweigh the number of LTAs, with the latter being more costly for institutions and thus approved with more caution. Resources such as library access, institutional affiliation and email, and extended health benefits are only valid during the term of the contract, and often instructors experience waves of access then denial. Per course instructors usually must apply for every course, every time, while LTAs may or may not be eligible for renewal without re-application. The time required just to compile applications and apply for jobs is often daunting and adds another dimension to the invisible labour required of contract workers (Cattapan 2017).

There are many ripple effects with this type of insecure university work. For example, contract instructors are often charged with teaching the biggest classes under the most trying conditions while also being the first targets when accusations of sub-optimal teaching arise (Foster and Birdsell Bauer 2018). Moreover, research time and outputs by these instructors are not remunerated, which has long-term but easy-to-overlook impacts regarding the university's capacity to advance knowledge (Turk 2017). And yet, contingent instructors still experience pressure to publish if they hope to secure permanent work, sometimes even to maintain their temporary positions. Accordingly, under these conditions, research activities can start to resemble a "hobby" – an unpaid activity pursued outside of your usual workday – more than a profession (Black 2016). The contradictions are clear: contingent instructors are expected to realize teaching excellence despite their second-tier status, often without office space or enough paid preparation time, marking time, or student contact time. Research productivity is a metric for employability, but it is not usually supported or remunerated by the institution. These clashing expectations heighten the conditions of insecurity.

Universities in Canada are straining to keep up with major transitions in the funding and delivery of higher education. Contract instructors regularly fulfil ongoing teaching gaps as "permanent, but precarious, fixtures in most departments" (Foster 2016, 27). It has been hard to determine the exact number of contract instructors in Canada because institutions are not eager to share data – it is not generally in their best interest (Brownlee 2015b).[2] Contract instructors, most hired on part-time contracts, teach more than 50 per cent of university courses in Canada (Pasma and Shaker 2018, 5), with a more precise snapshot becoming available because of freedom of information requests sent to seventy-eight universities (14). Researchers have tracked steady growths in enrolment and declines of permanent hires, so this also demonstrates that reliance on contract instructors has generally grown (Brownlee 2015b; Field and Jones 2016; Pasma and Shaker 2018). During interviews, administrators prefer to present faculty numbers in terms of full-time equivalents; this is a way to cite a higher full-time faculty number without having to explain how many per course instructors or LTAs are used to construct this full-time equivalent.[3] That said, because studio courses are time and resource intensive, the faculty-to-student ratios are very good compared to comprehensive universities.[4]

One of the most detailed studies of contract work in Canadian universities to date remains Rajagopal's *Hidden Academics* (2002). Although based on research conducted in 1991–2, key insights from this book remain valid. Rajagopal details how declining government support and a growing entrepreneurial spirit in administration supported the growth of contract positions, yet the experiences and contributions of this workforce are widely marginalized. The publications of major professional bodies, such as the Canadian Association of University Teachers' (CAUT) *Bulletin* and Universities Canada's *University Affairs*, regularly feature stories and debates around insecure work, and often with many recommendations for change (CAUT 2016; Faucher 2014, 2015; Fullick 2015, 2016a, 2016b; Riddell 2017). However, this topic often veers towards contention because disagreements are so value-charged. While university administrators highlight the many advantages of the model and its virtues for programs and part-time workers, some critics focus more on the devaluation of higher education overall, where it is a sign of declining resources and decreasing public commitment. Others still are more critical of the tenure system itself, which requires the labour exploitation of many to provide privilege for a relative few. Media stories (often written by contract faculty) regularly provide a range of perspectives on the issue, usually translating to a wider audience how and why this is an issue of public concern (Black 2016; Chiose 2018; Grant 2018; Wunker 2015a, 2015b).

Despite the challenge of securing exact employment numbers, a number of recent studies and reports have sought to capture current contract working conditions and experiences. With responses from 227 contract workers, *Precarious U: Contract Faculty in Nova Scotia Universities* (Foster 2016) contributes to our understanding of both the provincial context of Nova Scotia and that of smaller institutions in general.[5] This research identifies a key concern within the evaluation of employment insecurity: is this employment essential or supplemental? I had many participants holding tenured or administrative roles refer to the "myth" that everyone aspires to a tenure-track position, so how do we assess this idea? In Foster's survey, 32 per cent of respondents stated that they did not want a tenure-track job. However, the reasons cited in the qualitative responses often turned to barriers such as qualifications, competitiveness, and age, and respondents suggested that they did not want a position because they did not believe they were competitive; as one responded said, "I prefer to be realistic" (as cited in Foster 2016, 19).[6] The average respondent had applied for thirteen tenure-track jobs and five limited-term appointments. Thus, claims that people do not want tenure-track work cannot be entirely taken at face value and are harder to measure once multiple factors are taken into account. The overall findings of the survey demonstrate that most workers desire more security and certainty within their contracts. As Foster argues, "Given the overwhelming desire for security evident in the survey data … the most meaningful and impactful thing that university administrators could do to make life better for their contract employees is to reduce the insecurity they face as a result of their contingency" (27). What remains poorly addressed at the administrative level are the temporal dimensions of insecurity. The most difficult aspects of contingent work are not necessarily the actual duties of the job, as one instructor makes clear:

> It isn't necessarily the work itself. It's dealing with past, present, and future all at the same time that makes things stressful. In some regards, I am still dealing with my previous course at a different university, my current job, and also trying to secure employment for the winter term. (as cited in Foster 2016, 10)

While this report captures contingent work at a cohort of (generally) smaller universities in one province, it is a further challenge to assess what is specific to the art and design experience.

Drawing on results from a national survey of academic contract work in Canada ($n = 2{,}606$), we can glean some insights into contract instructors teaching in the arts (Foster and Birdsell Bauer 2018). According to unpublished data provided by lead author Karen Foster, there were 270 respondents who taught in the area identified as "visual and performing arts, and communication technologies." This is the category best aligned with art and design teaching areas, and there were some respondents from art and design universities.[7] There are a few observations we can make about this group compared to the larger sample of contingent university workers; for instance, they are more likely to work other jobs, they are more likely to hold course-to-course contracts, they are more likely to feel insecure in a way that impacts long-term decision-making, they have generally taught as contract workers within the system for longer, and they tend to teach more courses on average. So, for example, 16.3 per cent of this subset reported working three or more jobs in addition to their contract work; this is compared to 4.2 per cent for those in other subject areas. Also, 65.6 per cent have taught for six or more years, compared to 51.1 per cent of those in other areas; 71.8 per cent were teaching course-to-course at one or more institutions, whereas this number was only 61.7 per cent for those teaching in other areas. In terms of job security, 67.1 per cent reported feeling too insecure about their prospects of being rehired to make significant financial commitments compared to 54.1 per cent for other areas. Similarly, contract instructors teaching in the arts were more uncertain about long-term plans (55 per cent vs. 44.4 per cent). They were also less likely to have a doctorate (73 per cent vs. 55.2 per cent), though I would advise against interpreting this finding as an explanation for why this group experiences more insecurity overall. As discussed elsewhere in this book, an MFA or MDes is usually the credential requirement for studio-based practices. In sum, this recent survey suggests that contingent instructors at art and design universities are more susceptible to the impacts of job insecurity.

Recently, the Canadian academic art journal *RACAR* (*Revue d'art canadienne/Canadian Art Review*) produced a themed section on contract academic work (Terry and Wark 2018) that addresses arts-specific dimensions to unremunerated and insecure labour in Canadian academia with a general call for solidarity and a radical reimagination of the status quo (Black and Burisch 2018; Cowan 2018). In keeping with the above survey results, these articles further reinforce that employment insecurity at the crossroads of art and academia is especially pronounced for contract instructors. As Black and Burisch readily connect, "Artists and academics are a surplus labour force, that is, we are highly exploitable, and the functioning of both the art market and academia depend on it" (2018, 98). Importantly, this themed section also documents the growing expectation that academic art associations like the University Art Association of Canada (and publisher of *RACAR*) should be meaningfully intervening in these contemporary debates and issues. Likewise, Terra Poirier (2018) produced an art project and book on contract faculty experiences, *Non-Regular Precarious Academic Labour at Emily Carr University of Art + Design* (see figs.

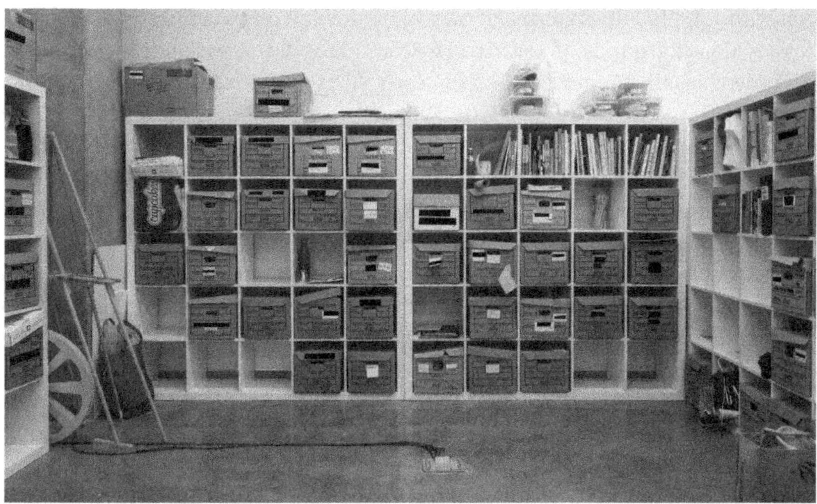

6.2   Storage cubicles in 864-square-foot office shared by more than eighty sessional instructors at ECUAD, 2018. From the book and art project by Terra Poirier, *Non-Regular: Precarious Academic Labour at Emily Carr University of Art + Design*. Photo credit: Terra Poirier.

6.1 and 6.2). The book and project – which included a photo installation set up outside of the president's office at ECUAD – pinpoints the impacts of employment insecurity. Poirier collaborated with contract faculty on this project to capture their perspectives on the many features of insecurity including inadequate office space, degrading application processes, low wages, and a culture of under-recognizing and devaluing contract labour. As one contract faculty member summed it up, "When it comes to the way I am treated by the institution – in terms of communication, transparency and a sense of being rewarded with stability for good work and excellent reviews – it's literally the worst job I've ever had" (as cited in Poirier 2018, 6). In light of the mounting critiques of contract teaching arrangements filtering into art and design discourses, the next section develops more insight into how these conditions are explained at Imagination University.

Redeeming Insecurity: Distancing Strategies and Associations

The concept of permanent, tenured positions at Imagination University comes with a history of dispute that participants occasionally mentioned. Generally, a more standardized system of tenure comparable to a comprehensive university steadily emerged in tandem with becoming a degree granting institution, but not without difficulty in terms of managing the different qualifications and professional backgrounds of instructors. Dominic spoke to me about some of the arguments against tenure during his early years at the institution; it was often cast as the "antithesis" of creativity and experimentation, considered to be the key to "lethargy in the institution." Other long-standing faculty recalled similar concerns around the idea of tenure early in their careers, while also adding that there was less anxiety about where or how one would work because there were, as Patrick said, "so many more jobs, more options. It was less make or break in terms of chances." Further, hiring was often very informal. Dominic recalled a sort of comical attempt to institute formality around the hiring process for his permanent position, with people trying to imitate what they thought a formal process should look like, but without one clearly in place. There is a history of suspicion around job security particular to these schools that stems from associations with the ideal conditions for artistic creativity as mobile, spontaneous, and distinct from "a regular job that meant permanently doing the same thing, all the time" (Nate). It is not inconsequential, for instance, that art critics attribute NSCAD's celebrated conceptual art contributions to its informal creative culture and the currency of visiting artists: "Most of the innovation happened after hours and not in day-to-day classes, and … most of the innovators – in addition to core NSCAD administrative and teaching staff … were freelance artists" (Eyland 2012, 127).[8] Originality is identified as something produced by movement through, not permeance within, the institution. Jack's assessment at the start of this chapter identifies this as a still present perception: too much time at the institution diminishes your creative currency.

As described in the introduction, this book focuses primarily on permanent faculty and administrators – that is, those who have attached their creative careers to the institution and who have participated in all facets of university activity (teaching, service, and research/professional practice). There are limitations to this design – an obvious one being that it does not account well for the contributions and experiences of contingent faculty workers. That said, four individuals who held ongoing, yet limited term, faculty appointments met the inclusion criteria and responded to my invitation to participate. Although a small group, their comments align with the research discussed above, addressing how, as contract faculty members, their contributions remained economically and symbolically marginalized through a range of both formal and informal practices, from the maddeningly inefficient application processes required for every course to exclusion from social events and hallway conversations. Their responses identified a persistent undervaluing of their time and skills at multiple points in the system.

Drawing on his experiences and those of fellow contract teaching staff, Jack captured these dimensions in many of the observations he made during our interview. With teaching, he said, you have to perform "better" than faculty, just to be regarded "equally as good," yet when the administration piles on new courses for which you do not have time to prep, this is regarded as your own "personal failing." You have to be careful socially, too. "Don't be too critical or vocal and don't offend anyone," he said; you never know who might be involved with the next round of hiring. There is also the burden of not knowing what to expect or how to plan for the future (for example, whether you have enough work to hold onto a childcare spot). Locating per course work from semester to semester, a process which "you repeat, all over again, every year," is extremely time consuming and brings unexpected highs and lows. Also, sudden changes in circumstances in a department create unanticipated needs that contract instructors feel obligated to meet in order to maintain good relations: "You say 'yes,' even when you are way too busy." But on the flipside, unpredictability was also a matter of unfilled promises – courses that should be available, but in the end were not, or LTAs that were waiting to be approved that somehow never materialized. "The chair will be so apologetic," Jack said, "but you still won't have work." Using the example of his friend and colleague, Jack also explained how you might be tasked with developing a new course, but then "admin will go out of their way to exclude you, even if you are the one with the most direct experience." In this case, Jack suspected that his colleague was not allowed to participate in conversations about the course and new subject area because the administration did not want it to seem like she "owned" or was "owed" the course, and they would not compensate her for her time. So instead, "you are abruptly shut out," which, Jack noted, feels "professionally insulting" on many levels.

These insights about contingent work suggest that it is not just important to gather data on the experiences of this sub-set of contract academic workers; we need to explore other sides of the conversation as well. For instance, how are these difficulties understood by permanent employees at Imagination University, especially given the prevalence of work insecurity within the creative and cultural industries overall?

Against this wider context, I am focusing on offhand comments by tenured faculty and administrators about the nature of contingent work and workers at Imagination University. The comments cited below emerged unsolicited – that is, a question about participants' thoughts on contract teaching was not part of my interview guide. Instead, the subject came up as part of other commentaries around everyday issues and challenges or when recounting one's personal work history. However, I did ask follow-up questions once the topic emerged, especially during interviews with upper administrators. By attending to representations mobilized in offhand comments, I am tracing out how this work is understood and justified within the everyday landscape at Imagination University. This compilation of unguarded moments illustrates many of the contradictions noted by contract instructors above, and my analysis points to common strategies permanent faculty use to explain and create distance from the emotional, economic, and social toll of work insecurity. Some faculty did acknowledge the key contributions of contract instructors to the institution, but comments that thoughtfully reflected on the conditions and experiences of contract staff were relatively uncommon during interviews.[9] The fact that it was largely unmentioned is perhaps as notable as the ways it does surface in the discussion below. When the topic did emerge, faculty and especially administrators were keen to envision contract work as the perfect marriage between the university and the creative, flexible artist.

Everyone Is an Artist

Participants often commented that "everyone is an artist" at the art and design university. By this, they meant that employees in all sorts of paid positions identified as being a creative type of some sort. As Anita explained to me as we walked around campus, "it's just a matter of whether or not you are explicitly paid to be an artist." She referred to the different artistic activities and careers of employees in student services, communications, and maintenance services. During interviews, employees in non-teaching roles were also identified as sculptors, painters, photographers, film-makers, musicians, crafters, and dancers. There is something appealing about this portrayal of Imagination University as a gathering place for creative individuals, where a faculty position and its recognition of your identity as an artist or designer is just the top tier. But since there are many points below this bar for artists in non-art roles in the school, this further complicates how contract work is understood. Len posed the dilemma as follows: "What is worse? Temporary work in your area, secure work outside of art altogether, or secure work outside of your area, yet inside the arts still?"

Perhaps the most telling aspect of this assessment is that the very idea of employment prospects is one of worst-case scenarios. Marnie admitted to me that she had made her peace with the ongoing tension in her faculty over the issue: "This is the consequence of being an artist – you cannot expect regular work." She continued to explain: "We have had all sorts of discussions around precarity of labour for teaching but there is a bigger question in terms of just the precarity of being an artist or designer, like, in the field, right?" This sort of comment functioned to turn the question back to the field overall, which works to the benefit of the university because it offers "at least some security." This point about the inevitability of work scarcity at the school was also made more jokingly by Darryl through the expression "live the life, pay the price." As he went on to say, "It's not just the faculty members who are artists and designers, it is our technicians who don't have year-round work with us! Some of them have MFAs and they come in at a much lower salary scale." While this type of comment is a way to recognize employees' skills beyond job title, at the same time, it can derail a more detailed conversation about job security in terms of teaching and research at the institution. It is a way to minimize the significance of the temporary–permanent divide because *everyone* is an artist, and some are even worse off – they are not hired to be artists and they are paid even less. This comment is another version of Len's "which would you rather?" scenario above, but with a more moralistic undertone. Given that some people are artists and not even working as artists, the implication is that contract instructors should be a bit more grateful given their comparatively higher status in the institutional hierarchy.

Managing Insecure Labour

Darryl, drawing on his years of experience as an upper administrator, portrayed the disgruntled contract worker type as follows: "Behind the committed artist-PhD, who after so many years can't find employment, you'll find a very bitter person … she has two or three kids … and she still doesn't have a full-time job." While this portrayal was not offered in reference to one individual in particular, the details brought to the scenario are telling. While Darryl presented this image to critique the anger and bitterness of contract instructors who do not seem to recognize that you are "not guaranteed a job," it is hard not to notice that this worker is a woman, she has extra caretaking responsibilities, and she is upset that her credentials are not recognized or rewarded. There is little reflexivity from Darryl on conditions and contexts of insecure work, even while he accurately identifies key issues of social location.

Darryl's representation demonstrates one of the many ways that administrators' accounts expressed remove from the experiences of contingent faculty. My analysis discerns recurring components to descriptions from those in administrative positions. While these surface in various combinations, the first set of explanations concentrates on the instructor: contract instructors desire flexible work; they are naive about the nature of academic work; they are just not competitive (for any number of reasons); they have chosen this insecure life course. The second set of explanations concentrates on wider contexts: insecure work is an inevitable by-product of government funding; these courses must be taught by active professionals in the field (not underemployed artists or designers); flexibility is mistakenly labelled as insecure work by labour activists.

A host of phrases surfaced in reference to contract teachers: they were referred to as "too dependent" (VP+), "unrealistic about opportunities" (Dean), and full of "unreasonable expectations" (Dean). [10] One chair described it as having a "poor sense" of the academic job market, where individuals think "hanging around" will increase their overall employability. And to be clear, the most dreaded type is the one who thinks "the institution owes him[/her] something" because they have taught "a few courses" (Dean). When this sort of language and characterization of contract workers surfaced, it was never paired with language that stressed the value of their contributions. Instead, in the passing descriptions and judgments, contract employees are often characterized as somehow flawed, but in curiously inconsistent ways. They are sometimes trained too much – "having a PhD doesn't help" (Dean) – and at other times, not enough – "they *only* had an MA" (Chair). Moreover, the conventional line by administrators is that per course instructors are hired because of their professional creative practice and experiences in the industry. This version also implies that those searching for job security within the institution are viewed with suspicion; their practice, whatever it is, is not successful enough. If you are explicit about needing work, your currency within the institution is diminished. In sum, the existing literature is not wrong on this point. This range of offhand comments made by administrators about contingent instructors does present how they are readily dismissed in everyday conversations, which, in turn, helps to legitimate existing practices – there is something wrong with *them* to need these courses to survive, and not with *us* for relying so heavily on their labour to operate as a university.

The emphasis on being current and active is also central to these discussions, and this confirms Jack's suspicion voiced at the start of this chapter that perceptions around creative currency and professional success inform administrative perspectives on this work. Taken together, employment security is identified as a misplaced request that spills into the university from the wider field. This is explained as follows:

> I can't say for sure but I am speculating that there is more pressure on an institution to provide stability in fields that are precarious and that's not something we're capable of for lots of different reasons: financially capable, structurally capable … it makes me a little bit nervous people think we could. I think we can improve some of our own labour practices. As always, I think there is always room for improvement, but I don't think we have the ability or the resources to provide such stability that we can anchor the cultural fields in this province or even just in the city. (VP+)

From an administrative perspective, having so much per course work and people looking for work is a combined headache. It is very time consuming to fill the positions. As one chair explained to me, the university often has trouble filling courses in areas that promise higher paying salaries in the industry. She cited animation and film as more uneven because prospects change suddenly, and the school will lose instructors with short notice. This is even more likely to happen in times of overall economic upswing. She noted that as the economy improves, filling per course teaching jobs in certain areas becomes harder. This also implies that the institution is advantaged by fewer opportunities in the industry because it improves the pool of per course applicants and the likelihood that they will accept work. But there is a double bind at work. A strong cultural economy can be an inconvenience of sorts to the institution, and yet as established above, a weak economy makes the applicants seems potentially weak, too, because they need the work and because their professional practice might seem less robust. As a potential solution, one VP+ discussed how the university could become better at securing its ideal contract employee. This ideal type is readily imagined by administrators as a flexible, well-employed professional with a skill for teaching:

> I mean, I think what we really need to look at is ways of identifying [contract] faculty who are more interested in teaching as an aspect of their practice and career and they are really good at it. How do we commit to them, as they commit to us? I see some people say they love it and it is kind of a break from their regular job, like "I am not going to do the tenure track but I would love some security" versus people who are just kind of like, maybe not even good at it, but feel they have a right to do it. (VP+)

This description summarizes the situation well – contract workers are not well regarded if they express a desire to hold a tenure-track position, and locating employees who both desire impermanence and have a talent for teaching solves this problem. Questions of insecurity can be overwritten when phrased as just a matter of institutional fit. And, clearly, administrators believe this type of undemanding, well-employed professional is out there – they just have to be better at finding them. Elsewhere, a chair explained, "I feel like sessional means something different here because there are so many artists who don't want to teach full-time. They just want an occasional [course], and that was certainly my position when I was sessional." Similarly, an upper administrator characterized it as bonus, not essential, income: "It's a really supplementary approach. I feel like a lot of people have that here. They are like, 'I have an additional chunk of money once a year, twice a year that still leaves time for my project.'" Another chair speculated that per course work was preferable because "most people want to retain their independence around their art practices." These comments are referring to "classic sessionals," who are defined as current or retired professionals who want to "give back," "teach for fun," or earn "extra cash on the side" (Field and Jones 2016, 3). They generally do not have a PhD or aspirations for full-time work within the university. However, this classic sessional is no longer representative. As Field and Jones demonstrate, the "precarious sessional" now predominates. For precarious sessionals, teaching is a central source of income; they have PhDs/advanced qualifications and desire permanent work in academia (4).[11] What the above comments express is a desire to return to the classic sessional that is now out of step with wider education and labour contexts – in essence, a return to the past and a different labour market.

However, this supplemental approach is accurate for some, and this is in part why making sense of the art and design context is challenging – it does work well for some in their creative practices, and professional currency in the field is important and valuable for students. Administrators are not wrong in saying that supporting only tenure-track positions is not appropriate. They spoke with a genuine commitment to students' enthusiasm for learning from individuals working in the industry; these "stories from the weeds" (Chair) make an important impression and enable a range of mentorship pathways. Limited contracts are a way that the value of non-academic expertise and credentials are recognized, and the expansiveness of creative knowledge supported. Yet while both contract faculty and administrators would agree on this point, administrators seem reluctant to discuss the disadvantages for the short-term employees. Nate, given his union experience, noted that the supplemental approach is more common in design and related professional programs, where instructors have a full-time job but are interested in teaching and engaging with students. These individuals sometimes act, I was told, in the spirit of "not quite volunteerism … I mean a lot of those people, like a senior creative director, is probably losing two or three times the income you are getting to teach." This limited term instructor is motivated "because they feel like it's a way to give back and all that kind of stuff." While this type of contract instructor does exist, he also explained that "most people who are teaching here hope at some point that they will get a permanent tenure-stream gig for sure."

Often, upper administrators characterized the desire for a permanent position by contingent faculty as a fundamental misunderstanding of the nature of academic and creative work. As one dean put it, "don't expect a job," by which she meant that it is a very competitive market, and if you are not actively achieving at all levels, you will not be visible within the competition. It is not that there is a "stigma" against hiring known employees, and certainly "sometimes" existing part-time faculty get work, but as another dean explained, "it's totally unreasonable to think this [course] will lead to the tenure track." Importantly, this is "not guaranteed and really shouldn't be." The dean continued to explain that everyone has to "trust hiring" – meaning, trust in the merit of the applications and their evaluation. Certainly, there is a patronizing component to comments around the image of the uninformed contract worker who does not understand the competitive nature of university work. Further, these justifications lean on a belief in the robustness of merit and competition, one that aligns well with previous comments that insecure work is a product of individual-level shortcomings – the university just requires more of the right type of contract worker. Yet, as I explore below, the desire for the "classic sessional" operates in parallel with a nostalgia for contract work by permanent faculty, one which contributes to their assessment of it in the present.

Nostalgia and Bureaucracy

In some ways, the boundary between permanent and temporary employees is not that clear cut, especially given that almost every tenured faculty member has some experience with contract teaching work in the past, even if only as a graduate student or only very briefly. When individuals recounted their employment histories, it was a common feature. However, there is often a distinct gap between how contingent work is understood by current contract employees versus current tenured professors who have benefited from years, and at times decades, of stable employment. When I was talking with Patrick, he described his start at the institution teaching design studio courses while still employed with a design firm. He said he "missed those days ... it was sort of great. I had more time, more energy to *do* design. I was connected." He spoke fondly of being able to benefit from the institution without having to "take it all on." Patrick summed up his time working per course as "very positive, very good all around." In contrast, the most challenging features of his current job are the endless administrative tasks and service obligations that take him away from his teaching and design interests.

This sentiment resonated across many of my conversations with faculty members, especially those with tenure – this group most consistently referred to missing the distance from service work, administration, and bureaucracy that contract work provided. Others explained this early period before they had a permanent position as one of "more freedom ... and exploration" and "much better than you'd think in many ways" (Len). Mel described it in terms of a different sort of wealth, as being "so very rich, even when you are poor, because you could do many different things at once ... Somehow, things were easier because you weren't responsible for everything. You could just leave without having to hold the school up." With a laugh, Claire declared, "Sometimes I miss it." This positive interpretation was present even when the descriptions themselves were not very encouraging. For example, Marnie characterized her overall experience under contract as "very beneficial" and "an asset ... real essential" to her professional development, but in her actual description of her time as a contract instructor she discussed feeling very isolated and disconnected from the department ("I never meet a soul ... the building was so empty"; "No one knows you"). She explained her isolation as circumstantial – a matter of her teaching time slot – rather than a pervasive experience within contract work. Together, these characterizations of contract work were set alongside descriptions of burdensome institutional responsibilities in the present and notable uncertainty around managing transitions (see chapter 7). Within these dynamics, contract work comes to symbolize a longing for another time – a time when individuals have a strong memory of being very active creatively, younger, and relatively unburdened institutionally. Accordingly, individuals cast this time as one focused on artistic development and pursuing diverse creative activities. They spoke fondly of teaching as "only supplemental" (Mel) and "a total bonus … whatever you needed it to be" (Len); it was "a chance for artistic exchange [with students], but you get paid" (Shaina). Put simply, permanent employees described their memories of contract work with a tinge of nostalgia and a sort of longing for their energetic creative pasts.

Nostalgia, to be sure, is multifaceted. As Pickering and Keightley explain, "as a specifically modern concept nostalgia has been used to identify both a sense of personal loss and longing for an idealized past, and a distorted public version of a particular historical period or a particular social formation in the past" (2006, 922). In practice, there are many "modalities" of nostalgia, and these can concurrently invite analytical reflections on the past and conservative revisioning. As a form of cultural expression, nostalgia strives to suture many existing tensions, but often with a cost. It can serve to erase complex power dynamics by pinpointing only one dimension of a situation – the one that presents the most appealing view in the present. As illustrated in the above accounts, tenured faculty were more likely to identify the advantages rather that the disadvantages of contract work in their employment histories. Insecure work is more likely to be viewed from the perspective of those with permanent work as a career stage issue – something that will pass. This retroactive vision allows for a more positive interpretation when you have followed the tenured career trajectory and have employment stability in the present. When it is regarded as a career stage, and not an enduring condition, it is easier to dismiss as a current problem, which creates distance from the many negative implications of insecure work. These positive accounts of individuals' experiences in the past can serve to reject serious engagement with the issue of contract work in the present. These examples are reminders that nostalgia can be indulgent; it has its own peculiar pleasure. There is a pleasure to recounting one's creative past – celebrating a time of heightened activity that is also proof of your creative worth and, at times, your artistic dedication through struggle. Your creative endurance is on display in these accounts of time in the trenches before your permanent position.

Yet despite this tone of artistic longing, I would also argue that these examples of work nostalgia are not totally devoid of critical insight. Much of the academic literature on nostalgia grapples with how to balance nostalgia's potential for criticality with that of distortion or sentimentality (Boym 2008; Pickering and Keightley 2006; Smith 2000; Tannock 1995). In this case, contract work is cast as appealing because it means freedom from paperwork, needless bureaucracy, and service commitments – all things regularly identified by faculty as especially draining and part of wider organizational issues. Thus, nostalgia for contract work is a response to overwork in the present rather than the experience of employment insecurity in the past. The institutional-artistic critique in this example does not focus on the obvious target: insecure labour. Instead, permanent employees talk about contract work in order to critique everyday bureaucracy and work overload. Thus, while my conversations with faculty at Imagination University around insecure work expressed insensitivity to the current plight of contract workers, these nostalgic interpretations of past experiences were not without some critical content, but these centred on heightened administrative and service expectations that diminished their creative activities. The complaint is one that has already surfaced in other chapters; there is less time to fulfil what is supposedly the most important parts of one's job: teaching and creative practice. This nostalgia for temporary work is not pure arrogance. These interviews illustrate how nostalgia emerges as a response to overwork and frustration. However, this focus on present work frustrations disrupts the potential for stronger collective acknowledgments of the importance of employment security and heightened recognition of the contributions of those in temporary positions. Nostalgia serves to sanitize and displace the force of what could be a much different critique of organizational inequities.

The Hazards of Critique

This chapter demonstrates how the new spirit of creativity celebrates flexibility within the institution while practically promoting its much less likeable cousin, insecurity. Here, the hazards of institutional-artistic critique become clear: the target of analysis can be easily switched and opportunities for creative solidarity diminished. This case builds on our understanding of contract work within art universities by examining how ideas about cultural work in general intersect with ideas about contingent work within the contemporary university. Insecure work puts workers in a compromised position, and this chapter illustrates different ways vulnerability is produced and explained at Imagination University. More specifically, it examines how narratives of artistic currency and creative professions are used to justify insecure work.

The institution creates distance from precarious work via many strategies, but in a more everyday sense it is supported by permanent employees' ambivalent identifications with those in insecure circumstances. In unguarded moments, rather than widespread recognition of key difficulties, we see various techniques for displacing the immediacy of the employment issue. Insecure work is considered to be the way of the world in art and design – be it inside or outside of the institution. It is cast as both a professional risk (the cost of being an artist) and a benefit (the advantages of flexibility). And, as Jack's story illustrates, artistic currency becomes just another part of the measurement. Even tenured faculty's nostalgic accounts of contract work tie the experience to creative identity and youthful vitality; it is a sign of being creatively current, which, when it resolves itself into permanent work, can be fondly remembered. This chapter establishes how artistic creativity's capacity for insight and the force of the institutional-artistic critique can become displaced in unsettling ways under the new spirit; nostalgia for more freedom and less bureaucracy protests increasing institutional demands in the present. However, this nostalgia recognizes one problem while minimizing another: the negative consequences of insecure work for current contract faculty. This chapter is another example of how inequities in compromise relations between artistic creativity and the new spirit can intersect with vulnerability – a vulnerability that Imagination University is able to easily justify because flexibility is one of the new spirit's core creative values.

Chapter Seven

Rocks and Bubbles: Descriptions of Institutional Duress

The big issue is our poor operating funds. It's a nightmare, and we're in trouble next year.

– Anita, study participant

There was very low morale for the most part. I mean there was kind of gallows solidarity, which was great.

– Nate, study participant

[The] bubble will burst … it's just a matter of time.

– Maretta, study participant

During my conversation with Anita, the word "bubble" repeatedly surfaced in her descriptions. She spoke of how most faculty members approached the "university as a bubble." She adamantly critiqued what she called a "bubble mentality" while painting a vivid picture of, well, a very soapy ivory tower. Her mission, as she portrayed it, was "to burst the bubble," especially since students "don't want this bubble." In her account, the bubble is a barrier and limitation; it is how the university remained isolated from the everyday world of cultural work and entrepreneurship that she also spoke of during our interview. This situation at Imagination University, she maintained, was "unsustainable."

In contrast to the fragility of the bubble, the unyieldingness of the rock was also used to describe a challenging institutional landscape, but with a very different emphasis. The recurring use of the phrase "stuck between a rock and a hard place" by multiple participants describes the difficult place of the university in light of a number of circumstances including dramatic funding cuts; escalating operating costs, particularly for studio-based programs; reductions in faculty appointments; increasing administrative loads and committee work; and fruitless labour negotiations.

In these descriptions, both the rock and the bubble are used to account for concerns over institutional sustainability. Curiously, the fragile bubble and the enduring rock each point to concerns over stability. This chapter thus tackles how growing uncertainty is an abiding concern at Imagination University. Uncertainty is a thread throughout the previous chapters; it rears its head when creative research is defined (chapter 3), when creative practices are evaluated (chapter 4), when professional identities are expressed (chapter 5), and when employment security is in question (chapter 6). Institutional strain is part of previous descriptions of the university's uncoordinated parts, but in this final chapter, uncertainty receives its due attention. Here, I disentangle the role of uncertainty within the institutional life of cultural work to understand another dimension of the new spirit of creativity: the new spirit's expansiveness challenges the stability and worth of artistic creativity. Accordingly, as the imagery of rock and bubble suggests, uncertainty is produced through dual conditions of vulnerable arrangements and inflexible circumstances.

In this chapter, I explore three dimensions to how institutional actors express and navigate this uncertainty – that is, how they respond to moments when institutional stability comes under threat, and how this response impacts planning and decision-making in the present. In the first section, I review crisis narratives within higher education in general and consider how these apply to the context of the art university specifically. NSCAD provides ample proof that the contemporary art and design university can, in fact, be threatened with elimination. In the second section, I explore how the imagery of both the rock and the bubble identifies the distinct temporalities of institutional constraint. In the third section, I focus on how constraints in the present impact perceptions of both past and future, including the imagination of creative identity. Together, this analysis argues that uncertainty is diversely expressed as a feature of institutional time with recourse to the past, present, and future of creative potential. Institutional uncertainty invites disagreement around the temporality of creativity and value. Graeber argues that academics do not analyse enough the bureaucratic landscapes that they are, inescapably, also actively shaping (2015, 54) – this somehow remains outside of the standard research agenda. Instead, he argues, it becomes the focus of office small talk to no end. While I agree with his overall line of concern, I would counter that this small talk is how faculty try to make sense of the demanding, tedious, and often absurd features of the institution, but to varying degrees of success and full-bodied critique. Thus, in this chapter, I use everyday examples to demonstrate how the institutional-artistic critique is resolutely muddy given the rise of uncertainty within the new spirit of creativity.

Describing Institutional Landscapes in Times of Uncertainty

Public institutions are usually associated with permanence. There is a belief that while change (for better or worse) is inevitable, universities are not prone to ready erasure.[1] So, in this regard, is instability or uncertainty of serious consequence at Imagination University? The short answer is yes. Faculty and administrators expressed concern over the stability of the institution, and there was a distinct perception among those interviewed that sustainability is an issue at multiple points in the system. The longer answer, however, touches on two further questions that require contemplation: (a) What are the shared circumstances across higher education (notably, the evidence for perpetual and normalized crisis)? and (b) What is specific to this university type?

The sense of unending crisis in higher education has become a cliché, a staple description of the status quo of austerity. The language of crisis refers to any number of concerns (e.g., student debt and job prospects, institutional funding arrangements, deteriorating infrastructure, diminished teaching and learning), while often glancing to wider contours of social inequality. Slater (2015) argues that the higher education system relies on crisis politics and a dialectic of calamity and reform that displaces recovery onto schools, students, and instructors. Or, as Letizia (2016) reasons, the steady incorporation of business models within higher education has created a disaster capitalism logic that rests on a hollowing out of the university's public mission as it scrambles from crisis to crisis.[2] Crisis is no longer a singular event but part of the everyday work of navigating ongoing limitations that impact teaching and research quality. While the crisis narrative can overshadow the slow and steady accomplishments of higher education over time (Tight 1994), the term is an expression that provocatively captures the concern that society is unable to protect high quality, accessible higher education. Broadly, a sense of crisis emerges when institutional actors regularly confront a disjuncture between quality of education versus available resources and fiscal responsibility, and when issues are almost always resolved in favour of the latter. Curiously, this language of crisis is used at all points of the political spectrum, which results in different strategic recommendations. For example, the straightforward policy and management version advises universities to deal with uncertainty by enhancing prestige and market share, embracing entrepreneurialism, and expanding interactions and co-creation with all stakeholders (Pucciarelli and Kaplan 2016, 311). Or, in a very different vein, crisis is foregrounded to inspire and grow student and faculty commitments to activism and transformative pedagogy within the university (Kapitulik, Kelly, and Clawson 2007).

Foust and Lair (2012) differentiate between ways the discourse of crisis unfolds in education scholarship. The discourse of what they term "administrative realism" rests on unavoidability; it is "couched in the premise that university administrators must accept the fact that the economic environment surrounding their institutions has irrevocably changed … all seem to accept some version of neoliberal economics as the warrant for reform, and even a primary justification for maintaining higher education itself" (161). Elsewhere, however, crisis discourse is an inroad for producing institutional and economic critiques of the contemporary university's divisions and inequities. And another version is rooted in the realm of culture, with many academics concerned about ideologically driven, conservative attacks on the purpose and value of universities. This approach frames disputes over how to best realize public responsibility, access, and democracy. Together, Foust and Lair argue that each crisis narrative provides a different explanation for uncertainty and leads to a different list of possible remedies, where addressing the unpredictability of uncertainty becomes embedded in the workforce, in strategic planning, in curriculum, and in economic forecasting. Alongside the many insightful commentaries within this crisis-themed work, there is a dark undertone. As academic and higher education advocate Turk puts it, "the degradation of the university continues" (2017, 9). But this is not just a feature of critical theory influenced scholarship in higher education; even research coming out of higher education management acknowledges, "there is a general consensus that the future of academia is and will be complicated, challenging, and uncertain" (Pucciarelli and Kaplan 2016, 311).

During my interviews, examples of the university in crisis emphasized how quality pedagogy and the creative expertise of faculty are unable to centre or drive change. For instance, students regularly report feeling lost and anonymous in large intro classes, but attempts to reduce these class sizes are futile because they are big earners for the university. Or the administration will refuse to replace faculty who have resigned, retired, or, sadly, even died on the job, but departments are expected to grow their programs and activities nonetheless. Maretta depicted her worst dealings with academic capitalism's decision-making priorities when she held an interim role as chair as follows:

> How do we keep the bums on the seat, keep the revenue flow in …? [T]hey were never interested in pedagogy, never ever asked me about the course content, and never wondered what was going on pedagogically or intellectually. They did not give a damn. It was about spreadsheets and cost … and hence is presented as a successful model to itself and to its government agencies because [higher education] is a money-making industry. It is a full articulation of that: the commodification of universities.

While she explained that things had improved somewhat in light of a number of administrative transitions, the experience weighed on her as a demonstration of the institution's disregard for meaningful content.

While Maretta's account might apply to any university, there is a vulnerability specific to Imagination University. And this is not just a matter of perception on behalf of faculty members. This point has surfaced in previous chapters, but I will briefly review here the specific challenges posed by delivering studio-based education. These programs are costly in terms of materials, space, and teaching time, and the higher cost of delivering studio programs is not well recognized by provincial funding formulas based on student enrolment. Further, it can be hard to place these practices within the existing grant models. So design is considered too applied for humanities and social sciences funding but "not science enough" for science and technology funding, while art and media practices risk being "not academic enough" for humanities and social sciences funding. Similarly, as relatively new universities, these schools have limited potential for alumni donations, and they have not had a chance to build substantial investment portfolios and endowments.

While the above underscores some factors common to art universities, NSCAD's very public battle over autonomy (see chapter 2) becomes the model case for how difficult circumstances can consolidate into dire circumstances – and with the overriding sense that it was an easier target because of its art and design specialization. For example, universities carrying long-term debts is the norm, not the exception in Nova Scotia. Many faculty from NSCAD expressed that singling out the institution seemed punitive and appeared motivated by a baseline government disrespect for the value of art education in the province. The stress and pace of change that was required during this period had a pronounced impact, largely because there were so many unknowns being projected, and all at once. Public accounts repeated again and again that "NSCAD's fate remains precarious" (CAUT 2012), with much accompanying speculation over its prospects for independence and/or the possibility of a merger. Alongside this were practical measures being rapidly implemented such as making course offerings as lean as possible, cutting contract teaching positions, and finding staffing reductions. In this scenario, faculty were the most secure employees, but they acutely felt the ongoing burden of changes within what was described to me as "a demoralizing climate ... of regular degradations" (Chair) and "impossible options" (Associate Professor).[3] Yet, equally, there was also a sense that it "could have been worse," and there was "considerable community, even solidarity around struggle" (Assistant Professor). When I asked what, exactly, could have been worse, the response was consistent: permanent faculty had not lost their jobs and the institution had not totally collapsed (yet – at least – was the unspoken implication). However, over a dozen administrative support staff and custodial staff were not so lucky; they did not keep their jobs, and this was readily cited as an institutional failure. When I pressed participants about what made this particular experience so dispiriting, it was not only the drain of uncertainty but also the readiness to dismiss non-economic values of artistic creativity. This can be summarized as follows: a disregard for the importance of cultural history and context; interest in art and design practices only within the small purview of the creative economy; and a reluctance to expand concepts of research and knowledge in higher education. Together, this experience reinforced a view of organizational relations where faith in institutional stability is not taken for granted. In fact, if anything, it inflected future prospects as well: "If it can happen once … it can for sure again" (Professor). Or as one academic plan rather ominously warned, "NSCAD may close programs, or modify areas of study," especially, it continues, if enrolments are low or if faculty are unavailable to teach in certain areas (NSCAD 2016a, 28).

NSCAD's tribulations are a reminder that even a public university can be mortal, fragile – a lesson not lost on observers. NSCAD's plight frequently came up during my conversations at the other schools; individuals acknowledged that this example was disheartening even from a distance. In this regard, the "could have been worse" stance of those at NSCAD served as a "could be worse" scenario for those at sister art and design universities. More than once I heard variations on this phrase when participants discussed key challenges: "It could be worse – we are not NSCAD!" Instability becomes framed via both past examples and future unknowns; appropriately, the next two sections will further analyse the institutional temporality of uncertainty.

Stuck between a Rock and a Hard Place

Imagination University's status was often portrayed through descriptions of hardship, with the phrase "stuck between a rock and a hard place" deftly capturing the sense of limited options and irresolvable circumstances. While this exact phrase dates from the early twentieth century (Hirsch, Kett, and Trefil 2002), its origins trace back to Homer's *Odyssey*, where the hero Odysseus must pass between Scylla and Charybdis – two equally treacherous monsters (Gagarin and Fantham 2010). In Greek mythology, one's only hope of safe passage is with the intervention of the gods. When faced with two impossible options, with neither the rock nor the hard place likely to yield, a solution is unlikely to present itself, but action must be taken nonetheless. In the case of Imagination University, faculty used variations of this phrase in a number of instances – "we are between rock and a hard place"(Marnie); "it's like a rock and hard place" (Heath); "it's a hard spot and a hard place" (Kat) – as well as a number of related expressions that convey difficulty and duress in a similar way: "impossible circumstances" (Anita); "troubling developments" (Ayana); and just the simple declaration "it's been too difficult" (Saeed).

In these various conversations, uncertainty was expressed in terms of halted temporality and action – the inability to plan or to find remedies amidst considerable ambiguity. It is found within suspended or forever delayed decision-making in light of seemingly insurmountable challenges. For example, Mel explained that "there is a lot of flux right now for sure," while Saeed assessed more forcefully, "I feel like nothing ever is possible." Marnie, on the other hand, cast the situation as follows: "Everybody is overworked and overworking. It's not really sustainable for the institution. So I don't know where that all leads, right? I am constantly trying to look for relief." Heath speculated, "I feel like there is a collective decision to just flow through the next year … and not worry too much about the sense of crisis, because there is a sense of crisis, but things have also really changed." While Heath expressed cautious optimism about the "improving crisis," others were less optimistic, stating quite clearly their concerns that things are deteriorating and will continue to do so. For instance, Shaina said, "I think it has gotten worse in the last two or three years," speaking not just of financial challenges, but in terms of collegiality and co-operation, too. She continued to refer to the day-to-day struggle to get things accomplished as outright bizarre: "It's a weird dynamic and it has gotten weirder since I've been here for sure." When I queried her use of the term "weird," her response indicated a mix of the strange and other worldly – a disbelief in the normalized insecurity across the university.

In terms of brief explanations offered to account for intractable circumstances, the responses hinged foremost on financial restriction, which was a point of commonality across faculty and administrators: "It's money. It's 100 per cent money. Yeah, 100 per cent. Everything else is great" (Anita). Or, as Darryl predicted, "If we had more money … that would pretty much solve all the points of pain that we have." While upper-level administrators expressed such sentiments in regard to any number of circumstances (see chapter 3) – complaints around inadequate resources are a default refrain – there are some important qualifications to be offered here. So while administrators identified specific challenges posed by their institutional type, faculty also stressed that they are identifying an issue above and beyond the regular jostling for resources in higher education. They are not expecting unlimited resources. A number of participants were careful to express that there is a need for reasonable resources. As Mel explained of her experiences of institutional scarcity, "it's got to get down to, like, normal levels." It is understood that some level of need is normal, yet the need has now ballooned to an untenable extreme. Alongside these financial limits, faculty identified flaws within the organizational structure and the distribution of decision-making; it can be "near impossible to act on everything" (Kat). As Chianne explained, "The other challenge is the administrative structure here. The deans really don't have anybody … they even have less power than a chair." Being a dean was regularly marked as "undesirable" (Len) by a number of faculty, precisely because of an imbalance between a heightened responsibility that is met with a near incapacity to respond to needs and make changes. Heavy reliance on interim administrative appointments was also identified as an issue that prevented long-term thinking, stability, and planning. Numerous acting positions assumed a symbolic dimension too. Interim appointments represented an inability to act in the present or commit to future planning because of a lack of resources, including recruiting for such administrative positions to begin with. These all compounded to create an overriding sense, sometimes, that "nothing is ever impossible."

Bubbles

While the rock and the hard place articulated tensions around institutional stability and stalled possibilities – the crush of dilemmas in the present – the imagery of the bubble is another way the temporality of uncertainty was expressed. The ivory tower has long been a way to describe privileged seclusion and abstract intellectualism, with connotations of impracticality and escapism, if not arrogance. The bubble emerged in some conversations to describe the separation of formal education from "the actual contexts of creative professions" (Patrick). Yet institutional actors characterized the university bubble of privilege as either an asset or detriment, depending on their perspective and focus. Some participants used bubble imagery to capture the positive dimensions of the school's creative freedoms. For example, it meant feeling lucky to have a stable job to support one's creative practices. Or it meant being removed from commercial demands to make art work and not having the strain and frustrations of independent creative work: "Not everyone gets these jobs ... it is a privilege to be removed from commercial competition and burdens" (Shaina). Faculty spoke with a sense of relief about the capacity to retain some freedom and distance from a commercial world of work that did not allow for the same untethered exploration within individual creative practices.

But at the same time, Anita was concerned that faculty wanted to keep students within "a bubble" as a form of unrealistic protection. She represented the position of many of her colleagues as follows: students should have the freedom and space to experiment because they have plenty of time to pursue the chore of work later. However, Anita was presenting this position to refute it. She wanted to *burst* the bubble. Her point was that this protective enclosure was not helping students adapt to "real world exercises" and the business of art and design that is required of almost everyone in order to develop a successful practice. Many others with extensive non-academic work experience also expressed discontent with the protected environment of Imagination University. They missed the pace and stimulation of their previous professional practices before they had become faculty members: "There is this energy, like, of need and motivation" (Patrick). Or as Len described it, there is "less paper and procedures" outside of the protected university environment. In this version, the bubble is a container that demarcates the inability to be distant from university bureaucracy.

The accusation that somebody lives in a bubble has always been a way to critique a perceived reluctance to engage with the real world, one often directed towards both artists and academics alike. Yet it is worth noting that bubbles are forms with a well-recognized, underlying instability. They always pop; they do not endure. So to take refuge in a bubble is to invite uncertainty, and to claim that someone is hiding in a bubble is also grounded in that understanding. It will not last! The world will always intervene.

Fear of Creative Erosions

Widespread institutional uncertainty has consequences for creativity at Imagination University. Participants identified the impacts of uncertainty on the ability to cultivate relationships, sustain creative communities, and nurture collaborative practices. Saeed described this as a "structural inability to collaborate" that is undergirded by financial limitations and organizational practices. A recurring example participants cited was that there is no capacity for faculty to cross departments or faculties to teach a course, despite the high demand for such exchanges. When recounting this diminishment of creative exchanges, Maretta explained, "It's just too tight to collaborate now" (Maretta); or as Nate put it in reference to sustaining key relationships, "I think … our togetherness … has gotten worse in the last two or three years." There is ample evidence of successful collaborations at Imagination University, so individuals do cultivate and grow practices together regularly; yet organizational structure was often identified as an inhibitor rather than facilitator of such exchanges. It was something to be overcome. As Chianne explained of her experience of trying to get an interdisciplinary project off the ground, "collaborations are the hardest thing within the university … building effective collaborations for something is very difficult right now." This produces its own range of effects, referred to as the "course release economy," which trades in begging for favours and widespread scepticism that releases are unfairly distributed. As Jack put it, the small size of the university appears to reduce many requests to interpersonal dynamics: "It's very difficult to not see these things [course releases] almost as personal favours." This, in turn, makes establishing one's need both an issue of creative productivity but also social intelligence. And, no matter what the scenario, the perception is that to actually receive one of these treasured releases creates animosity because everyone feels so strapped for time. As Patrick noted, "I didn't manage until I got myself into release time." In his case, this was achieved by rigorously pursuing private-public funding for projects. This sort of private funding, by his account, was the only way. Certainly, this emerged as the only type of collaboration easily able to flourish within an otherwise difficult climate for sustained cooperation in research or teaching. Alongside disputes around economic responsibility for collaboration, time as a scarce resource is its shadow: "When you dig deeper, mostly it comes down to time … the fear of lost time" (Dominic). Or as Chianne characterized it, "if only time wasn't always on the line." When artistic collaboration or community engagement is framed at the organizational level in terms of lost or wasted time, it can easily start to seem outside of the frame of one's day-to-day artistic work.

Underlying these discussions is an overriding concern for the creative consequences. This is another facet of uncertainty: the erosion of artistic creativity. Because of her active role in coordinating artistic research projects, Mel was able to aptly summarize this concern: "I think the big fear right now is that people lose their artistic expression, right? They don't want to lose that. There is fear around that. That's *the* big fear." Losing artistic vibrancy and autonomy in this context is twofold. As Mel continued to explain, concern swirled around unreasonable teaching expectations, including everything from teaching load, project supervision, curriculum and learning outcomes, and unreasonable research expectations – including the devaluation of certain types of practice while elevating commercial outputs and private partnerships. These are the ways that institutional practices can have a deleterious impact on creative diversity. In this regard, however, commercialization is not a blanket enemy or inhibitor to creativity. Patrick for instance, was adamant that commercial applications were able to "stimulate" and "inspire" him to work well. Ayana clarified that everyone has "moved past" old tensions where "artists never talk about money." In truth, money was often a topic of conversation, from union meetings to hallway conversations. Ayana used the example of university salaries to support her point. The healthy salaries of faculty members were key to nurturing their wider creative endeavours: "Let's not forget what keeps us all afloat." But participants' anxieties around sustaining and nurturing creativity hinged on how commercialization initiatives were so often tied to conservative economic and cultural perspectives that were potentially limiting diversity within creative practices and contributions, especially within the type of community and collaborative contexts outlined above. As Mel elaborated, "Everybody has been sitting, watching the last decade, and watching the conservative, creeping conservative, framework around commercialization." Likewise, when Dominic spoke of a new position established to spearhead a creativity and business management curriculum, he noted his "deep suspicion" of the new hire; this person was smart and talented but had no experience or real interest in working with artists and designers. This new leader was discernibly "not getting the art community" and "not very creative or knowledgeable about actual artistic practices and process … but very entrepreneurial." If entrepreneurialism not even rooted in artistic communities starts to take over, this is bound to have creative consequences over time.

The Fragility of Creative Past and Future

They're trying to re-build the past … and I don't know if it will be better or worse.

– Jack, study participant

In the above quotation, Jack aptly captures a temporal dilemma. Rebuilding the past has many dimensions. In the context of this discussion, Jack argued that the university wanted to return to a perceived "golden age" of art and design education that allowed for intense, creative, practice-based developments with more expansiveness and less formal regulation. He identified this position as being blind to the context of the present and its myriad challenges – looking to the past was a way to ignore the present. But at the same time, he did see the appeal of a past institution that was less bureaucratic and more open to diverse creative experimentation – more committed to artistic creativity – whether or not it was actually part of the past or just a perception of the past. However, as his quotation stresses, the overall implications of this backward-looking orientation remain uncertain. For others, an interest in resurrecting the past surfaced as a way to protect the independence of the art and design university – to ensure that it will not lose its unique character and resemble, what Nate termed, "any old university." This, it seems, is at the heart of these conversations about the robustness of creativity in the past; as Marnie argued, "There aren't many of these only art schools around … this can't be lost." The distinctive identity of the school and artistic creativity seems under threat with so many pressures, and one solution to the present predicament is to return to the past.

Consequently, in this version of institutional-artistic critique, the past is used to highlight and counter the restrictions of the present and call into question the core principles of the new spirit of creativity. This was especially marked when participants expressed apprehension over the heightened management of artistic practices under the new spirit (see also chapters 3 and 4). The past is freer, actually more creative, despite claims within and outside the institution that we have entered a "so-called imagination age" (Nate). Longer serving faculty identified how the past was less constrained by "administrative bloat" (Len), "burgeoning administration" (Nate), and an overall "more corporate look and feel" (Claire). The university was able to dedicate itself exclusively to art and design. As Saeed described, "The great thing about [Imagination University] is it used to be an institute just for art – meaning all art and design." Now, as he continued, the increase in academic faculty and course expectations for all degrees has "shifted the culture" to be "more academic, less artistic." He recalled that decades ago, faculty and students argued against becoming degree granting for this reason. While Saeed's comments might seem antagonistic to the contemporary school, as a professor he is widely identified as successful and well-funded. He is regularly featured when the school showcases its achievements. But even though he is considered a leader, this did not diminish the anxiety he expressed in our conversation that the institution is not able to sustain what is valuable and specific to the arts. The university is diversifying its activities more and more, which curiously risks diminishing its uniqueness because it starts to resemble standard academic or business – not creative – trajectories. The fact that he had successfully navigated these new requirements did not minimize his concern.

Creative Identities in and out of Fashion

Although many faculty at Imagination University feared that the past was more open to creative experimentation, higher education discourse in general hinges on a future orientation. As Clegg identifies, higher education's focus on future promise means that "temporality is coded as future time for the person, their achievements, and their employability" (2010, 345). This emphasis serves to limit types of reflexivity within higher education and enable discourses of personal failure instead of analysis in the present. Not surprising, narratives of individual-level shortcomings are inseparable from conceptions of time and age. Certainly, youth and currency are widely identified as central characteristics within the wider cultural industries (McRobbie 2015) and part of art school lore specifically (Frith and Horne 1987; Tickner 2008). Within the creative university, a clear contradiction arises: the past might have been more creative, but the individuals associated with that past are not. The value of one's creative identity is less certain over time.

There is a fear of being perceived by others as passé – as part of a past legacy of the school and not its active future. This surfaced within discussions of research as well as insecure work, but here I will align it with wider issues of institutional time and uncertainty. Senior faculty members were variously characterized by research participants. At times, these representations were not especially flattering. Jack was miffed by "the regular challenges posed by more senior faculty," especially during his program's strategic planning exercises. His concern was that long-term decisions are more determined by those who are not especially committed to the future; they have a "shorter runway to the door" but exercise considerable reach in future planning. On the one hand, Jack was dismissing the importance of institutional memory and expertise because of proximity to retirement; on the other hand, he was expressing his frustration with decision-making hierarchies. Elaborating on this point, Jack explained how he felt "muffled" and often unable to voice his perspective because of his junior and contractually limited status. This dynamic had two dimensions. First, he described the culture of the institution as "less receptive" to all sorts of ground-up changes, with resistance to new ideas increasing if the person suggesting them was new to the institution. The university was too inflexible. Second, there could be future job security repercussions for him if an adamant disagreement were to arise. So this was the main source of his discontent and concern: there are unintended consequences around the peer-review process specifically and status in general. While these critiques are legitimate, they become packaged with shades of ageism. This also suggests there is something else at work in terms of the perception of age and creative identity.

There were many terms used to describe senior faculty members such as "mature" and "older." As an upper administrator, Anita switched from the term "older faculty" to "mature faculty" mid-interview; with this, she expressed a moment of uncertainty around how to be most respectful. Occasionally, the term "legacy faculty" or "previous faculty" was used to describe those who were inherited from the university's past – the long serving instructors who some-times do not neatly fit the contemporary faculty member profile. Legacy faculty was employed to capture the spectre of the less qualified, less active individu-als who do not contribute in the same way as those hired more recently. This usage relies on a purposeful misuse of the meaning of *legacy*. It deploys a term with connotations of prestige to justify dismissal in practice. For example, when Anita later explained that Imagination University "still has a number of legacy faculty," this was not presented as something to celebrate. Rather, this is how she made sense of differences between the professional activities of faculty members. Nate explained the origins of the term as follows: it was designed to entice retirement of faculty members who were not well aligned with new strategic plans and research mandates; it was a "formal … cover term" to target those perceived to be "dead weight" within the institution. For example, the term legacy faculty was used to ground complaints about faculty who lacked "an ability to stay involved" (Patrick) in current trends, or "had almost no pro-fessional practices" (Heath).

Importantly, no one spoke of themselves as a legacy faculty member, even though I interviewed many individuals who had decades of service and had weathered numerous transitions. It is an image that provides definition through contrast. It was a way to elaborate upon what the speaker is not and to demonstrate one's own currency. Thus, while the term legacy purportedly bestows respect, its use in practice is the opposite: their legacies are dead to the institution. This is the other undertone to being referred to as dead weight – one's contributions will not be remembered. More rarely, the term was used to illustrate the university's disrespectful attitude towards its faculty, ageism in tow; that is, it was used to critique the conflation of creative value with youth. This is why Nate brought the term into the conversation; it was an example of the institution's disrespect towards employees, with another recognition at play: administrative processes can house an inhumanity that occasionally boils up to the surface. Specifically, as Sennett (2007) elaborates, value seems to decrease with time of service within the new culture of workplaces, where professional knowledge and commitments over time are more readily disregarded.

These characterizations of time spent within the university also raise a companion issue: when does one leave? A number of participants referred to their plans to leave Imagination University, in no small part because of the issues raised above. While switching jobs was cast as a desire for career advancement, it was also fuelled by, as Marnie phrased it, "some, ahh, concerns over university stability and day-to-day stress." Kat admitted that she was actively applying for positions elsewhere. She had taught studio art for two years as an LTA at a comprehensive university, but she found herself questioning the wisdom of moving to an art and design school for a permanent position. She noted with irony that her temporary appointment had been better than her tenure-track position – the union was stronger, the salary higher, and the teaching load lower. She had taken her current position because of its permanence – because of its supposed certainty – without realizing the hit she would take in terms of overall conditions. Over coffee, Darryl confessed towards the end of our interview that he was planning to leave his position in the next few years. He said that after carefully considering the "time-remuneration puzzle," he was confident that returning to commercial design work would maintain, if not grow, his income and give him "a much-needed break from bureaucratic red tape."

Generally, retirement was the most common reason to leave, but I had a number of senior faculty members make offhand remarks about their concern for retirement security, and the need to delay or reconsider their existing retirement strategy because it was "unaffordable" and there was a "tremendous retirement hit" (Saeed) with the economic insecurity ushered in by the global financial crash in 2008. As Dominic plainly assessed, "I am going to be here longer than even I expected." Plans to depart the institution have taken an unexpected turn for these faculty, many of whom find they need to keep working because of wider economic uncertainty. Even more recent appointments seemed to be aware of this; as Shaina ruefully declared, "I am never going to be able to retire." In so many ways, a future orientation is always undergirding these conversations about time already served. An emerging peril of the future is that individuals will no longer be valued as committed workers to the institution, while at the same time, employees must work longer and cannot exit the university when they feel the time is right. Longevity has always been a pronounced issue within cultural labour because of the youthful image and make-up of the workforce (McRobbie 2015), but the university context creates a different sort of dilemma for workers when they have stability: these members of faculty have survived longer than many in this line of work, but they must continue to work while watching their perceived creative value and currency diminish.

Same Difference

This chapter has identified the ways institutional actors grapple with the instabilities ushered in under the new spirit of creativity, including doubt around how to manage the future with limited resources and anxiety around how to manage mushrooming expectations and workloads with seemingly less support and less clarity. Participants enumerated many discouraging and difficult aspects to their everyday work lives while expressing little expectation that things will improve. The metaphor "stuck between a rock and a hard place" represents impossible scenarios and a pervasive sense of inhospitable conditions, and the idea of the bubble provides an image of fragility and protection – but without consensus around what or who needs to be protected. If we combine these descriptions, conditions of austerity and uncertainty have a curious flattening effect, where both bubble and rock become indistinguishable under an organizational model that demands more for less. Both images respond to the underlying concern that artistic creativity and creative diversity face more dramatic constraints and will not be sustainable. The multiplying uncertainties under the new spirit of creativity, despite its creative flexibility and expansiveness, risk pushing artistic creative work into sameness.

This chapter nuances the portrait of instability at Imagination University by tying creative value to contradictions within the representation of institutional time and characterizations of creativity in the past, present, and future. In many respects, institutional-artistic critique in this chapter rightfully identifies conditions that facilitate uncertainty and its deleterious effects, but prospects for mutual compromise and collaboration seem exhausted due to internal and external organizational constraints; there is no room to budge. This becomes clear in the ways legitimate critiques are displaced (similar to chapter 6) or stalled within the tempo of uncertainty. For example, Jack's frustration with some senior faculty members articulates relevant critiques of organizational hierarchies, but these become overshadowed by ageist overtones that reinforce narratives of creativity and youth. Or in the example of efforts to leave Imagination University, employees became stalled, feeling unable to leave and unable to stay. Senior faculty members risk feeling more and more devalued, but because of wider financial uncertainties, they have to retire later and later. Similar to the previous chapter, replacing one inequity with another leaves the new spirit of creativity's negative repercussions intact and ensures that compromises with artistic creativity remain in the domain of the new spirit's third compromise relation: vulnerability.

The Terms of Compromise

It's all in how the terms of compromise are defined.

– Mel, study participant

They say artists don't know how to compromise, but they don't work here.

– Kat, study participant

This book has explored a major shift in how creativity is understood and valued at Imagination University. I have traced changes in organizational practices, examined contestations over meaning, and pinpointed a range of effects on an art/higher education institution that finds itself caught somewhere between artistic creativity and a new spirit of creativity. From the perspective of day-to-day operations, it is not a question of whether one needs to compromise – it is just a matter of how. But while the emergence of the new spirit of creativity is connected to rising uncertainties at Imagination University, rather than position this new spirit as wholly antithetical to artistic creativity, I make a different sort of argument. Here, I identify both shared concerns and key distinctions, and I theorize how artistic creativity intersects with compromise; artistic critique is by no means dead at Imagination University, but it is complicated. Creativity requires compromise, and this has always been the case if we read it sociologically, embedded as it is within social practices and relationships – structurally shaped yet socially contingent and mutually produced. Professional artistic creativity and everyday creative work as it is managed by the university and practiced by participants demonstrates how creativity involves compromises, but the forms and terms vary. Accordingly, compromise is not necessarily weakening; rather, it depends on social and organizational contexts. By elaborating on creativity as compromise, my critical-interpretive framework for the sociology of creativity is put to work in ways attentive to status, structure, and authority without losing sight of questions of meaning and interpretation at the core of work and organizational life.

Here, I briefly revisit the different compromise relations threaded throughout the chapter case studies. The first relation, recombination, is an intermediate ground between two different things: a compromise between forms, a hybrid. This version underscores the importance of establishing novel perspectives and relationships within artistic creativity and work. Recombination is one way that Dominic and others located compromise as crucial to sustaining successful artistic careers at Imagination University. Consider, for example, how many participants employed hyphens to describe their professional identity and practices; the hyphen is a way to combine the academic, teaching, and art worlds. This sort of compromise presents in the multiple definitions and versions of artistic research circulating at Imagination University, and in how participants identified ways their practices hinged on collaborations between areas or communities inside and outside of the university. A central part of creativity within everyday work is engaging with diverse possibilities and outcomes – a willingness to connect things and to forge relations of recombination. Not one interview participant portrayed creativity as fidelity to one perspective or an isolated vision; instead, it is cast as a test of endurance, cooperation, and openness. With recombination there is a striving for a common ground that can productively inform creative experimentation; however, successful recombination requires some equivalence between parts. Experimentation falls short if, in practice, research plans only devote resources to certain models; this is the complaint behind the "department for non-applied creativity." Likewise, paperwork and procedures can serve to limit how collaborations can take shape. While the art and design university is well equipped to be the intermediary that supports aesthetic experimentations and creative interconnections, participants also described various challenges to such mergers. The work of both compromise and critique remains unfinished and ongoing, which brings me to the second compromise relation: mutual concession.

Mutual concession refers to the mutual giving up required to reach accord. This form of compromise highlights the importance of reciprocity and mutual benefit within creative work arrangements. In general, participants expressed unmistakable dedication to their work; they are sincere about the importance of aesthetics and creativity within higher education and research. The starting compromise for almost all participants in this study is that by committing to the bureaucratic weight of creative regulation and evaluation, job security and considerable artistic freedom are offered in return. This is the overarching compromise an artist or designer engages with when they enter Imagination University, and, in its ideal form, it is an arrangement of mutual benefit. Unionized work is an essential backdrop to this conversation – one that is important because of what participants did not have to talk about in terms of working conditions and remuneration (for permanent employees, at least). It provides job security that is in scant supply in most artistic creative work. Further, collective agreements are often where theoretical commitments to greater equity are given some teeth, but as labour negotiations have it, this is by no means a straightforward process, and how to measure fair concessions on both sides is a considerable source of dispute and discontent. This form of compromise is key to strengthening existing arrangements, yet true mutuality requires reciprocity and a share in resources and benefits, and this is why this form of compromise is likely to falter. Besides unionization and the provision of general artistic autonomy, there are other emergent ways that mutual arrangements of creativity and compromise might work at the institutional level. For example, consider the growing support for and responsiveness to artistic research at Imagination University and higher education overall. While participants discussed making some adaptations to their writing and practices to better fit shifts in funding and academic discourses, they also identified many creative, professional, and institutional benefits. Here, the concession is made not only on the part of the artist or designer; the university and granting bodies, too, have transformed their definitions of research to better recognize and evaluate artistic research. The acknowledgment and funding of artistic research has expanded contemporary definitions of knowledge and extended, as well as diversified, research possibilities within the university. Yet, overall, compromise as mutual concession has difficulty flourishing because of existing arrangements of authority, resources, and decision-making. And this is where the collective compromises around expanding and funding artistic research, for example, quickly become imbalanced when funding is used to undergird hierarchies of value, recognition, and creative identity. This brings us to my final compromise relation: vulnerability.

Vulnerability, as a compromise relation, describes situations where practices of artistic creativity, as well as their valuation, are jeopardized. This version brings issues and consequences of organizational structure and hierarchy to the forefront. There are legitimate reasons to fear that artistic creativity is under threat at Imagination University. My analysis shows how the new spirit of creativity informs a new model worker at Imagination University – one who can capably navigate the demands of an active academic career and creative practice – and sees a growing emphasis placed on academic credentials, research, and funding. There is a sense of fragility and anxiety around being up to date; institutional documents and administrative accounts sketched out this ideal employee, and participants recognized new hierarchies of creative practices. Faculty are more easily divided into "fundable" and "unfundable" employees, and this too has consequences for how service to the institution is remembered and valued. Further, there are a number of techniques that mobilize diversity to uphold a progressive, creative institutional image, yet at the same time Ayana was penalized for being "too creative," a designation only applied negatively to a racialized pre-tenure woman – someone more vulnerable within the (permanent) employment order. In another case, Jack's contract was not renewed despite his artistic accomplishments. Shades of this sort of debilitating alignment of creativity and compromise are found elsewhere as well – for example, in the blurring of institutional and artistic identities, in the exclusions of policy and planning, and in informal and formal practices of judgment and evaluation. There are many instances where too many concessions and compromises are required of faculty, fueling fatigue and uncertainty. Yet even as creativity and compromise merge into vulnerability, they are not totally reducible to it. That is why these different forms of creativity and compromise coexist. While under the current arrangements of the new spirit of creativity, the balance tips towards vulnerability, this is not a static or absolute condition. This is important to keep in mind as art and cultural organizations of all types continue to face uncertain times.

Institutional-artistic critique features throughout the case studies: creative practices are generally maintained in diverse and exuberant ways. Despite many constraints, organizational flaws are often readily recognized and sometimes resisted, and possible remedies are identified and sometimes even realized. The art school remains one of the most creative and critical sites within contemporary culture, and this is in no small part because critique is also central to the job, with substantial autonomy around artistic creative practices. As Chris Burden, a boundary-pushing performance artist of the 1970s, reasoned much later in his career, "People think collectors support artists … But it's universities that support artists" (as cited in Solomon 1999). This point is woven throughout this book: Imagination University provides a crucial avenue of support for diverse artistic practices and careers. The fact that I have stressed the complexity of these dynamics and, ultimately, the various types of compromise they engender, is not a symptom of creativity's failure or insufficiency. Through a sociology of creativity lens, I have attended to the nuanced ways that institutional-artistic critique can be insightful, contradictory, and sometimes miss the mark considerably. I fear that the analysis presented in this book will, if not carefully read, lead to snap judgments about the shortcomings of artistic creativity's arrangement within institutional life. Rather, what I have documented is that despite being stalled by various organizational challenges, uncertainties, and inequities, creativity persists. The commitments to creativity captured in this book are forceful and genuine, even while some comments appear callous. Without doubt, every faculty member and upper administrator I spoke with was sincere about the importance of Imagination University within Canadian higher education. And while artistic creativity informs the institutional-artistic critique, it does not centre on authenticity, autonomy, or anti-commercialization in the ways one might expect. Instead, as I have shown, it is contextually responsive, critically reflective, and collectively oriented. Through this analysis, I show how a vital and renewed artistic creativity might emerge within art institutions like Imagination University.

I do not want to be overly prescriptive – I will not finish with a series of bullet point recommendations – but Imagination University must uphold strong commitments (financial, social, and cultural) to artistic creativity in diverse forms, contexts, and communities and prioritize non-economic contributions and values. Yet sustaining vibrant forms of artistic creativity within a complex organization requires more, not less, compromise. We need compromise relationships of reciprocity that are grounded in mutual concession and hybrid arrangements – ones that engage more and more at an organizational level with non-economic values to the benefit of artistic creativity, critical practices, and epistemic diversity. This can, as I see it, neutralize the new spirit's more detrimental effects. More alignments with artistic creativity and compromises of the right sort, not only via formalized collective labour agreements, will ensure that the institutional-artistic critique remains valid, robust, and creative. Instead of dismissing or obscuring it, if we better understand the multifold role compromise plays in creativity and cultural work, we can more meaningfully support diverse creative practices from all areas of art, media, and design within art schools, universities, cultural institutions, and other organizational contexts.

The wider contributions of this research – those beyond this particular case study – are threefold. First, this research establishes the new spirit of creativity as a well-defined, wide-reaching concept that is open to additional development, applications, and modifications in future research. Second, it develops an original argument around creativity and compromise relevant to the sociology of creativity and broader studies of cultural work and organizational research (e.g., artist-run centres, community maker studios, museums, design firms). Third, by demonstrating some of the effects of restructuring and austerity agendas on already marginalized and less well understood disciplines, this research adds further empirical support to critical scholarship on contemporary higher education.

The art school, as a mediating institution, plays a crucial role in the wider project of reimagining cultural labour, solidarity, and creative justice for contemporary times (Banks 2017). While I have focused my attention on the centre of authority and decision-making, this is only one aspect. Students are essential to maintaining the vibrancy of artistic creativity, critique, and change. The future of these schools as provocative and heterogeneous institutions depends on them too – a point that becomes all the more pressing as I write the conclusion of this book. Current political trends are witness to a rise in anti-academic *and* anti-culture sentiments, which are further complicated by an ongoing global pandemic with unknown long-term consequences for the arts, cultural work, and artists' employment trajectories. If there is a renewed devaluing of artistic creativity altogether on the horizon, the dynamics of creativity and compromise will be more confined to circumstances of vulnerability. If so, even the voracious new spirit of creativity may become a ghost.

Methodological Appendix

As a qualitative research project, this book leans on a number of underlying principles about the value and purpose of qualitative research. This perspective foregrounds depth over generalizability, and it values the insights drawn out of a contextualized, multifaceted case study that centres on participants' insights and experiences, analyses key themes, and develops concepts that help to forge connections between this work and other research. While I addressed the overarching roots of this methodology in the introduction, I will spend some time here elaborating on details and decision-making processes.

This book emerged from my place as a sympathetic insider–outsider to both the art and design university and the world of cultural work. While I currently work in a sociology and anthropology department, I have an interdisciplinary background that bridges art history, cultural theory, and sociology, which I bring to the study of many different things, including art and artists. I have written about art in both popular and academic contexts and have dabbled in curatorial work and creative practice, but I am on the whole a fairly conventional academic. However, I have crossed paths with the universities central to this study in different ways, and a number of experiences shaped my interest in this material. I am originally from the West Coast of Canada, and I have associations with ECUAD's Granville Island campus from my youth. I can still picture my incomplete application to transfer to Emily Carr as an undergraduate student sitting on my very messy desk. I lived in Toronto for a decade and attended various events at OCAD (artist's talks, symposiums, public lectures, and exhibitions) during this time; plus, I have a hazy memory of working as a TA for a year during graduate school for a visual culture course. Comments from others about the institution really stuck with me from that brief teaching stint – the way people would interject unsolicited comments questioning the quality of the institution and the calibre of its contributions, and from academics, artists, and people not part of either world. I could tell that the school seemed to rattle individuals because it challenged a readily accepted boundary of what was and was not considered academically valuable higher education. I have a much sharper memory of the SSHRC postdoctoral fellowship I held at NSCAD, which provided the initial groundwork for this book. Many academics advised against this choice of institution for my postdoctoral fellowship (the award can be held at any university), thinking it a risky gamble for my future prospects, yet I located myself at an art and design school very intentionally, and I have no doubt that this project would have been harder and less successfully realized if I had not been situated at one of these schools. So I want to be clear that an animating premise of this book is that the art and design university remains poorly understood and recognized within Canadian higher education.

The research for this project was gathered over a five-year period (2013–18). During the first year, I spent time on two of the three university campuses, attending talks and various events, as part of my preparatory research, but I did not begin data collection proper until 2014. After that, I treated all of my time on these campuses as field visits, observing, taking fieldnotes, and interviewing participants systematically. For each university, I conducted some archival research, mainly reviewing institutional documents (course calendars, reports, self-produced histories, planning documents). Between 2014 and 2018, I had home bases in both Nova Scotia and Ontario, so I had regular access to NSCAD and OCAD. With ECUAD, I had to plan my travel more carefully; my total time on the ECUAD campus was shorter but more intense (three visits in total), with one trip to the new university campus in 2018. Although I draw on some ethnographic principles in this approach, I do not describe this project as an ethnography – to do so would have required even more sustained periods of observation and participation on these campuses. I received ethics approval for this research first from NSCAD via St. Mary's University Research Ethics Board, and then from Acadia University's Research Ethics Board once I started a faculty position at Acadia University (Wolfville, Nova Scotia) in the fall of 2015.

My interview guide covered four areas: education and training; work experiences; institutional consistency and change; and workplace culture and interactions. First, I asked participants to describe their professional biography and discuss their education and training. Here, I would ask how they describe their creative practice and/or research practice and get a sense of their general interests and career trajectory. Next, I asked about work experiences within and outside of the school and gathered details about each participant's history and position(s) at the university. Third, I asked questions about what had remained the same and what, if anything, had changed during their time at the university. I solicited as many concrete examples as possible in these discussions to support claims, especially in terms of descriptions of turmoil or transition. And, when applicable, I would ask about comparable experiences at other institutions. Finally, I asked participants how they would characterize the workplace culture and everyday interactions of their institutions, and I solicited stories and experiences describing the pleasures and challenges of the workplace. This is where individuals would often talk about issues around work/creativity balance and elaborate on relationships and organizational dilemmas.

The overall interview dynamic with participants was conversational – collegial yet spirited (participants often questioned my questions). In terms of rapport, I benefited from my status as a sort-of-hard-to-place colleague (generic-looking white, somewhat arty female academic and postdoc). In my analysis, I paid extra attention to the types of examples and imagery people used to communicate their points during interviews. These examples are a form of storytelling and research is also storytelling. When I am listening to or transcribing interviews, I am always reminded of the many different types of shorthand that we use in everyday conversation. I never lose my sense of surprise about how many missing words, pauses, breaks, and incomplete thoughts occur that we do not notice during the conversation precisely because a conversation is held together by two participants. In terms of the presentation of the interview data in the analysis, I include some of the most representative quotations as demonstrations of a main point under discussions, but found it most effective to use a combination of the participants' descriptions and my own paraphrasing to capture the meaning and context. Generally, I do not quote long sections from interviews. While such sections do help convey participants' voices, I often found longer chunks did not represent well all of the dimensions of the point being made, especially given the non-linear and non-verbal content of many conversations. I did conduct some interviews via video chat (seven) and by telephone (three) to accommodate participants' preferences.

During interviews, I had to find a balance between allowing participants to direct the conversation and being responsive to their interests, while also maintaining comparability in terms of the interview guide. With some of the questions, there are other sources of information (institutional documents, media reports, public profiles) that support participants' responses. For example, in terms of key changes, I was able to draw on both participants' assessments as well as supporting documents that verify such changes. The responses about change were surprisingly consistent. For example, it might seem, at a glance, that the discussions around uncertainty were more heavily drawn from NSCAD participants because of their higher profile struggle, but this was not the case: evidence of uncertainty was produced across the research sites. For the interviews, I listened to, transcribed (I hired students to help with some of the transcription), read, and reread the interviews many times before I started coding. There are three levels of coding at work here: first, an overarching one that centres on the two versions of creativity (artistic and new spirit); second, individual chapter themes that take shape around this wider tension; third, the composite profiles that carve out different artistic work experiences, attitudes, and career trajectories. For this number of interviews (fifty-four), I preferred not to use dedicated data analysis software; I find the interface fragments the interviews and disconnects me from the content, so I developed a process that I feel maintains the integrity of the entire context and conversation. First, I open code on paper; then, in a word-processing program, I use search functions and develop tables as themes (or composites) emerge, and then cross-check again against the first open round to compare my assessment. I like to hang out with the material, and even after a chapter was "finished," I would go back to reread certain transcripts to check the representation and interpretation.

In terms of interpretation and analysis, I will discuss my approach to creating composites some more, especially as they are likely to be misunderstood, even under the big tent of qualitative research. A researcher creates a composite account "through careful attention to the context, the questions, and the purpose of the report" (Markham 2012, 342). It is a way for a researcher to organize and analyse large quantities of qualitative interview and observational data while removing loss of privacy risks that emerge (Willis 2019). In this case, privacy was an issue because of the small size of the schools, the small Canadian art scene, the public identities of many of the participants, and the extra risks for faculty artists from under-represented groups. All quotations, paraphrasing of positions, and observational details come directly from the interview transcripts and observations. This method retains clear links between the original interview transcripts and the final narratives, but instead of presenting each interview individually, it presents data from several interviewees via one composite. Overall, I believe this approach enhanced the readability of the entire manuscript and more effectively represented participants' experiences. Each composite participant profile I developed was drawn from three (and occasionally two or four) participants, with an eye to capturing what were a combination of relevant features that I identified as follows: career stage, training/education, practice/area of specialization, attitudes, concerns, and social identity. I should note that in terms of socially ascribed identities, I did not ask participants to do a demographic survey; this felt too intrusive, especially given the professional and collegial context of the interviews. Instead, I drew on self-descriptions during the interview and publicly available professional profiles. I wanted individuals to tell me what they felt was important about their work experiences in relationship to their social identity and location. This means that participants did talk about their identity and experiences in intersectional terms (e.g., gender, race, ethnicity, sexuality, language, citizenship, disability), but I do not have a comprehensive overview of such for the entire sample. Moreover, characteristics like class background, for example, were almost never discussed. Likewise, whiteness generally featured as an unnamed aspect of identity in self-descriptions. While I believe this approach is appropriate for an interpretive, qualitative project of this sort, the clear limitation is that many discussions around stigmatized identities – for example, chronic or invisible disabilities – did not happen, and for good reason on the part of participants. Further, discussions around how privilege shapes creative careers and employment remain underexplored. This study cannot, unfortunately, claim to address many important questions around the failures of diversity and belonging in cultural work and higher education, but it does give evidence to how some examples of discrimination and exclusion are maintained and justified at an organizational level.

By identifying common themes that arose across the research sites, I developed a composite portrait of the art and design university as an institutional type in Canada. However, one risk of this approach is that any one of these schools may be unrecognizable in a specific sense, especially for my participants or other employees of one of the universities in this study. It might be possible to have never encountered some of the ideas and perspectives discussed in this book, especially if you are not spending much time with individuals working in different areas. In my Informed Consent letter given to each participant, I listed disagreeing with my analysis as a potential risk of participation – a very real possibility given the expertise of my participants and their capacity for perceptive critiques. While I very much hope that readers connected to these schools or like institutions identify with features of this analysis, I sadly cannot promise this will be the case.

In total, I conducted fifty-four in-depth semi-structured interviews, plus nine follow-up interviews (three per school, for updates and clarifications), and six informational interviews with staff to clarify and fact-check points of information. Generally, interviews were between 60 and 120 minutes long. Although the management and organization of specialty areas is not exactly the same at each of the three schools, I identified potential participants based on information provided on each university's website, moving through the different areas and sub-specialties specific to each institution. I contacted seventy-five individuals in total based on the following criteria: the individual is a permanent faculty member,[1] the individual shows evidence of recent (within the past five years) participation in professional practice/research, and the individual has a record of teaching and service within the institution. The total number of individuals who occupy permanent positions across the three schools is just over 300 (chapter 6 discusses inconsistencies in numbers). However, to narrow this even more, I prioritized people who are or have been involved with research planning or research projects, new programs, or other recent institutional initiatives. My requests were organized to keep a balance across participant backgrounds, faculties, and areas at each school (i.e., art, craft, media, design, art history/curatorial studies). I use "administrators" to refer to school presidents, vice-presidents, and deans (including all variations like interim and associate), and I treated this group as its own area because of its significance to decision-making. With this design, I tried to recreate the size and scale of the smallest of the universities in this study, NSCAD, with its lean organization of fifty or so permanent full-time faculty members and key administrators.[2] While other staff positions are also very valuable to the operation of these schools, I did not include part-time faculty, studio technicians, or the many other important staff positions. Rather, this project is a study of the centre, and I focused on those who are most responsible for organizational activities and decision-making.

I used publicly available profile information to ensure invitations were sent out to a diverse range of participants. With the exception of some information on gender (see chapter 5), I did not have institutional numbers on faculty diversity, such as faculty who identify from the four designated groups as defined by Canada's Employment Equity Act (women, Indigenous Peoples, members of visible minorities, and persons with disabilities). According to Universities Canada, however, Canadian universities are expected to start producing diversity statistics over the next few years. The response rate to my interview requests was higher for women-identified participants, with a total of thirty-one (57 per cent) women and twenty-three (43 per cent) men. I had three participants self-identify as members of the LGBTQ2I+ community, and two that discussed how their work was impacted by a disability. In terms of Black, Indigenous, and People of Colour (BIPOC) – groups that are by all accounts under-represented at these schools and in arts careers more widely – I had nine (16.6 percent) faculty participants. With the exception of an OCAD labour force survey from 2011 that stated that 13 per cent of its faculty members identified as part of a racialized group (as cited in OCAD 2017, 6), I did not have concrete numbers to work with. For universities in Canada overall, full-time faculty representation for racialized and Indigenous groups hovered just over 22 per cent in 2016 (Statistics Canada 2018). However, based on the glimpse available from OCAD and my own estimate, the art and design universities are below this average (OCAD is the closest); further, it should be noted that the arts, humanities, and social sciences are disciplines that have a reputation for being more white compared to the sciences in Canada (Henry et al. 2017). Moreover, racialized women especially are more likely to hold insecure contracts rather than full-time positions (CAUT 2018). Although there are some important changes in process, my data collection concluded before these initiatives were implemented. For example, OCAD's Presidential Task Force on the Under-Representation of Racialized and Indigenous Faculty and Staff has launched a number of initiatives, including the gathering of accurate data and changing hiring processes and retention of BIPOC members; since 2017, there have been Black and Indigenous cluster hires. In addition, NSCAD announced in 2020 that it will establish the Institute for Canadian Slavery. Under the directorship of Dr. Charmaine Nelson (Tier 1 Canada Research Chair in Transatlantic Black Diasporic Art and Community

Engagement), this is the first research and education centre at any Canadian university dedicated to the study of the transatlantic slave trade in Canada.

There were a few additional challenges in terms of securing participation from BIPOC faculty members that I would like to mention, such as their almost complete absence from upper administrative roles. Also, BIPOC faculty are frequently called upon to "represent" or account for institutional diversity. Not only is this burdensome in so many ways, but it also often happens alongside a heightened struggle for professional recognition and respect (Ahmed 2012; Henry et al. 2017). I recognize that, for the above reasons and more, my invitation was probably not very appealing to many BIPOC faculty members. My research findings indicated there are good reasons to be cautious about such requests. That said, there was consistency around the issues described by BIPOC participants, and these were very important to my overall analysis and align well with current research within higher education as well as the cultural industries.

I cannot thank my participants enough for their time and their openness to this project, nor for their willingness to share and talk at length about their careers, work experiences, and creative practices.

Notes

Introduction

1   A note on terms is necessary here. *Artistic creativity*, with its emphasis on aesthetic processes and products, is a specialized domain of creativity. It is a way to capture the centrality of aesthetic practice and knowledge within art, media, craft, and design. Unless otherwise stated, when I refer to *creativity* throughout this book, I mean it in this specialized way. I recognize that many participants in this study, as well as many people working in art, media, or design fields, do not refer to themselves as artists – they might use *designer, creative, creative practitioner*, or other more specific job titles. While I shorten this for readability reasons to *artist* or *artists and designers*, I mean to include this full range of ways individuals describe their roles. However, regardless of preferred labels or identifications, I see the art, design, and media fields engaging in artistic creative practices as defined here.

2   *Oxford Dictionary of English*, 3rd ed. (2010), s.v. "compromise."

3   To be clear, there are also many relevant works from the wider domain of the social sciences interested in contemporary creativity. For example, scholarship from cultural geography on the often-fraught relationship between artists and creative city discourses of urban development and processes of gentrification (e.g., Mathews 2010; McLean 2014, 2017; Zukin 1982, 1995) and scholarship from anthropology on the creativity of everyday life and improvisation (e.g., Hallam and Ingold 2007; Lavie, Narayan, and Rosaldo 1993).

4   The fourth university in Canada is the Alberta University of the Arts (formerly Alberta College of Art and Design). It achieved university status on 1 March 2018 and its new name passed in the Alberta legislature in December 2018. Its university transition was still in process when I started this project in 2013, so I did not include it in this study; it was not yet comparable – for example, in terms of research development – to the other art and design universities.

There is also the related domain of a school or faculty of fine art or art and design located within a comprehensive university. While many of the conflicts and debates I address are relevant to these contexts, the stand-alone nature of the art and design university provides a focused lens on the arrangements between art and academia.

5   Certainly, this employment security does not apply to all employees, and insecure workers are also crucial to the everyday operation of the art and design university (see chapter 6).

6   For example, a recent statistical portrait of artists and cultural workers in Canada (Hill 2019) demonstrates the size, range, and significance of this category to the overall labour market based on Statistics Canada data. The report notes the high rates of self-employment and lower rates of income typical of artistic professions, with some variation between areas. However, this sort of study does not include artists who teach in the elementary, secondary, or post-secondary systems; because of occupational classifications, these artists would be classified as teachers or professors.

1 Our New Spirit and the Dilemmas of Artistic Critique

1   I follow the succinct definition provided by Boltanski and Chiapello of the minimal formula of capitalism as "an imperative to unlimited accumulation of capital by formally peaceful means" (2007, 4).

2   Because of the importance of this previous book to the argument made in *The New Spirit of Capitalism*, I will provide more background here. In *On Justification*, Boltanski and Thévenot identify six common orders of worth (polities) on which agreements or disagreements emerge – as noted above – to which Boltanski and Chiapello add the project-based. While the polity is the abstract model of justification, the six common worlds (e.g., inspired world, market world) that correspond to these orders of worth refer to the concrete unfolding of worth as objects and are qualified according to a specific polity (world = polity + objects; Jagd 2011, 347).

3   The orders of worth approach has been productively applied to the arts, including Thévenot's (2015) own writing on participatory art and political engagement. Daigle and Rouleau (2010) examined three performing arts organizations in Quebec. Based on an analysis of their strategic plans, they found that the industrial world of economic rationality and value dominated, but with some space for micro-compromises with artistic values emerging. Together, this mix of certainty and ambiguity helped to "seduce, persuade and mystify the organization's different stakeholders" (13). Also drawing on Boltanski and Thévenot, Gerber's *The Work of Art* (2017) provides an elegant investigation into how artists negotiate questions of value in art making and identifies the multidimensional accounts artists use to make sense of art as symbolic production, work, and economic activity. Based

on interviews with art world elites to small scale hobbyists, Gerber identifies four accounts artists use to explain the value of their artistic practice: pecuniary, vocational, credentialing, relational. Her research carefully dismantles the still prevalent notion that artistic identity and production is incompatible with economic values, and her approach is more open to combined orders of worth and compromise than Boltanski and Thévenot envision (153–4n1, 155–6n2).

4   Sometimes I shorten this is to "artistic critique" in the coming chapters for readability, but I always mean "institutional-artistic critique" in the sense developed here.

5   While some participants in this study are artists who have worked within the lineage of institutional critique, the critical insights of these works of art are not part of my analysis.

6   Students at Hornsey College of Art were protesting changes in art and design curriculum geared to standardization and institutionalization; essentially, changes that are now commonplace.

2 What Could Be More Creative Than an Art School?

1   This includes the whole gamut of art, craft, media, and design. Media and craft are not in the formal institutional titles but should be acknowledged as a clear focus at these schools. This does not include the performing arts (music, theatre, and dance). Lines between art and design are not always easily drawn and are organized a bit differently at each school. Many interview participants quibbled around the organization of areas. This is not exhaustive, but here is a list of general areas, with some examples for each, that fall under the art, media, and design umbrella: craft (ceramics, jewelry, textiles); media (film, photography, animation; digital media); art (painting, sculpture, installation; performance art, community art, curatorial studies, mixed media); design (industrial design, interactive design, health design, graphic design). And you can add to this list academic specialties relevant to the study of art, design, media, and culture including art history and criticism, film studies, social and political theory, cultural studies, and communications.

2   I address in more detail these sources in my overview of the individual schools below.

3   Contrary to the US, Canada has relatively few private universities (many are faith related) and little appetite for a private system. Public universities in Canada operate at an arm's length from the government as non-profit institutions that receive substantial public funds (albeit subject to government budgets and priorities) and for whom tuition revenue is crucial. Tuition fees for full-time undergraduate students for the 2018–19 school year per semester were as follows: ECUAD: $2,709.96; NSCAD: $4,049.00; OCAD: $3,568.80. Many well-known private art schools in the US charge tuition fees exceeding USD$20,000 per semester.

4 The year 2010 represented a peak of 66 per cent, and 2012 a low of 48 per cent, which is a considerable drop, but one representing the financial renegotiations between the institution and the province at this time. The other years are between 54 per cent and 59 per cent. Since 2015, the provincial operating grant, as a proportion of NSCAD's total income, has been steadily declining. It was 48.5 per cent in 2017, 47.5 per cent in 2018, and 42.8 per cent in 2019.

5 For example, revenue from donations, endowments/investment, and non-government contracts were reported to CAUBO as follows: in 2013–14, 3 per cent for OCAD, 5.2 per cent for NSCAD, and 10.7 per cent for ECUAD; in 2014–15, 5.4 per cent for NSCAD, 9.4 per cent for OCAD, and 11.5 per cent for ECUAD.

6 Preliminary enrolment numbers have been posted every year for NSCAD since 2000 as part of the Association of Atlantic Universities' data. All yearly reports are available at https://www.atlanticuniversities.ca/statistics /aau-survey-preliminary-enrolments.

7 After her time in Asia, Leonowens settled in Halifax. Importantly, women played a central role in NSCAD's early history. For example, in addition to its founding team, Elizabeth Styring Nutt was the principal when it became a college in 1925.

8 Kennedy comments that after checking the university's charter, he realized they could award degrees. He thought it was a good idea, especially because of OCA's antipathy to awarding degrees: "We were also 25 years ahead of most art colleges in Canada in giving degrees … I looked at the school's charter and low and behold it gave us permission to hand out degrees. So we gave the BFA and then the MFA" (as cited in McLaughlin 2016).

9 See Kennedy (2012) for the full list of regular teaching faculty from 1968 to 1978. Visiting artists came to the school through a number of mechanisms – from giving artist talks to working with NSCAD press to occupying formal visiting faculty positions to designing an assignment for the legendary Projects class.

10 This is a term used in Canada to refer to how provinces rely on equalization payments from the federal government to reduce fiscal disparities between provinces in the country. British Columbia, where Emily Carr is located, is a "have province," and Ontario has moved in and out of the "have" category in the recent past.

11 While the NSCAD Board of Governors (2020) sent out a statement to address this situation and the backlash it received, including a public protest, many unanswered questions remain.

12 Referred to as a "cross word puzzle on stilts" (Goldberger 2007, 184), the Sharp Centre for Design launched Alsop's international profile and has been named as evidence of Toronto's architectural revival.

13 When a university uses an FTE (full-time equivalent) number to capture faculty positions, it is not distinguishing between contract or permanent positions. See chapter 6 for more discussion.

14 At issue was not only the process around the third-term appointment, but also the bonus in Diamond's contract of $50,000 per year for five years after retirement.

Ian Tudhope, the private-sector finance professional and former chair of the OCAD Board of Governors who helped broker the deal, spoke about the contract as follows: "I'm glad we are doing something that doesn't have a whole number of precedents … I think we are fortunate to be able to pay so little to get such insight" (as cited in Choise 2015).

15 In some interviews with longer-serving faculty at OCAD, this history of suspicion surrounding the concept of tenure did come up. How this relates to perceptions of temporary work within the institution is discussed in chapter 6.

16 This gamble did not appear to resonate as intended, and the MAA degree was changed to an MFA in 2017.

17 Great Northern Way Campus Trust is jointly owned by Vancouver's four universities (University of British Columbia, Simon Fraser University, British Columbia Institute of Technology, and ECUAD). Emily Carr's relocation is key to the revitalization of previous industrial land into a cultural and creative sector hub. It is just over four kilometers from the former Granville Island campus.

18 ECUAD is already an outlier in this group of institutions in BC. For example, it has a provincial mandate compared to smaller regional mandates of the other "special purpose, teaching universities." And in addition to its specialized offerings, Emily Carr was already smoothly operating as a university-like institution, even before its designation as such, while the others were operating more like colleges. This designation acts as a constraint that does not respond well to the provincial context and contributions of the university.

3 Welcome to the Department of Non-applied Creativity

1   This first section of chapter 3 includes some revised material from a previously published article (see Liinamaa 2018).

2   This variation on terms can be confusing. Borgdorff uses "research on the arts" to refer to the more traditional types of academic inquiry (and most closely corresponds to Frayling's use of "research into art and design"). His "research for the arts" corresponds with Frayling's idea of "research through arts and design," and Borgdorff's "research in the arts" is his way of explaining the impossibility of separating theory and practice in the arts.

3   Certainly, some faculty members have practices that sometimes, if not regularly, involve working with a commercial client, while others not at all; thus, some qualification of this statement is required. When the question of commercialization and research emerged, individuals were more or less comfortable with the idea. But there is an important distinction to be made for even those directly involved with product development – commercial or market interests cannot be the most important component of advanced research. As Patrick put it, "it's a by-product, not the whole pie."

4   This was a well-developed focus of Getzels and Csikszentmihalyi (1976; see Part 2) that is now widely used.

5   See Wohl (2021, 43–71) for a relevant parallel discussion of how emotions feature strongly within artists' aesthetic decision-making and experimentation, and Fine (2018, 113–16) on the role of emotion within MFA training.

6   As Bourdieu argues in the introduction of *Distinction*, "social subjects, classified by their classifications, distinguish themselves by the distinctions they make, between the beautiful and the ugly, the distinguished and the vulgar, in which their position in the objective classifications is expressed or betrayed" (1984, 6).

7   Dominic credited this metaphor to Marcel Duchamp (1887–1968), which also points to a conceptual art history and lineage for artistic research.

4 Audit Culture

1   SSHRC is a widely drawn upon funding source, and its "research-creation" category has been a way to extend funding to a range of artistic research activities and practices. Research-creation is defined as "an approach to research that combines creative and academic research practices, and supports the development of knowledge and innovation through artistic expression, scholarly investigation, and experimentation. The creation process is situated within the research activity and produces critically informed work in a variety of media (art forms)" (SSHRC 2021a).

2   Only the limited group of participants who identified as more conventional academics cited peer-reviewed journal articles or books published by a university press.

3   To be clear, my research demonstrates that the conventional language of the individual-level creative genius or vision was only very rarely employed by artists or administrators in their everyday talk about creative practices.

4   In terms of insecure work, I return to Jack's case in chapter 6. Here, he suggested that his insecure status is one of the factors that contributed to this review. Mainly, because he was not a permanent employee, the school did not want to celebrate his achievements in quite the same way, even though he had been on a recurring contract for many years.

5   This legendary conceptual art piece by Baldesarri is directly connected to NSCAD, where it was produced based on instructions Baldesarri sent to students; he was not actually in attendance during its production (see Kennedy 2012, 96).

5 Performing at the "Shit Show"

1   In 2016, Statistics Canada reinstated its survey, University and College Academic Staff System – Full Time Staff (FT-UCASS), which had not been conducted since 2010–11. Numbers for ECUAD and NSCAD are not released, however, because

they have fewer than 100 full-time teaching staff. OCAD's numbers indicate gender parity for full-time staff at the rank of assistant professor or above, with eighty-one women and eighty-one men in 2016–17 and seventy-eight women and seventy-eight men in 2017–18. CAUT's review of the first survey (CAUT 2016a, Table 2.6) places the overall number of full-time women university teachers for 2016–17 at 39.52 per cent. For the area of Visual and Performing Arts specifically, the number is higher at 45.51 per cent. In 2020–1, OCAD reported slightly more full-time women faculty than men (seventy-eight women, seventy-five men).

2   Drawing on Deleuze and Guattari (1987), *agencement* shares an etymological root with agency that is important here. Callon describes this as "arrangements endowed with the capacity of acting in different ways depending on their configuration. This means that there is nothing left outside of *agencements*: there is no need for further explanation, because the construction of its meaning is part of an *agencement*" (2007, 321).

3   Because of the higher education context, participants demonstrated a fluency with critical concepts such a neo-liberalization and would use it to describe the logic of many activities and decisions.

4   And Hochschild does cite classrooms as one of the many sites of emotional labour ([1983] 2012, ix).

5   Despite decades of well-documented evidence of racism, the scale and depth of systemic racism in Canadian universities is only now, at the time of writing, starting to become the focus of more public and institutional discourse (see Deckard, Akram, and Ku 2021). Current activism and scholarship are developing both practical and conceptual strategies for growing the anti-racist university.

6   In addition, statements like "fucking disaster" (Kat) served the same function but are an even more provocative profanity in terms of social scripts. As Nate put it, "As an institution this place is, to use a technical term, so fucked up." In general, participants were more likely to swear when we had a stronger rapport.

7   But as Tyler (2013) emphasizes, it is important not to idealize abjection to the point where we eschew its implications for social identities that experience the only too real consequences of its symbolic violence.

6 Navigating the Permanent–Temporary Divide

1   There is no one preferred term in Canada, and many researchers have struggled with how to be consistent and account for different usages and associations. For example, *sessional* is a term widely used in Ontario to refer to contract teachers. Terms like *contract academic staff* (CAS) or *contract academic faculty* (CAF) are being more widely used, but there is some uncertainty over what type of work is included by the term *staff*, and thus it is not as commonly used here as it is in the UK. I am using the term *contract faculty* as the most general description of temporary work in the institution, but I think it is important to emphasize the

temporary dimension to these arrangements, so I often use *insecure, contingent,* or *temporary.* I do not discuss the wider range of impermanent positions possible in the university (e.g., graduate teaching assistants, researchers/project coordinators, technicians). It is worth noting that, because of the history of the schools involved in this study, there are in some cases permanent yet not tenure-track positions in this category of full-time faculty. Canadian universities do not widely use the term *adjunct faculty* to refer to contract academic faculty (as is the case in the US).

2   Brownlee discusses the many challenges of collecting data on workers in Ontario universities, arguing that "the idea that universities are unable to assemble hiring data on their contract employees seems implausible. A more likely explanation is that these institutions have no particular interest in compiling or releasing the information" (2015b, 789). He filed numerous Access to Information requests at eighteen Ontario universities under the Freedom of Information and Protection of Privacy Act in 2010. With many delays and difficulties working around institutional gatekeeping, it was challenging but not impossible to verify that there has been a steady increase in part-time appointments overall at these universities. OCAD, not yet a university, was not included in Brownlee's research.

3   Statistics Canada's survey, "University and College Academic Staff System," is based on full-time employees defined as those with appointments of not less than twelve months or longer. Brownlee recounts Statistics Canada's failed attempts to accurately collect part-time data (2015b, 788–9). Based on the definition, this number could include those on full-time multi-year contracts.

4   The need for instructor intensive teaching is not well recognized in the government funding formulas for art and design institutions. This was frequently noted by administrators during my research because it puts extra strain on teaching needs.

5   This survey potentially had respondents who were employed at NSCAD, but it did not break down respondents' teaching areas or institutions. With the exception of Dalhousie University, with about 19,000 students, and St. Mary's University, at about 7,000, the other seven universities in Nova Scotia have 5,000 or less full- and part-time students each, with Université Sainte-Anne, King's College, and NSCAD at less than 1,000 students each (based on numbers from the 2018 Association of Atlantic Universities data).

6   Similarly, Field and Jones found that three-quarters of respondents (76.4 per cent) in their survey of sessional faculty in Ontario would prefer to have a permanent position yet were generally pessimistic about their chances of acquiring such (2016, 20).

7   The response rate was too small to report findings from only those who had worked at the art and design universities in this study (personal communication with Karen Foster, June 2018). Many thanks to Karen Foster and CAUT for sharing this data.

8   This is also well captured by the history of conceptual art in Canada as defined by the concept of "traffic" between cities and regions (see Arnold and Henry 2012).

9   Active union members were most likely to express concern for the rise of contract labour and note its links to shifting management culture and governance. Dominic noted how disheartening it was to see long-serving and qualified contract faculty overlooked for a tenure-track position, and with no remedy in sight to recognize their commitments. Mel readily admitted that "if all of the sessionals quit tomorrow, we would be toast, basically," and Nate assessed the future ramifications of the rise of contract work: "The situation of high reliance seems unsustainable."

10   For the rest of this section only, I break with my usual format of presenting interview quotations. I use "Chair," "Dean," and "VP+" (vice-president or above) to better capture all comments that emerged from an administrator's perspective and role.

11   This is how Field and Jones (2016) adapt what Rajagopal (2002) calls the "contemporary instructor" to current circumstances.

7 Rocks and Bubbles

1   There are, however, some very concerning possibilities of university restructuring emerging in Canada in light of the unprecedented situation at Laurentian University in Sudbury, Ontario. In April 2021, the university eliminated over 100 faculty positions and cut dozens of programs after the university had declared itself insolvent and filed for creditor protection two months earlier (Flaherty 2021).

2   *Disaster capitalism* treats economic uncertainty as the fuel for opportunity (Klein 2008); *academic capitalism* is a term used to refer to universities as market-like entities (Slaughter and Rhoades 2004).

3   Again, this is a rare instance where I cannot use the composite profiles because of the specificity to NSCAD.

Methodological Appendix

1   This included those faculty members who had moved into upper administrative roles.

2   Based on staff numbers provided in annual reports. For example, in 2017–18, NSCAD had forty-three individuals listed as faculty (which includes librarians) and five listed in key upper administrative roles (president, vice-presidents, associate vice-presidents). NSCAD does not have deans; chairs are included under faculty.

References

Abbott, Andrew Delano. 1988. *The System of Professions: An Essay on the Division of Expert Labor.* Chicago: University of Chicago Press.

Abery, Elizabeth, and Jessica Shipman Gunson. 2016. "The Cycle of Student and Staff Wellbeing: Emotional Labour and Extension Requests in Higher Education. A Practice Report." *Student Success* 7, no. 1 (March): 65–71. DOI: 10.5204/ssj .v7i1.326.

Adams, Suze. 2014. "Practice as Research: A Fine Art Contextual Study." *Arts and Humanities in Higher Education* 13, no. 3 (July): 218–26. DOI: 10.1177/1474022213514549.

Adler, Judith E. 1979. *Artists in Offices: An Ethnography of an Academic Art Scene.* New Brunswick, NJ: Transaction Publishers.

Afonso, Alexandre. 2016. "Varieties of Academic Labor Markets in Europe." *PS: Political Science & Politics* 49, no. 4 (October): 816–21. DOI: 10.1017 /S1049096516001505.

Ahmed, Sara. 2004. *The Cultural Politics of Emotion.* New York: Routledge.

– 2012. *On Being Included: Racism and Diversity in Institutional Life.* Durham, NC: Duke University Press.

Ainsworth-Vincze, Cameron. 2011a. "Emily Carr: Cool and Energetic." In *Maclean's Guide to Canadian Universities.* Toronto: Rogers Media.

– 2011b. "OCAD: It's All about Imagination." In *Maclean's Guide to Canadian Universities.* Toronto: Rogers Media.

Alacovska, Ana. 2018. "'Keep Hoping, Keep Going': Towards a Hopeful Sociology of Creative Work." *The Sociological Review* 67, no. 5 (June): 1118–36. DOI: 10.1177/0038026118779014.

Alacovska, Ana, and Rosalind Gill. 2019. "De-Westernizing Creative Labour Studies: The Informality of Creative Work from an Ex-Centric Perspective." *International Journal of Cultural Studies* 22, no. 2 (January): 195–212. DOI: 10.1177/1367877918821231.

Alberro, Alexander, and Blake Stimson, eds. 2011. *Institutional Critique: An Anthology of Artists' Writings*. Cambridge, MA: MIT Press.

Alexander, Jeffrey C. 2004. "Cultural Pragmatics: Social Performance between Ritual and Strategy." *Sociological Theory* 22, no. 4 (December): 527–73. DOI: 10.1111/j.0735-2751.2004.00233.x.

– 2006. *The Meanings of Social Life: A Cultural Sociology*. Oxford: Oxford University Press.

– 2011. *Performance and Power*. Cambridge: Polity.

Alexander, Victoria D., and Anne E. Bowler. 2014. "Art at the Crossroads: The Arts in Society and the Sociology of Art." *Poetics* 43 (April): 1–19. DOI: 10.1016/j.poetic.2014.02.003.

Alfoldy, Sandra. 2005. *Crafting Identity: The Development of Professional Fine Craft in Canada*. Montreal: McGill-Queen's University Press.

Allen, Felicity, ed. 2011. *Education*. London: Whitechapel Gallery.

Amabile, Teresa. 1996. *Creativity in Context*. Boulder, CO: Westview Press.

Anderson, Elijah. 2015. "The White Space." *Sociology of Race and Ethnicity* 1, no. 1 (January): 10–21. DOI: 10.1177/2332649214561306.

Anderson, Gina. 2006. "Carving out Time and Space in the Managerial University." *Journal of Organizational Change Management* 19, no. 5 (September): 578–92. DOI: 10.1108/09534810610686698.

Appadurai, Arjun. 1996. *Modernity at Large: Cultural Dimensions of Globalization*. Minneapolis: University of Minnesota Press.

Arnold, Grant, and Karen Henry, eds. 2012. *Traffic: Conceptual Art in Canada 1965–1980*. Vancouver: Vancouver Art Gallery.

Arya, Rina, and Nicholas Chare, eds. 2016. *Abject Visions: Powers of Horror in Art and Visual Culture*. Manchester: Manchester University Press.

Ascott, Roy. 1971. *Aug. 3rd: Roy Ascott Talks About Curriculum for Year 2*. Vinyl Record. Toronto: Ontario College of Art.

Ashton, Daniel. 2010. "Productive Passions and Everyday Pedagogies: Exploring the Industry-Ready Agenda in Higher Education." *Art, Design & Communication in Higher Education* 9, no. 1 (October): 41–56. DOI: 10.1386/adch.9.1.41_1.

– 2011. "Media Work and the Creative Industries: Identity Work, Professionalism and Employability." *Education + Training* 53, no. 6 (July): 546–60. DOI: 10.1108/00400911111159494.

– 2013a. "Cultural Workers In-the-Making." *European Journal of Cultural Studies* 16, no. 4 (August): 468–88. DOI: 10.1177/1367549413484308.

– 2013b. "Industry Practitioners in Higher Education: Values, Identity and Cultural Work." In *Cultural Work and Higher Education*, edited by Daniel Ashton and Caitriona Noonan, 172–92. London: Palgrave Macmillan.

– 2015. "Creative Work Careers: Pathways and Portfolios for the Creative Economy." *Journal of Education and Work* 28, no. 4 (July): 388–406. DOI: 10.1080/13639080.2014.99768.

Ashton, Daniel, and Caitriona Noonan, eds. 2013. *Cultural Work and Higher Education*. London: Palgrave Macmillan.

Bailey, Kerry A. 2016. "Racism within the Canadian University: Indigenous Students' Experiences." *Ethnic and Racial Studies* 3, no. 7 (May): 1261–79. DOI: 10.1080/01419870.2015.1081961.

Bain, Alison L. 2013. *Creative Margins: Cultural Production in Canadian Suburbs*. Toronto: University of Toronto Press.

Baldwin, Roger G., and Jay L. Chronister. 2001. *Teaching without Tenure: Policies and Practices for a New Era*. Baltimore: Johns Hopkins University Press.

Banks, Mark. 2007. *The Politics of Cultural Work*. London: Palgrave Macmillan.

– 2014. "Being in the Zone of Cultural Work." *Culture Unbound: Journal of Current Cultural Research* 6, no. 1 (February): 241–62. DOI: 10.3384/cu.2000.1525.146241.

– 2017. *Creative Justice: Cultural Industries, Work and Inequality*. London: Rowman & Littlefield International.

Banks, Mark, Rosalind Gill, and Stephanie Taylor, eds. 2013. *Theorizing Cultural Work: Labour, Continuity and Change in the Cultural and Creative Industries*. London: Routledge.

Banks, Mark, and Katie Milestone. 2011. "Individualization, Gender and Cultural Work." *Gender, Work & Organization* 18, no. 1 (January): 73–89. DOI: 10.1111/j.1468-0432.2010.00535.

Banks, Mark, and Kate Oakley. 2016. "The Dance Goes on Forever? Art Schools, Class and UK Higher Education." *International Journal of Cultural Policy* 22, no. 1 (January): 41–57. DOI: 10.1080/10286632.2015.1101082.

Barbalet, Jack M. 2010. *Weber, Passion and Profits:* The Protestant Ethic and the Spirit of Capitalism *in Context*. Cambridge: Cambridge University Press.

Barber, Bruce. 2006. *NSCAD: The 80's*. Halifax: Anna Leonowens Gallery.

– 2009. "The Question (of Failure) in Art Research." In *Rethinking the Contemporary Art School: The Artist, the PhD, and the Academy*, edited by Brad Buckley and John Conomos, 45–63. Halifax: NSCAD Press.

Barkley, Alan. 1994. "The Exhibition, the Catalogue and Two Short Sagas." In *64–94: Contemporary Decades*, edited by Sam Carter, 11–15. Vancouver: Charles H. Scott Gallery/ECIAD.

Barone, Tom, and Elliot W. Eisner. 2012. *Arts Based Research*. Los Angeles: SAGE.

Bataille, Georges. 1985. *Visions of Excess: Selected Writings, 1927–1939*. Translated and edited by Allan Stoekl. Minneapolis: University of Minnesota Press.

Bauman, Zygmunt. 2011. *Wasted Lives: Modernity and Its Outcasts*. Reprint. Cambridge: Polity.

Baxter, Kristin, Hugo Ortega López, Dan Serig, and Graeme Sullivan. 2008. "The Necessity of Studio Art as a Site and Source for Dissertation Research." *International Journal of Art & Design Education* 27, no. 1 (January): 4–18. DOI: 10.1111/j.1476-8070.2008.00553.x.

Beck, John, and Matthew Cornford. 2012. "The Art School in Ruins." *Journal of Visual Culture* 11, no. 1 (May): 58–83. DOI: 10.1177/1470412911430467.

Beck, Ulrich. 2000. *The Brave New World of Work*. Malden, MA: Polity.

Becker, Howard Saul. 1982. *Art Worlds*. Berkeley: University of California Press.

Belcher, Shaun D. 2014. "Can Grey Ravens Fly? Beyond Frayling's Categories." *Arts and Humanities in Higher Education* 13, no. 3 (July): 235–42. DOI: 10.1177/1474022213514548.

Belfiore, Eleonora. 2014. "'Impact,' 'Value' and 'Bad Economics': Making Sense of the Problem of Value in the Arts and Humanities." *Arts and Humanities in Higher Education* 14, no. 1 (February): 95–110. DOI: 10.1177/1474022214531503.

Beljean, Stefan, Phillipa Chong, and Michèle Lamont. 2015. "A Post-Bourdieusian Sociology of Valuation and Evaluation for the Field of Cultural Production." In *Routledge International Handbook of the Sociology of Art and Culture*, edited by Laurie Hanquinet and Mike Savage, 38–48. New York: Routledge.

Bell, Katherine. 2008. "The MFA Is the New MBA." *Harvard Business Review*, April 14, 2008. https://hbr.org/2008/04/the-mfa-is-the-new-mba.

Benjamin, Walter. 2002. *The Arcades Project*. Translated by Howard Eiland and Kevin McLaughlin. Cambridge, MA: Harvard University Press.

Berry, Ellen E. 2016. *Women's Experimental Writing: Negative Aesthetics and Feminist Critique*. London: Bloomsbury Academic.

Berry, Karen, and Simon Cassidy. 2013. "Emotional Labour in University Lecturers: Considerations for Higher Education Institutions." *Journal of Curriculum and Teaching* 2, no. 2 (January): 22–36. DOI: 10.5430/jct.v2n2p22.

Biggs, Michael, and Henrik Karlsson, eds. 2010. *The Routledge Companion to Research in the Arts*. New York: Routledge.

Black, Anthea, and Nicole Burisch. 2018. "Still Performing Austerity: Artists, Work, and Economic Speculation." *RACAR* 43, no. 1 (August): 85–9. DOI: 10.7202/1050823ar.

Black, Stephen. 2016. "When Tenure Never Comes." *The Walrus*, July 18, 2016. https://thewalrus.ca/when-tenure-never-comes/.

Blair-Loy, Mary. 2003. *Competing Devotions: Career and Family among Women Executives*. Cambridge, MA: Harvard University Press.

Bodnar, Christopher. 2006. "Taking It to the Streets: French Cultural Worker Resistance and the Creation of a Precariat Movement." *Canadian Journal of Communication* 31, no. 3 (July): 675–94. DOI: 10.22230/cjc.2006v31n3a1768.

Boltanski, Luc. 2011. *On Critique: A Sociology of Emancipation*. Malden, MA: Polity.

Boltanski, Luc, and Eve Chiapello. 2007. *The New Spirit of Capitalism*. Translated by Gregory C. Elliott. London: Verso.

Boltanski, Luc, and Laurent Thévenot. 2006. *On Justification: Economies of Worth*. Princeton: Princeton University Press.

Borgdorff, Henk. 2010. "The Production of Knowledge in Artistic Research." In *The Routledge Companion to Research in the Arts*, edited by Michael Biggs and Henrik Karlsson, 44–63. London: Routledge.

– 2012. *The Conflict of the Faculties: Perspectives on Artistic Research and Academia.* Leiden: Leiden University Press.

Born, Georgina. 1995. *Rationalizing Culture: IRCAM, Boulez, and the Institutionalization of the Musical Avant-Garde.* Berkeley: University of California Press.

– 2005. *Uncertain Vision: Birt, Dyke and the Reinvention of the BBC.* London: Vintage.

– 2010. "The Social and the Aesthetic: For a Post-Bourdieuian Theory of Cultural Production." *Cultural Sociology* 4, no. 2 (July): 171–208. DOI: 10.1177/1749975510368471.

Bourdieu, Pierre. 1984. *Distinction: A Social Critique of the Judgement of Taste.* Cambridge, MA: Harvard University Press.

– 1993. *The Field of Cultural Production: Essays on Art and Literature.* New York: Columbia University Press.

Boyle, David, and Kate Oakley. 2018. *Co-Operatives in the Creative Industries.* Manchester: Co-operatives UK. https://culturalworkersorganize.org/wp-content /uploads/2018/10/Cooperatives-and-Creative-Industries-Boyle-and-Oakley.pdf.

Boym, Svetlana. 2008. *The Future of Nostalgia.* New York: Basic Books.

Bradshaw, James. 2010. "OUAD Just Didn't Have Right Ring for the Soon-to-Be Dubbed OCAD University." *Globe and Mail*, April 27, 2010. https://www.theglobeandmail.com/news/toronto/ouad-just -didnt-have-right-ring-for-the-soon-to-be-dubbed-ocad-university /article4316577/.

– 2011. "Storied Nova Scotia Art College Faces Hard Choices to Stay Afloat." *Globe and Mail*, December 12, 2011. https://www.theglobeandmail.com/news/national /education/storied-nova-scotia-art-college-faces-hard-choices-to-stay-afloat /article4180705/.

Bradshaw, James, and Oliver Moore. 2011. "Nova Scotia Art School Avoids Forced Merger." *Globe and Mail*, December 13, 2011. https://www.theglobeandmail.com /news/national/nova-scotia-art-school-avoids-forced-merger/article4097419/.

Brenneis, Don, Cris Shore, and Susan Wright. 2005. "Getting the Measure of Academia: Universities and the Politics of Accountability." *Anthropology in Action* 12, no. 1 (Spring): 1–10. DOI: 10.3167/096720105780644362.

Brownlee, Jamie. 2015a. *Academia, Inc.: How Corporatization Is Transforming Canadian Universities.* Halifax: Fernwood Publishing.

– 2015b. "Contract Faculty in Canada: Using Access to Information Requests to Uncover Hidden Academics in Canadian Universities." *Higher Education* 70, no. 5 (November): 787–805. DOI: 10.1007/s10734-015-9867-9.

Bryan-Wilson, Julia. 2009. *Art Workers: Radical Practice in the Vietnam War Era.* Berkeley: University of California Press.

Buchloh, Benjamin. 1990. "Conceptual Art 1962–1969: From the Aesthetics of Administration to the Critique of Institutions." *October*, no. 55 (Winter): 105–43. DOI: 10.2307/778941.

Buckley, Brad, and John Conomos, eds. 2009. *Rethinking the Contemporary Art School: The Artist, the PhD, and the Academy*. Halifax: NSCAD Press.

Bunzl, Matti. 2014. *In Search of a Lost Avant-Garde: An Anthropologist Investigates the Contemporary Art Museum*. Chicago: University of Chicago Press.

Burns, Tom R., Ugo Corte, and Nora Machado. 2015a. "The Sociology of Creativity: Part I: Theory: The Social Mechanisms of Innovation and Creative Developments in Selectivity Environments." *Human Systems Management* 34, no. 3: 179–99. DOI: 10.3233/HSM-150839.

– 2015b. "The Sociology of Creativity: Part II: Applications: The Socio-Cultural Contexts and Conditions of the Production of Novelty." *Human Systems Management* 34, no. 4: 263–86. DOI: 10.3233/HSM-150850.

Butler, Judith. 1988. "Performative Acts and Gender Constitution: An Essay in Phenomenology and Feminist Theory." *Theatre Journal* 40, no. 4: 519–31. DOI: 10.2307/3207893.

– 2006. *Precarious Life: The Powers of Mourning and Violence*. London: Verso.

– 2015. *Notes Toward a Performative Theory of Assembly*. Cambridge, MA: Harvard University Press.

Butt, Danny. 2017. *Artistic Research in the Future Academy*. Bristol: Intellect.

Cahnmann-Taylor, Melisa, and Richard Siegesmund, eds. 2008. *Arts-Based Research in Education: Foundations for Practice*. New York: Routledge.

Callon, Michel. 1998. "An Essay on Framing and Overflowing: Economic Externalities Revisited by Sociology." *The Sociological Review* 46, no. S1 (May): 244–69. DOI: 10.1111/j.1467-954X.1998.tb03477.x.

– 2007. "What Does It Mean to Say That Economics Is Performative?" In *Do Economists Make Markets? On the Performativity of Economics*, edited by Donald MacKenzie, Fabian Muniesa, and Lucia Siu, 311–57. Princeton: Princeton University Press.

Campbell, Miranda. 2013. *Out of the Basement: Youth Cultural Production in Practice and in Policy*. Montreal: McGill-Queen's University Press.

Canadian Association of University Business Officers (CAUBO). n.d. "Financial Information of Universities and Colleges." Accessed April 17, 2019. https://www .caubo.ca/knowledge-centre/surveysreports/fiuc-reports/.

Canadian Association of University Teachers (CAUT). 2012. "NSCAD's Fate Remains Precarious following Release of Consultant's Report." *Bulletin*, January 2012. https://bulletin-archives.caut.ca/bulletin/articles/2012/01/-nscad-s-fate -remains-precarious-following-release-of-consultant-s-report.

– 2016. "The Precarious Life of Contract Academic Staff." *Bulletin*, October 2016. https://www.caut.ca/bulletin/2016/10/precarious-life -contract-academic-staff.

– 2018. *Underrepresented & Underpaid: Diversity & Equity among Canada's Post-Secondary Education Teachers*. Ottawa: CAUT. https://www.caut.ca/sites/default /files/caut_equity_report_2018-04final.pdf.

Canadian Press. 2013. "B.C. Invests $113 M for New Home of Too-Full Emily Carr University." *Global News*, January 23, 2013. https://globalnews.ca /news/382627/b-c-invests-113-m-for-new-home-of-too-full-emily-carr-university/.

Candlin, Fiona. 2001. "A Dual Inheritance: The Politics of Educational Reform and PhDs in Art and Design." *International Journal of Art & Design Education* 20, no. 3 (October): 302–10. DOI: 10.1111/1468-5949.00279.

Canel-Çınarbaş, Deniz, and Sophie Yohani. 2019. "Indigenous Canadian University Students' Experiences of Microaggressions." *International Journal for the Advancement of Counselling* 41, no. 1 (April): 41–60. DOI: 10.1007/s10447-018-9345-z.

Cattapan, Alana. 2017. "Have They Thought about What They're Asking? The Inequity of Job Applications." *Hook & Eye* (blog), March 16, 2017. https:// hookandeye.ca/2017/03/16/guest-post-have-they-thought-about-what-theyre -asking-the-inequity-of-job-applications/.

Chait, Richard, ed. 2002. *The Questions of Tenure*. Cambridge, MA: Harvard University Press.

Chalmers, F.G. 1993. "Who Is to Do This Great Work for Canada? South Kensington in Ontario." *Journal of Art and Design Education* 12, no. 2 (June): 161–78. DOI: 10.1111/j.1476-8070.1993.tb00584.x.

– 1998. "Teaching Drawing in Nineteenth-Century Canada – Why?" In *Curriculum, Culture and Art Education: Comparative Perspectives*, edited by Kerry Freedman and Fernando Hernandez, 47–58. Albany, NY: SUNY Press.

– 2006. "Learning to Draw at the Barrie Mechanics' Institute." In *From Drawing to Visual Culture*, edited by Harold Pearse, 31–46. Montreal: McGill-Queen's University Press.

Chan, Janet. 2011. "Towards a Sociology of Creativity." In *Creativity and Innovation in Business and Beyond: Social Science Perspectives and Policy Implications*, edited by Leon Mann and Janet Chan, 134–53. London: Routledge.

Chapman, Owen B., and Kim Sawchuk. 2012. "Research-Creation: Intervention, Analysis and 'Family Resemblances.'" *Canadian Journal of Communication* 37, no. 1 (January): 5–26. DOI: 10.22230/cjc.2012v37n1a2489.

Charbonneau, Leo. 2008. "Five New Universities in B.C." *University Affairs*, June 9, 2008. https://www.universityaffairs.ca/news/news-article/five-new-universities-in-bc/.

Chiapello, Eve. 1998. *Artistes versus managers: Le management culturel face á la critique artiste*. Paris: Métailié.

– 2004. "Evolution and Co-optation: The 'Artist Critique' of Management and Capitalism." *Third Text* 18, no. 6: 585–94. DOI: 10.1080/0952882042000284998.

Childress, Clayton. 2017. *Under the Cover: The Creation, Production, and Reception of a Novel*. Princeton: Princeton University Press.

Chiose, Simona. 2014. "Tensions between President, Faculty Grow at Ontario College of Art and Design." *Globe and Mail*, October 8, 2014. https://www.theglobeandmail .com/news/national/education/tensions-mounting-at-ontario-college-of-art -and-design/article20999108/.

– 2015. "Behind the Scenes at OCAD: With Acclaimed Status, Comes Strife." *Globe and Mail*, February 13, 2015. https://www.theglobeandmail.com/arts/art-and -architecture/behind-the-scenes-at-ocad-with-acclaimed-status-comes-strife /article22989232/.

– 2018. "York University, Union at Odds over Temporary Instructors." *Globe and Mail*, March 5, 2018. https://www.theglobeandmail.com/news/national /york-university-contract-faculty-go-on-strike-as-negotiating-breaks-down /article38205801/.

Chong, Phillipa K. 2020. *Inside the Critics' Circle: Book Reviewing in Uncertain Times*. Princeton: Princeton University Press.

Christophers, Brett. 2014. "Wild Dragons in the City: Urban Political Economy, Affordable Housing Development and the Performative World-Making of Economic Models." *International Journal of Urban and Regional Research* 38, no. 1 (January): 79–97. DOI: 10.1111/1468-2427.1203.

Clark, Roger. 1994. *Art Education: A Canadian Perspective*. Toronto: Ontario Society for Education through Art.

Clegg, Sue. 2010. "Time Future – the Dominant Discourse of Higher Education." *Time & Society* 19, no. 3 (November): 345–64. DOI: 10.1177/0961463X10381528.

Clews, Antonia, and David Clews. 2011. "And I Also Teach: The Professional Development of Teaching Creatives." *Journal of Arts and Communities* 1, no. 3 (May): 265–78. DOI: 10.1386/jaac.1.3.265_1.

Coates, Kenneth, and William R. Morrison. 2013. *Campus Confidential: 100 Startling Things You Don't Know about Canadian Universities*. Toronto: Lorimer.

Cohen, Nicole S. 2016. *Writers' Rights: Freelance Journalism in a Digital Age*. Montreal: McGill-Queen's University Press.

Cohen, Nicole S., and Greig de Peuter. 2018. "I Work at Vice Canada and Need a Union." In *Labour Under Attack: Anti-unionism in Canada*, edited by Stephanie Ross and Larry Savage, 114–28. Halifax: Fernwood Press.

– 2020. *New Media Unions: Organizing Digital Journalists*. New York: Routledge.

Coles, Amanda. 2016. "Creative Class Politics: Unions and the Creative Economy." *International Journal of Cultural Policy* 22, no. 3 (June): 456–72. DOI: 10.1080/10286632.2014.994612.

Collini, Stefan. 2012. *What Are Universities For?* London: Penguin.

Comunian, Roberta, and Abigail Gilmore, eds. 2016. *Higher Education and the Creative Economy: Beyond the Campus*. Abingdon, UK: Routledge.

Conor, Bridget, Rosalind Gill, and Stephanie Taylor, eds. 2015. *Gender and Creative Labour*. Malden, MA: Wiley-Blackwell.

Constanti, Panikkos, and Paul Gibbs. 2004. "Higher Education Teachers and Emotional Labour." *International Journal of Educational Management* 18, no. 4 (June): 243–9. DOI: 10.1108/09513540410538822.

Côté, James E., and Anton Allahar. 2007. *Ivory Tower Blues: A University System in Crisis*. Toronto: University of Toronto Press.

– 2011. *Lowering Higher Education: The Rise of Corporate Universities and the Fall of Liberal Education.* Toronto: University of Toronto Press.

Cowan, T.L. 2018. "Insubordinate, Indiscrete, Interdisciplinary: Cabaret Methods, Adjunct Methods, and Technologies of Fabulous." *RACAR* 43, no. 1 (August): 95–8. DOI: 10.7202/1050827ar.

Csikszentmihalyi, Mihaly. 1996. *Creativity: Flow and the Psychology of Discovery and Invention.* New York: HarperCollins.

Currie, Brooklyn. 2020. "NSCAD President Removed after 1 Year on the Job." *CBC News*, June 28, 2020. https://www.cbc.ca/news/canada/nova-scotia /nscad-president-removed-1.5630533.

Cushen, Jean. 2013. "Financialization in the Workplace: Hegemonic Narratives, Performative Interventions and the Angry Knowledge Worker." *Accounting, Organizations and Society* 38, no. 4 (May): 314–31. DOI: 10.1016/j.aos.2013.06.001.

Dafoe, Taylor. 2020. "Faculty at One of Canada's Top Art Schools Demand to Know Why the University's Progressive-Minded President Was Let Go." *Artnet*, August 18, 2020. https://news.artnet.com/art-world /nova-scotia-college-of-art-and-design-macnamara-1902386.

Daigle, Pascale, and Linda Rouleau. 2010. "Strategic Plans in Arts Organizations: A Tool of Compromise between Artistic and Managerial Values." *International Journal of Arts Management* 12, no. 3 (Spring): 13–30. https://www.jstor.org /stable/41065025.

Dault, Gary Michael. 2008. "The Once and Future Art School: NSCAD Then and Now." *Canadian Art*, December 1, 2008. https://canadianart.ca/features /once-and-future/.

Deckard, Natalie, Ayesha Akram, and Jane Ku. 2021. "Canadian Universities: 10 Years of Anti-racist Reports but Little Action." *The Conversation*, February 23, 2021. https://theconversation.com /canadian-universities-10-years-of-anti-racist-reports-but-little- action-153033.

Deem, Rosemary, and Kevin J. Brehony. 2005. "Management as Ideology: The Case of 'New Managerialism' in Higher Education." *Oxford Review of Education* 31, no. 2 (June): 217–35. DOI: 10.1080/03054980500117827.

Deleuze, Gilles, and Félix Guattari. 1987. *A Thousand Plateaus: Capitalism and Schizophrenia.* Minneapolis: University of Minnesota Press.

Deschamps, Tara. 2014. "OCAD U Ex-Teacher Alleges 'Systemic' Discrimination by School." *Toronto Star*, September 3, 2014. https://www.thestar.com/yourtoronto /education/2014/09/03/ocadu_exteacher_alleges_systemic_discrimination_by _school.html.

– 2015. "OCAD U Discrimination Case Prompts Moves to Boost Diversity." *Toronto Star*, March 16, 2015. https://www.thestar.com/yourtoronto /education/2015/03/16/ocad-u-discrimination-case-prompts-moves-to- boost-diversity.html.

Deuze, Mark, and Nicky Lewis. 2013. "Professional Identity and Media Work." In *Theorizing Cultural Work: Labour, Continuity and Change in the Cultural and Creative Industries*, edited by Mark Banks, Rosalind Gill, and Stephanie Taylor, 161–74. London: Routledge.

Dhoest, Alexander, Steven Malliet, Barbara Segaert, and Jacques Haers, eds. 2015. *The Borders of Subculture: Resistance and the Mainstream.* New York: Routledge.

DiMaggio, Paul. 1991. "Constructing an Organizational Field as a Professional Project: U.S. Art Museums, 1920–1940." In *The New Institutionalism in Organizational Analysis*, edited by Walter W. Powell and Paul DiMaggio, 267–92. Chicago: University of Chicago Press.

– 2000. "Social Structure Institutions and Cultural Goods: The Case of the United States." In *The Politics of Culture: Policy Perspectives for Individuals, Institutions, and Communities*, edited by Gigi Bradford, Glenn Wallach, and Michael Gary, 38–62. New York: New Press.

Dixon, Guy. 2015. "Art School at Centre of Redrawn Vancouver Neighbourhood." *Globe and Mail*, November 30, 2015. https://www .theglobeandmail.com/report-on-business/industry-news/property-report /art-school-at-centre-of-redrawn-vancouver-neighbourhood/article27537978/.

Donoghue, Frank. 2008. *The Last Professors: The Twilight of the Humanities in the Corporate University and the Fate of the Humanities.* New York: Fordham University Press.

Douglas, Kitrina, and David Carless. 2018. "Engaging with Arts-Based Research: A Story in Three Parts." *Qualitative Research in Psychology* 15, no. 2–3 (July): 156–72. DOI: 10.1080/14780887.2018.1429843.

Douglas, Mary. (1966) 2002. *Purity and Danger: An Analysis of Concepts of Pollution and Taboo.* London: Routledge.

Douglas, Stan. 1991. *Vancouver Anthology: A Project of the Or Gallery.* Vancouver: Or Gallery.

Druick, Zoe, and Danielle Deveau. 2015. "Cultural Production in Canada." *Canadian Journal of Communication* 40, no. 2 (April): 157–63. DOI: 10.22230 /cjc.2015v40n2a3027.

Du Gay, Paul. 1996. *Consumption and Identity at Work.* Thousand Oaks, CA: SAGE.

Du Gay, Paul, and Glenn Morgan, eds. 2013. *New Spirits of Capitalism? Crises, Justifications, and Dynamics.* Oxford: Oxford University Press.

Duncan, Carol. 1995. *Civilizing Rituals: Inside Public Art Museums.* London: Routledge.

Dupree, Janet Rae. 2008. "Let Computers Compute. It's the Age of the Right Brain." *New York Times*, April 6, 2008. https://www.nytimes.com/2008/04/06 /technology/06unbox.html/.

Durkheim, Emile. 1995. *The Elementary Forms of Religious Life.* Translated by Karen E. Fields. New York: Free Press.

ECUAD. n.d. "Practice Based Research." Accessed August 2, 2018. https://www .connect.ecuad.ca/research/practicebasedresearch.

– 2010. *Strategic Plan 2010–2015*. Vancouver: ECUAD.

– 2013a. "BC Arts Philanthropist Gifts $5M to Emily Carr University to Benefit Future Generations of Visual Artists." *Cision Newswire*, March 7, 2013. https://www.newswire.ca/news-releases/bc-arts-philanthropist-gifts-5m-to-emily-carr-university-to-benefit-future-generations-of-visual-artists-512040151.html.

– 2013b. *CRC and CFI Strategic Research Plan 2013–2018*. Vancouver: Office of the Director of Research. https://www.ecuad.ca/assets/pdf-attachments/StrategicResearchPlan-2013-2018.pdf.

– 2014. "Reliance Properties' $7-Million Gift Launches Emily Carr University's Capital Campaign." *Cision Newswire*, May 2, 2014. https://www.newswire.ca/news-releases/reliance-properties-7-million-gift-launches-emily-carr-universitys-capital-campaign-514221311.html.

– 2018. *Eight Commitments to an Emergent Future: Emily Carr University's Strategic Plan to 2021*. Vancouver: ECUAD. https://www.ecuad.ca/assets/hero-images/ECU-Strategic-Plan-2021-Nov-2018.pdf.

ECUAD Faculty Association. 2014. *Collective Agreement, 2014–2019*. Vancouver: ECUAD. https://www.ecuad.ca/assets/content-images/ECUAD-CUPE-April-1-2014-to-March-31-2019.pdf.

Elkins, James, ed. 2009. *Artists with PhDs: On the New Doctoral Degree in Studio Art*. Washington, DC: New Academia Publishing.

Eyland, Cliff. 2012. "Review: The Last Art College: Nova Scotia College of Art and Design, 1968–1978." *Border Crossings* 31, no. 3: 126–8.

Faculty Union of NSCAD. 2016. *Collective Agreement, 2016–2018*. Halifax: NSCAD. https://navigator.nscad.ca/wordpress/wp-content/uploads/2017/12/CollectiveAgreementUnit1.pdf.

Faucher, Kane X. 2014. "Six Myths about Contract Faculty in Canada." *University Affairs*, March 4, 2014. https://www.universityaffairs.ca/career-advice/contractually-bound/contractually-bound-six-myths-about-contract-faculty-in-canada/.

– 2015. "Let's Reconsider Our Hiring Practices for Contract Academic Staff." *University Affairs*, March 2, 2015. https://www.universityaffairs.ca/career-advice/contractually-bound/lets-reconsider-our-hiring-practices-for-contract-academic-staff/.

Field, Cynthia C., and Glen A. Jones. 2016. *A Survey of Sessional Faculty in Ontario Publicly-Funded Universities*. Toronto: Centre for the Study of Canadian and International Higher Education, OISE-University of Toronto. https://www.oise.utoronto.ca/hec/UserFiles/File/Sessional_Faculty_-_OHCRIF_Final_Report_-_July_2016.pdf.

Fields, Jill, ed. 2012. *Entering the Picture: Judy Chicago, the Fresno Feminist Art Program, and the Collective Visions of Women Artists*. New York: Routledge.

Fine, Gary Alan. 2004. *Everyday Genius: Self-Taught Art and the Culture of Authenticity*. Chicago: University of Chicago Press.

– 2017. "A Matter of Degree: Negotiating Art and Commerce in MFA Education." *American Behavioral Scientist* 61, no. 12 (November): 1463–86. DOI: 10.1177/0002764217734272.

– 2018. *Talking Art: The Culture of Practice and the Practice of Culture in MFA Education.* Chicago: University of Chicago Press.

Finkel, Rebecca, Deborah Jones, Katherine Sang, and Dimitrinka Stoyanova Russell. 2017. "Diversifying the Creative: Creative Work, Creative Industries, Creative Identities." *Organization* 24, no. 3 (May): 281–8. DOI: 10.1177/1350508417690167.

Flaherty, Colleen. 2021. "A University in Tatters." *Inside Higher Ed*, April 29, 2021. https://www.insidehighered.com/news/2021/04/29/ insolvency-declaration-laurentian-throws-much-limbo.

Florida, Richard L. 2004. *The Rise of the Creative Class and How It's Transforming Work, Leisure, Community and Everyday Life.* New York: Basic Books.

Foster, Hal. 1996. *The Return of the Real: The Avant-Garde at the End of the Century.* Cambridge, MA: MIT Press.

Foster, Karen. 2016. *Precarious U: Contract Faculty in Nova Scotia Universities.* Association of Nova Scotia University Teachers. https://ansut.caut.ca/wp-content /uploads/2016/09/ANSUT-Precarious-U-Final-Report.pdf.

Foster, Karen, and Louise Birdsell Bauer. 2018. *Out of the Shadows: Experiences of Contract Academic Staff.* Canadian Association of University Teachers. https:// www.caut.ca/sites/default/files/cas_report.pdf.

Foucault, Michel. 1980. *Power/Knowledge: Selected Interviews and Other Writings, 1972–1977.* Translated by Colin Gordon. New York: Pantheon Books.

Foust, Christina R., and Daniel J. Lair. 2012. "The Political, Cultural, and Economic Assault on Higher Education." *Review of Communication* 12, no. 2 (April): 159–74. DOI: 10.1080/15358593.2011.653505.

Fraser, Andrea. 2005. "From the Critique of Institutions to an Institution of Critique." *Artforum* 44, no. 1: 278–84. https://www.artforum.com/print/200507 /from-the-critique-of-institutions-to-an-institution-of-critique-9407.

Frayling, Christopher. 1993. "Research in Art and Design." *Royal College of Art Research Papers* 1, no. 1: 1–5. https://researchonline.rca.ac.uk/384/3/frayling _research_in_art_and_design_1993.pdf.

Freud, Sigmund. (1940) 2010. *An Outline of Psycho-Analysis.* Mansfield Centre, CT: Martino.

Friedland, Roger, and Robert R. Alford. 1991. "Bringing Society Back In: Symbols, Practices, and Institutional Contradictions." In *The New Institutionalism in Organizational Analysis*, edited by Walter W. Powell and Paul DiMaggio, 232–63. Chicago: University of Chicago Press.

Frith, Simon, and Howard Horne. 1987. *Art into Pop.* New York: Methuen.

Fulford, Robert. 1993. "The Trouble with Emily: How Canada's Greatest Woman Painter Ended Up on the Wrong Side of the Political Correctness Debate."

Canadian Art, December 15, 1993. https://canadianart.ca/features/1993/12/01
/the-trouble-with-emily-carr/.

Fullick, Melonie. 2015. "Past Is Prologue When It Comes to Contract Faculty."
University Affairs, March 11, 2015. https://www.universityaffairs.ca/opinion
/speculative-diction/past-is-prologue-when-it-comes-to-contract-faculty/.

– 2016a. "Confronting the Conditions of Contract Faculty." *University Affairs*,
February 26, 2016. https://www.universityaffairs.ca/opinion/speculative-diction
/confronting-conditions-contract-faculty/.

– 2016b. "Feeding the 'Crisis' Beast: How *The Walrus* Got It
Wrong on Contract Faculty." *University Affairs*, July 29, 2016.
https://www.universityaffairs.ca/opinion/speculative-diction
/feeding-crisis-beast-walrus-got-wrong-contract-faculty/.

Gagarin, Michael, and Elaine Fantham, eds. 2010. *The Oxford Encyclopedia of
Ancient Greece and Rome*. New York: Oxford University Press.

Gerber, Alison. 2017. *The Work of Art: Value in Creative Careers*. Stanford, CA:
Stanford University Press.

Gerber, Alison, and Clayton Childress. 2017. "The Economic World Obverse:
Freedom through Markets after Arts Education." *American Behavioral Scientist*
61, no. 12 (November): 1532–54. DOI: 10.1177/0002764217734275.

Getzels, Jacob W., and Mihaly Csikszentmihalyi. 1976. *The Creative Vision: A
Longitudinal Study of Problem Finding in Art*. New York: Wiley.

Ghosh, Peter. 2014. *Max Weber and* The Protestant Ethic: *Twin Histories*. Oxford:
Oxford University Press.

Gill, Rosalind. 2002. "Cool, Creative and Egalitarian? Exploring Gender in Project-
Based New Media Work in Euro." *Information, Communication & Society* 5, no. 1
(January): 70–89. DOI: 10.1080/13691180110117668.

– 2014a. "Academics, Cultural Workers and Critical Labour Studies." *Journal of
Cultural Economy* 7, no. 1 (January): 12–30. DOI: 10.1080/17530350.2013.861763.

– 2014b. "Unspeakable Inequalities: Post Feminism, Entrepreneurial Subjectivity,
and the Repudiation of Sexism among Cultural Workers." *Social Politics* 21, no. 4
(Winter): 509–28. DOI: 10.1093/sp/jxu016.

Gill, Rosalind, and Andy Pratt. 2008. "In the Social Factory? Immaterial Labour,
Precariousness and Cultural Work." *Theory, Culture & Society* 25, no. 7–8
(December): 1–30. DOI: 10.1177/0263276408097794.

Giroux, Henry A. 2014. *Neoliberalism's War on Higher Education*. Chicago:
Haymarket Books.

Glynn, Mary Ann, and Michael Lounsbury. 2005. "From the Critics' Corner:
Logic Blending, Discursive Change and Authenticity in a Cultural Production
System." *Journal of Management Studies* 42, no. 5 (July): 1031–55. DOI:
10.1111/j.1467-6486.2005.00531.x.

Goffman, Erving. 1990. *The Presentation of Self in Everyday Life*. New York:
Doubleday.

Gold, Kerry. 2014. "'The Flats' Rises from a Post-Industrial Cradle." *Globe and Mail*, March 14, 2014. https://www.theglobeandmail.com/real-estate /the-flats-rises-from-a-post-industrial-cradle/article17501907/.

Goldberger, Paul. 2007. "The Colorist." *The New Yorker*, October 22, 2007. https:// www.newyorker.com/magazine/2007/10/22/the-colorist.

Graeber, David. 2015. *The Utopia of Rules: On Technology, Stupidity, and the Secret Joys of Bureaucracy*. Brooklyn: Melville House.

Graham, Hugh Davis, and Nancy Diamond. 1997. *The Rise of American Research Universities: Elites and Challengers in the Postwar Era*. Baltimore: Johns Hopkins University Press.

Grant, Taryn. 2018. "Halifax Students Say Precarious Work for Faculty Is Hurting Their Education." *Toronto Star*, November 1, 2018. https://www.thestar.com /halifax/2018/11/01/halifax-students-say-precarious-work-for-faculty-is-hurting -their-education.html.

Grauer, Perrin. 2021. "ECU Ranked Top University in Canada for Art & Design (Again)." *Emily Carr University News*, June 28, 2021. https://www.ecuad.ca /news/2021/ecu-ranked-top-canadian-university-art-design-2021.

Greenfeld, Liah. 2003. *The Spirit of Capitalism: Nationalism and Economic Growth*. Cambridge, MA: Harvard University Press.

Grennan, Simon. 2015. "Arts Practice and Research: Locating Alterity and Expertise." *International Journal of Art & Design Education* 34, no. 2 (June): 249–59. DOI: 10.1111/jade.1776.

Griffin, Kevin. 2006. "Emily Carr's Media and Visual Arts Master's Program First of Its Kind." *Vancouver Sun*, October 21, 2006.

Griffith, Alison I., and Dorothy E. Smith, eds. 2014. *Under New Public Management: Institutional Ethnographies of Changing Front-Line Work*. Toronto: University of Toronto Press.

Griswold, Wendy. 1987. "A Methodological Framework for the Sociology of Culture." *Sociological Methodology* 17: 1–35. DOI: 10.2307/271027.

– 2000. *Bearing Witness: Readers, Writers, and the Novel in Nigeria*. Princeton: Princeton University Press.

Haiven, Max. 2012. "What Is the Value of an Art School?" *Art Threat*, January 7, 2012.

Hall, Stuart. 2018. *Essential Essays*. Edited by David Morley. Durham, NC: Duke University Press.

Hallam, Elizabeth, and Tim Ingold, eds. 2007. *Creativity and Cultural Improvisation*. New York: Berg.

Hancock, Ange-Marie. 2004. *The Politics of Disgust: The Public Identity of the Welfare Queen*. New York: New York University Press.

Hannula, Mika, Juha Suoranta, and Tere Vadén. 2005. *Artistic Research: Theories, Methods and Practices*. Helsinki: Academy of Fine Arts.

Hayot, Eric. 2014. *The Elements of Academic Style: Writing for the Humanities*. New York: Columbia University Press.

Hebdige, Dick. 1991. *Subculture: The Meaning of Style*. New York: Routledge.

Hedgecoe, A. 2016. "Reputational Risk, Academic Freedom and Research Ethics Review." *Sociology* 50, no. 3 (June): 486–501. DOI: 10.1177/0038038515590756.

Hegel, Georg Wilhelm Friedrich. (1807) 2017. *The Phenomenology of Spirit*. Translated by Terry P. Pinkard. New York: Cambridge University Press.

Heinich, Nathalie. 1996. *Glory of Van Gogh: An Anthropology of Admiration*. Translated by Paul L. Browne. Princeton: Princeton University Press.

– 2015. "Practices of Contemporary Art: A Pragmatic Approach to a New Artistic Paradigm." In *Artistic Practices: Social Interactions and Cultural Dynamics*, edited by Tasos Zembylas, 32–43. London: Routledge.

Hemer, Susan R. 2014. "Finding Time for Quality Teaching: An Ethnographic Study of Academic Workloads in the Social Sciences and Their Impact on Teaching Practices." *Higher Education Research & Development* 33, no. 3 (May): 483–95. DOI: 10.1080/07294360.2013.841647.

Hennekam, Sophie, and Dawn Bennett. 2017. "Sexual Harassment in the Creative Industries: Tolerance, Culture and the Need for Change." *Gender, Work & Organization* 24, no. 4 (July): 417–34. DOI: 10.1111/gwao.12176.

Henningsson, Malin, Anders Jörnesten, and Lars Geschwind. 2018. "Translating Tenure Track into Swedish: Tensions When Implementing an Academic Career System." *Studies in Higher Education* 43, no. 7: 1215–26. DOI: 10.1080/03075079.2016.1239704.

Henry, Frances, Carl James, Peter S. Li, Audrey Kobayashi, Malinda Sharon Smith, Howard Ramos, and Enakshi Dua. 2017. *The Equity Myth: Racialization and Indigeneity at Canadian Universities*. Vancouver: UBC Press.

Henry, Frances, and Audrey Kobayashi. 2017. "The Everyday World of Racialized and Indigenous Faculty Members in Canadian Universities." In *The Equity Myth: Racialization and Indigeneity at Canadian Universities*, edited by Henry Frances et al., 115–54. Vancouver: UBC Press.

Henry, Frances, and Carol Tator, eds. 2009. *Racism in the Canadian University: Demanding Social Justice, Inclusion, and Equity*. Toronto: University of Toronto Press.

Henry, Karen A. 2001. *Art Is All Over: Emily Carr Institute of Art + Design*. Vancouver: ECIAD.

Herbert, Anne, and Janne Tienari. 2013. "Transplanting Tenure and the (Re) Construction of Academic Freedoms." *Studies in Higher Education* 38, no. 2 (March): 157–73. DOI: 10.1080/03075079.2011.569707.

Hesmondhalgh, David, and Sarah Baker. 2008. "Creative Work and Emotional Labour in the Television Industry." *Theory, Culture & Society* 25, no. 7–8 (December): 97–118. DOI: 10.1177/0263276408097798.

– 2011. *Creative Labour: Media Work in Three Cultural Industries*. New York: Routledge.

Hill, Kelly. 2019. "A Statistical Profile of Artists in Canada in 2016." Hill Strategies, November 27. https://hillstrategies.com/resource/statistical-profile-of-artists-in-canada-in-2016/.

Hillman, Susan. 1994. "Vancouver School of Art to Emily Carr Institute of Art and Design 1964–1994." In *64–94: Contemporary Decades*, edited by Sam Carter, 143–9. Vancouver: Charles H. Scott Gallery/ECIAD.

Hirsch, E.D., Joseph F. Kett, and James Trefil. 2002. *The New Dictionary of Cultural Literacy*. Boston: Houghton Mifflin.

Hochschild, Arlie Russell. (1983) 2012. *The Managed Heart: Commercialization of Human Feeling*. Berkeley: University of California Press.

Hracs, Brian J., and Deborah Leslie. 2014. "Aesthetic Labour in Creative Industries: The Case of Independent Musicians in Toronto, Canada." *Area* 46, no. 1 (March): 66–73. DOI: 10.1111/area.12062.

Hudson-Miles, Richard, and Andy Broadey. 2019. "'Messy Democracy': Democratic Pedagogy and Its Discontents." *Research in Education* 104, no. 1 (August): 56–76. DOI: 10.1177/0034523719842296.

Hutter, Michael, and C.D. Throsby, eds. 2008. *Beyond Price: Value in Culture, Economics, and the Arts*. Cambridge: Cambridge University Press.

Jackson, Shannon. 2011. *Social Works: Performing Art, Supporting Publics*. New York: Routledge.

Jagd, Søren. 2011. "Pragmatic Sociology and Competing Orders of Worth in Organizations." *European Journal of Social Theory* 14, no. 3 (August): 343–59. DOI: 10.1177/1368431011412349.

Jagodzinski, Jan, and Jason J. Wallin. 2013. *Arts-Based Research: A Critique and a Proposal*. Rotterdam, NL: Sense Publishers.

Jermyn, Diane. 2010. "Ontario Art School Leader Comes Full Circle." *Globe and Mail*, April 13, 2010. https://www.theglobeandmail.com/report-on-business/small-business/sb-managing/ontario-art-school-leader-comes-full-circle/article1372160/.

Joas, Hans. 1996. *The Creativity of Action*. Translated by Jeremy Gaines and Paul Keast. Chicago: University of Chicago Press.

Jones, Candace, and Reut Livne-Tarandach. 2008. "Designing a Frame: Rhetorical Strategies of Architects." *Journal of Organizational Behavior* 29, no. 8 (November): 1075–99. DOI: 10.1002/job.556.

Jones, Caroline A. 1996. *Machine in the Studio: Constructing the Postwar American Artist*. Chicago: University of Chicago Press.

– 2016. *The Global Work of Art: World's Fairs, Biennials, and the Aesthetics of Experience*. Chicago: University of Chicago Press.

Jones, Deborah, and Judith K. Pringle. 2015. "Unmanageable Inequalities: Sexism in the Film Industry." *The Sociological Review* 63, no. S1 (May): 37–49. DOI: 10.1111/1467-954X.12239.

Jones, Glen, Julian Weinrib, Amy Scott Metcalfe, Don Fisher, Kjell Rubenson, and Iain Snee. 2012. "Academic Work in Canada: The Perceptions of Early-Career Academics." *Higher Education Quarterly* 66, no. 2 (April): 189–206. DOI: 10.1111/j.1468-2273.2012.00515.x.

Kapitulik, Brian P., Hilton Kelly, and Dan Clawson. 2007. "Critical Experiential Pedagogy: Sociology and the Crisis in Higher Education." *The American Sociologist* 38, no. 2 (September): 135–58. DOI: 10.1007/s12108-007-9005-y.

Kelly, Gemey. 1982. *Arthur Lismer: Nova Scotia, 1916–1919*. Halifax: Dalhousie Art Gallery.

Kennedy, Garry Neill. 2012. *The Last Art College: Nova Scotia College of Art and Design, 1968–1978*. Cambridge, MA: MIT Press.

Kenny, John. 2017. "Academic Work and Performativity." *Higher Education* 74, no. 5 (November): 897–913. DOI: 10.1007/s10734-016-0084-y.

Kerr, Aphra, and John D. Kelleher. 2015. "The Recruitment of Passion and Community in the Service of Capital: Community Managers in the Digital Games Industry." *Critical Studies in Media Communication* 32, no. 3 (August): 177–92. DOI: 10.1080/15295036.2015.1045005.

Kezar, Adrianna, and Cecile Sam. 2010. *Understanding the New Majority of Non-Tenure-Track Faculty in Higher Education: Demographics, Experiences, and Plans of Action*. San Francisco: Jossey-Bass.

Klein, Naomi. 2008. *The Shock Doctrine: The Rise of Disaster Capitalism*. Toronto: Vintage Canada.

Knowles, J., and Ardra Cole. 2008. *Handbook of the Arts in Qualitative Research: Perspectives, Methodologies, Examples, and Issues*. Thousand Oaks, CA: SAGE.

Koster, Shirley. 2011. "The Self-Managed Heart: Teaching Gender and Doing Emotional Labour in a Higher Education Institution." *Pedagogy, Culture & Society* 19, no. 1 (March): 61–77. DOI: 10.1080/14681366.2011.548988.

Kramer, Reinhold. 1997. *Scatology and Civility in the English-Canadian Novel*. Toronto: University of Toronto Press.

Kristeva, Julia. 1982. *Powers of Horror: An Essay on Abjection*. New York: Columbia University Press.

– 1991. *Strangers to Ourselves*. New York: Columbia University Press.

– 1993. *Nations without Nationalism*. New York: Columbia University Press.

Kuitenbrouwer, Peter. 2014. "Former OCAD University Teacher Passed Over for Promotion." *National Post*, September 2, 2014. https://nationalpost.com/news /toronto/former-ocad-university-teacher-passed-over-for-promotion-because-he -is-not-white-rights-complain-alleges.

Kunst, Bojana. 2015a. *Artist at Work: Proximity of Art and Capitalism*. Winchester, UK: Zero Books.

– 2015b. "The Institution between Precarization and Participation." *Performance Research* 20, no. 4 (July): 6–13. DOI: 10.1080/13528165.2015.1071032.

Kwon, Miwon. 2002. *One Place after Another: Site-Specific Art and Locational Identity*. Cambridge, MA: MIT Press.

Ladkin, Sam, Robert McKay, and Emile Bojesen, eds. 2016. *Against Value in the Arts and Education.* London: Rowman & Littlefield International.

Lamont, Michèle. 2009. *How Professors Think: Inside the Curious World of Academic Judgment.* Cambridge, MA: Harvard University Press.

– 2012. "Toward a Comparative Sociology of Valuation and Evaluation." *Annual Review of Sociology* 38, no. 1 (August): 201–21. DOI: 10.1146/annurev-soc-070308120022.

Lamont, Michèle, and Ann Swidler. 2014. "Methodological Pluralism and the Possibilities and Limits of Interviewing." *Qualitative Sociology* 37, no. 2 (June): 153–71. DOI: 10.1007/s11133-014-9274-z.

Lamont, Michèle, and Laurent Thévenot, eds. 2000. *Rethinking Comparative Cultural Sociology: Repertoires of Evaluation in France and the United States.* Cambridge: Cambridge University Press.

Landry, Mike. 2016. "The Next Art School." *Canadian Art,* November 30, 2016. https://canadianart.ca/features/nscad-university/.

Lavie, Smadar, Kirin Narayan, and Renato Rosaldo, eds. 1993. *Creativity/Anthropology.* Ithaca, NY: Cornell University Press.

Lazzarato, Maurizio. 2007. "The Misfortunes of the 'Artistic Critique' and of Cultural Employment." *Transveral* (blog), January 2007. https://transversal.at/transversal/0207/lazzarato/en.

Leavy, Patricia. 2009. *Method Meets Art: Arts-Based Research Practice.* New York: Guilford Press.

– ed. 2018. *Handbook of Arts-Based Research.* New York: Guilford Press.

Lederman, Marsha. 2008. "Emily Carr to Become University." *Globe and Mail,* April 29, 2008. https://www.theglobeandmail.com/news/national/emily-carr-to-become-university/article959033/.

– 2017. "Emily Carr's New Home Becomes a Catalyst for Urban Renewal." *Globe and Mail,* September 1, 2017. https://www.theglobeandmail.com/news/british-columbia/vancouvers-emily-carr-university-reshapes-itself-and-its-city-with-a-newcampus/article36153499/.

Lee, David. 2011. "Networks, Cultural Capital and Creative Labour in the British Independent Television Industry." *Media, Culture & Society* 33, no. 4 (May): 549–65. DOI: 10.1177/0163443711398693.

Léger, Marc James. 2010. "The Non-Productive Role of the Artist: The Creative Industries in Canada." *Third Text* 24, no. 5 (September): 557–70. DOI: 10.1080/09528822.2010.502774.

Lena, Jennifer C., and Danielle J. Lindemann. 2014. "Who Is an Artist? New Data for an Old Question." *Poetics* 43 (April): 70–85. DOI: 10.1016/j.poetic.2014.01.001.

Letizia, Angelo J. 2016. "The Hollow University: Disaster Capitalism Befalls American Higher Education." *Policy Futures in Education* 14, no. 3 (April): 360–76. DOI: 10.1177/1478210316633378.

Liinamaa, Saara. 2018. "Negotiating a 'Radically Ambiguous World': Planning for the Future of Research at the Art and Design University." *International Journal of Art & Design Education* 37, no. 3 (August): 426–37. DOI: 10.1111/jade.1214.

Liinamaa, Saara, and Malia Rogers. 2020. "Women Actors, Insecure Work, and Everyday Sexism in the Canadian Screen Industry." *Feminist Media Studies,* (May): 1–16. DOI: 10.1080/14680777.2020.1759114.

Littler, Jo. 2017. *Against Meritocracy: Culture, Power and Myths of Mobility.* New York: Routledge.

Lord, Barry. 1970. "Art College Begins a New Life." *Toronto Star,* March 14, 1970.

Lorenz, Chris. 2012. "If You're So Smart, Why Are You under Surveillance? Universities, Neoliberalism, and New Public Management." *Critical Inquiry* 38, no. 3 (Spring): 599–629. DOI: 10.1086/664553.

MacKenzie, Donald. 2008. *An Engine, Not a Camera: How Financial Models Shape Markets.* Cambridge, MA: MIT Press.

Macleod, Katy, and Neil Chapman. 2014. "The Absenting Subject: Research Notes on PhDs in Fine Art." *Journal of Visual Art Practice* 13, no. 2 (May): 138–49. DOI: 10.1080/14702029.2014.959722.

Macleod, Katy, and Lin Holdridge. 2004. "The Doctorate in Fine Art: The Importance of Exemplars to the Research Culture." *International Journal of Art & Design Education* 23, no. 2 (May): 155–68. DOI: 10.1111/j.1476-8070.2004.00394.x.

Madoff, Steven Henry, ed. 2009. *Art School: (Propositions for the 21st Century).* Cambridge, MA: MIT Press.

Margalit, Avishai. 2013. *On Compromise and Rotten Compromises.* Princeton: Princeton University Press.

Markham, Annette. 2012. "Fabrication as Ethical Practice: Qualitative Inquiry in Ambiguous Internet Contexts." *Information, Communication & Society* 15, no. 3 (April): 334–53. DOI: 10.1080/1369118X.2011.641993.

Marx, Karl, and Friedrich Engels. (1848) 2012. *The Communist Manifesto.* London: Verso.

Mason, Rachel. 2008. "Problems of Interdisciplinarity: Evidence-Based and/or Artist-Led Research?" *International Journal of Art & Design Education* 27, no. 3 (October): 279–92. DOI: 10.1111/j.1476-8070.2008.00586.x.

Matcham, David. 2014. "Practices of Legitimacy and the Problem of Artistic Research." *Arts and Humanities in Higher Education* 13, no. 3 (July): 276–81. DOI: 10.1177/1474022213514553.

Mathews, Vanessa. 2010. "Aestheticizing Space: Art, Gentrification and the City." *Geography Compass* 4, no. 6 (June): 660–75. DOI: 10.1111/j.1749-8198.2010.00331.x.

McClintock, Anne. 1995. *Imperial Leather: Race, Gender, and Sexuality in the Colonial Contest.* New York: Routledge.

McDonnell, Terence E., and Steven J. Tepper. 2014. "Culture in Crisis: Deploying Metaphor in Defense of Art." *Poetics* 43 (April): 20–42. DOI: 10.1016 /j.poetic.2014.01.002.

McLaughlin, Bryne. 2016. "Why the NSCAD Legend Mattered – and Still Matters." *Canadian Art*, March 1, 2016. https://canadianart.ca/features /why-the-nscad-legend-mattered-and-still-matters/.

McLean, Heather E. 2014. "Cracks in the Creative City: The Contradictions of Community Arts Practice." *International Journal of Urban and Regional Research* 38, no. 6 (November): 2156–73. DOI: 10.1111/1468-2427.12168.

– 2017. "Hos in the Garden: Staging and Resisting Neoliberal Creativity." *Environment and Planning D: Society and Space* 35, no. 1: 38–56. DOI: 10.1177/0263775816654915.

McNiff, Shaun. 2013. *Art as Research: Opportunities and Challenges.* Chicago: Intellect.

McRobbie, Angela. 1998. *British Fashion Design: Rag Trade or Image Industry?* London: Routledge.

– 2015. *Be Creative: Making a Living in the New Culture Industries.* Cambridge: Polity.

Meanwell, Emily, and Sibyl Kleiner. 2014. "The Emotional Experience of First-Time Teaching: Reflections from Graduate Instructors, 1997–2006." *Teaching Sociology* 42, no. 1 (January): 17–27. DOI: 10.1177/0092055X13508377.

Menger, Pierre-Michel. 2001. "Artists as Workers: Theoretical and Methodological Challenges." *Poetics* 28, no. 4 (February): 241–54. DOI: 10.1016/S0304 -422X(01)80002-4.

Mitchell, Timothy. 2005. "The Work of Economics: How a Discipline Makes Its World." *European Journal of Sociology* 46, no. 2 (August): 297–320. DOI: 10.1017 /S000397560500010X.

Möntmann, Nina, ed. 2006. *Art and Its Institutions: Current Conflicts, Critique and Collaborations.* London: Black Dog Publishing.

Moray, Gerta. 2006. *Unsettling Encounters: First Nations Imagery in the Art of Emily Carr.* Vancouver: UBC Press.

Morgan, George, and Pariece Nelligan. 2015. "Labile Labour – Gender, Flexibility and Creative Work." *The Sociological Review* 63, no. S1 (May): 66–83. DOI: 10.1111/1467-954X.12241.

Mould, Oliver. 2015. *Urban Subversion and the Creative City.* New York: Routledge.

Mullin, Morgan. 2021. "NSCAD Announces It Will *Not* Be Moving Next to the New Art Gallery of Nova Scotia." *The Coast*, May 7, 2021. https://www.thecoast.ca/halifax/nscad-announces-it -will-not-be-moving-next-to-the-new-art-gallery-of-nova-scotia /Content?oid=26374828.

Murphy, Peter, and Eduardo de la Fuente, eds. 2014. *Aesthetic Capitalism.* Boston: Brill.

Murray, Catherine, and Mirjam Gollmitzer. 2012. "Escaping the Precarity Trap: A Call for Creative Labour Policy." *International Journal of Cultural Policy* 18, no. 4 (July): 419–38. DOI: 10.1080/10286632.2011.591490.

Neff, Gina, Elizabeth Wissinger, and Sharon Zukin. 2005. "Entrepreneurial Labor among Cultural Producers: 'Cool' Jobs in 'Hot' Industries." *Social Semiotics* 15, no. 3 (December): 307–34. DOI: 10.1080/10350330500310111.

Nelson, Cary, ed. 1997. *Will Teach for Food: Academic Labor in Crisis*. Minneapolis: University of Minnesota Press.

Nelson, Robert. 2009. *The Jealousy of Ideas: Research Methods in the Creative Arts*. Melbourne: Ellikon.

Newfield, Christopher. 2011. *Unmaking the Public University: The Forty-Year Assault on the Middle Class*. Cambridge, MA: Harvard University Press.

Ngai, Sianne. 2009. *Ugly Feelings*. Cambridge, MA: Harvard University Press.

Noonan, Caitriona. 2013. "Smashing Childlike Wonder? The Early Journey into Higher Education." In *Cultural Work and Higher Education*, edited by Daniel Ashton and Caitriona Noonan, 133–53. London: Palgrave Macmillan.

NSCAD. 1999. *Strategic Research Plan 1999–2002*. Halifax: NSCAD. https://navigator.nscad.ca/wordpress/wp-content/uploads/2017/11/NSCAD-Strategic-Research-Plan-1999-2002.pdf.

– 2003. *Strategic Research Plan 2003–2006*. Halifax: NSCAD. https://navigator.nscad.ca/wordpress/wp-content/uploads/2017/11/NSCAD-Strategic-Research-Plan-2003-2006.pdf.

– 2006. *Strategic Research Plan 2006–2009*. Halifax: NSCAD. https://navigator.nscad.ca/wordpress/wp-content/uploads/2017/11/2013-2016-Strategic-Research-Plan.pdf.

– 2009a. *Strategic Research Plan 2009–2012*. Halifax: NSCAD.

– 2009b. *Building Opportunities: NSCAD University's Strategic Plan 2009–2012*. Halifax: NSCAD. https://www.yumpu.com/en/document/read/19205950/building-opportunities-nscad-universitys-strategic-plan-2009-2012.

2013a. *Strategic Research Plan 2013–2016*. Halifax: NSCAD. https://navigator.nscad.ca/wordpress/wp-content/uploads/2017/11/2013-2016-Strategic-Research-Plan.pdf.

– 2013b. *Bilateral Report*. Halifax: NSCAD. https://navigator.nscad.ca/wordpress/wp-content/uploads/2017/12/Bilaterial-Bilateral-Report-2013.pdf.

– 2016a. *NSCAD Academic Plan: Towards 2020*. Halifax: NSCAD. https://issuu.com/nscadadmissions/docs/nscad_academic_plan_towards_2020.

– 2016b. *Strategic Research Plan 2016–2019*. Halifax: NSCAD. https://issuu.com/nscadadmissions/docs/nscad_strategic_research_plan_digit.

– 2019. *Strategic Research Plan 2019–2022*. Halifax: NSCAD. https://issuu.com/nscadadmissions/docs/nscad_strategic_research_plan_2019-2022_online.

NSCAD Board of Governors. 2020 "Message to the NSCAD Community from the Board of Governors." NASCAD University, August 12, 2020. https://nscad.ca/bog-message-to-the-nscad-community/.

Oakley, Kate. 2009. "From Bohemia to Britart: Art Students over 50 Years." *Cultural Trends* 18, no. 4 (December): 281–94. DOI: 10.1080/09548960903268105.

Oakley, Kate, Brooke Sperry, and Andy Pratt. 2008. *The Art of Innovation: How Fine Arts Graduates Contribute to Innovation.* London: NESTA. http://openaccess.city .ac.uk/6704/.

O'Brien, Daniel. 2012. "Best Wishes for the Holidays." NSCAD. *President's Blog*, December 11, 2012. Accessed November 11, 2016. http://wordpress.nscad.ns.ca /president/holidays/.

– 2013. "Where We Stand." NSCAD. *President's Blog*, February 13, 2013. Accessed November 11, 2016. http://wordpress.nscad.ns.ca/president /where-we-stand/.

OCAD. n.d.a. "About: Vision and Mission Statements." Accessed April 17, 2019. https://www.ocadu.ca/about/vision-mission.

– n.d.b. "Preparing a Portfolio." Accessed April 17, 2019. https://www.ocadu.ca /admissions/preparing-a-portfolio.

– 2006. *Leading in the Age of the Imagination: OCAD Strategic Plan 2006–2012.* Toronto: OCAD. https://www.ocadu.ca/sites/default/files/legacy_assets /documents/leading-in-the-age-of-imagination-full.pdf.

– 2012a. *Strategic Research Plan 2012–2017.* Toronto: OCAD. https://www.ocadu.ca /Assets/content/research/strategic-research-plan.pdf.

– 2012b. *Advancing Excellence at OCAD University for the Age of the Imagination: OCAD University Strategic Plan 2012–2017.* Toronto: OCAD. https://www.ocadu .ca/Assets/documents/ocad-university-strategic-plan-advancing-excellence-at -ocad-university-for-the-age-of-imagination-2012-2017.pdf.

– 2017. *Presidential Task Force on Under-Representation of Racialized and Indigenous Faculty and Staff: Report and Recommendations.* Toronto: OCAD. https://www .ocadu.ca/Assets/documents/Presidential+Task+Force+on+the+Under -Representation+of+Racialized+and+Indigenous+Faculty+and+Staff.pdf.

– 2018a. *OCAD University Strategic Research Plan 2019–2024.* Toronto: OCAD. https://www.ocadu.ca/Assets/content/research/strategic-research-plan-2019-2024 .pdf.

– 2018b. *Annual Report 2017/2018.* https://www1.ocadu.ca/annual-report-2018/#/.

– 2019. "Statement from President Sara Diamond on the Creative City Campus." April 15, 2019. https://www2.ocadu.ca/news /statement-from-president-sara-diamond-on-the-creative-city-campus.

OCAD Board of Governors. 2015. "Communication from the Board Chair Re: *Globe and Mail* Article," February 15, 2015. Accessed November 29, 2016. http://www .ocadu.ca/about/governance/board-of-governors.htm.

OCAD Faculty Association. 2016. "Memorandum of Agreement, 2016–2020." Toronto: OCAD. https://www.ocadu.ca/Assets/content/hr/Memorandum %20of%20Agreement%202016-2020.pdf.

Omand, Geordon. 2015. "Dispute between Students Escalates to Stabbing at Emily Carr University: Police." *CTV News*, December 3, 2015. https://www.ctvnews.ca /canada/dispute-escalates-to-stabbing-at-emily-carr-university-police-1.2685199.

O'Neill, Paul, Lucy Steeds, and Mick Wilson, eds. 2017. *How Institutions Think: Between Contemporary Art and Curatorial Discourse*. Cambridge, MA: MIT Press.

O'Neill, Tim. 2010. *Report on the University System in Nova Scotia*. Halifax: Province of Nova Scotia. https://novascotia.ca/lae/HigherEducation/documents/Report _on_the_Higher_Education_System_in_Nova_Scotia.pdf.

"Ontario School of Art." *The Globe*, November 6, 1876.

"Ontario School of Art." 1880. *Canadian Illustrated News* 21, no. 20 May 15, 1880. https://www.canadiana.ca/view/oocihm.8_06230_548/8?r=0&s=1.

Orr, Susan, and Alison Shreeve. 2018. *Art and Design Pedagogy in Higher Education: Knowledge, Values and Ambiguity in the Creative Curriculum*. London: Routledge.

Paltridge, Brian, Sue Starfield, Louise Ravelli, and Sarah Nicholson. 2011. "Doctoral Writing in the Visual and Performing Arts: Issues and Debates." *International Journal of Art & Design Education* 30, no. 2 (June): 242–55. DOI: 10.1111/j.1476-8070.2011.01700.x.

Parker, Martin, and David Jary. 1995. "The McUniversity: Organization, Management and Academic Subjectivity." *Organization* 2, no. 2 (May): 319–38. DOI: 10.1177/135050849522013.

Pasma, Chandra, and Erika Shaker. 2018. "Contract U: Contract Faculty Appointments at Canadian Universities." Ottawa: Canadian Centre for Policy Alternatives. https://www.policyalternatives.ca/publications/reports/contract-u.

Pearse, Harold. 2006. *From Drawing to Visual Culture: A History of Art Education in Canada*. Montreal: McGill-Queen's University Press.

Peek, Jade Byard. 2020. "Is There a Credible Future for 'The Last Art College'?" *Canadian Art*, July 30, 2020. https://canadianart.ca/essays /is-there-a-credible-future-for-the-last-art-college/.

Peters, Michael. 2011. *Neoliberalism and After? Education, Social Policy, and the Crisis of Western Capitalism*. New York: Peter Lang.

de Peuter, Greig. 2011. "Creative Economy and Labor Precarity: A Contested Convergence." *Journal of Communication Inquiry* 35, no. 4 (October): 417–25. DOI: 10.1177/0196859911416362.

– 2014a. "Beyond the Model Worker: Surveying a Creative Precariat." *Culture Unbound: Journal of Current Cultural Research* 6 (February): 263–84. DOI: 10.3384/cu.2000.1525.146263.

– 2014b. "Confronting Precarity in the Warhol Economy: Notes from New York City." *Journal of Cultural Economy* 7, no. 1 (January): 31–47. DOI: 10.1080/17530350.2013.856337.

de Peuter, Greig, and Nicole S. Cohen. 2015. "Emerging Labour Politics in Creative Industries." In *The Routledge Companion to the Cultural Industries*, edited by Kate Oakley and Justin O'Connor, 305–18. London: Routledge.

de Peuter, Greig, Nicole S. Cohen, and Enda Brophy, eds. 2015. "Interrogating Internships: Unpaid Work, Creative Industries, and Higher Education." *TripleC:*

Communication, Capitalism & Critique 13, no. 2 (Special Issue): 329–602. DOI: 10.31269/triplec.v13i2.719.

Pickering, Michael, and Emily Keightley. 2006. "The Modalities of Nostalgia." *Current Sociology* 54, no. 6 (November): 919–41. DOI: 10.1177/0011392106068458.

Poirier, Terra. 2018. *Non-Regular: Precarious Academic Labour at Emily Carr University of Art + Design.* Vancouver: UNIT PITT Projects.

Pollard, Emma. 2013. "Making Your Way: Empirical Evidence from a Survey of 3,500 Graduates." In *Cultural Work and Higher Education*, edited by Daniel Ashton and Caitriona Noonan, 45–66. London: Palgrave Macmillan.

Postareff, Liisa, and Sari Lindblom-Ylänne. 2011. "Emotions and Confidence within Teaching in Higher Education." *Studies in Higher Education* 36, no. 7 (November): 799–813. DOI: 10.1080/03075079.2010.483279.

Pucciarelli, Francesca, and Andreas Kaplan. 2016. "Competition and Strategy in Higher Education: Managing Complexity and Uncertainty." *Business Horizons* 59, no. 3 (May–June): 311–20. DOI: 10.1016/j.bushor.2016.01.003.

Rabkin, Nick. 2012. "Teaching Artists and the Future of Education." *Teaching Artist Journal* 10, no. 1 (December): 5–14. DOI: 10.1080/15411796.2012.630633.

Rajagopal, Indhu. 2002. *Hidden Academics: Contract Faculty in Canadian Universities.* Toronto: University of Toronto Press.

Raunig, Gerald, and Gene Ray, eds. 2009. *Art and Contemporary Critical Practice: Reinventing Institutional Critique.* London: Mayfly.

Reckwitz, Andreas. 2017. *The Invention of Creativity: Modern Society and the Culture of the New.* Malden, MA: Polity.

Reuter, Monika. 2015. *Creativity: A Sociological Approach.* London: Palgrave Macmillan.

Rhoades, Gary. 1998. *Managed Professionals: Unionized Faculty and Restructuring Academic Labor.* Albany, NY: SUNY Press.

Richardson, Letia. 1994. "Art for People and Commerce: Vancouver School of Decorative and Applied Arts." In *64–94 Contemporary Decades*, edited by Sam Carter, 129–35. Vancouver: Charles H. Scott Gallery/ECIAD.

Richler, Noah. 2008. "Shape-Shifter in the City." *Canadian Art*, December 1, 2008. https://canadianart.ca/features/shape-shifter/.

Riddell, Jessica. 2017. "The Precarious Workforce: An Ongoing Threat to Quality Higher Education." *University Affairs*, December 1, 2017. https://www.universityaffairs.ca/opinion/adventures-in-academe /ongoing-threat-to-higher-education/.

Robbins, Wendy. 2012. "Critiquing Canada's Research Culture: Social, Cultural, and Political Restraints on Women's University Careers." *Forum on Public Policy* 2012, no. 2.

Roberts, David. 2012. "From the Cultural Contradictions of Capitalism to the Creative Economy: Reflections on the New Spirit of Art and Capitalism." *Thesis Eleven* 110, no. 1 (June): 83–97. DOI: 10.1177/0725513612444563.

Roberts, Peter. 2013. "Academic Dystopia: Knowledge, Performativity, and Tertiary Education." *Review of Education, Pedagogy, and Cultural Studies* 35, no. 1 (January): 27–43. DOI: 10.1080/10714413.2013.753757.

Rodgers, Paul A., and Joyce Yee, eds. 2015. *The Routledge Companion to Design Research*. New York: Routledge.

Ross, Andrew. 2004. *No-Collar: The Humane Workplace and Its Hidden Costs*. Philadelphia: Temple University Press.

– 2009. *Nice Work If You Can Get It: Life and Labor in Precarious Times*. New York: New York University Press.

Rüegg, Walter, ed. 2004. *Universities in the Nineteenth and Early Twentieth Centuries (1800–1945)*. Cambridge: Cambridge University Press.

Saha, Anamik. 2013. "The Cultural Industries in a Critical Multicultural Pedagogy." In *Cultural Work and Higher Education*, edited by Daniel Ashton and Caitriona Noonan, 214–31. London: Palgrave Macmillan.

– 2018. *Race and the Cultural Industries*. Malden, MA: Polity.

Sandals, Leah. 2017. "See Inside Canada's Newest Art-School Campus." *Canadian Art*, September 5, 2017. https://canadianart.ca /news/a-look-inside-canadas-newest-art-school-campus/.

Sandoval, Marisol. 2016. "Fighting Precarity with Co-Operation? Worker Co-Operatives in the Cultural Sector." *New Formations* 88, no. 88 (Spring): 51–68. DOI: 10.3898/NEWF.88.04.2016.

Satzewich, Vic. 2014. "Visa Officers as Gatekeepers of a State's Borders: The Social Determinants of Discretion in Spousal Sponsorship Cases in Canada." *Journal of Ethnic and Migration Studies* 40, no. 9 (September): 1450–69. DOI: 10.1080/1369183X.2013.854162.

Scaff, Lawrence A. 1989. *Fleeing the Iron Cage: Culture, Politics, and Modernity in the Thought of Max Weber*. Berkeley: University of California Press.

Schroeder, Ralph. 1992. *Max Weber and the Sociology of Culture*. London: SAGE.

Sennett, Richard. 2007. *The Culture of the New Capitalism*. New Haven: Yale University Press.

Shaker, Erika, and Robin Shaban. 2018. "No Temporary Solution: Ontario's Shifting College and University Workforce." Ottawa: Canadian Centre for Policy Alternatives. https://www.policyalternatives.ca/publications/reports/no-temporary-solution.

Sheikh, Simon. 2009. "Notes on Institutional Critique." In *Art and Contemporary Critical Practice: Reinventing Institutional Critique*, edited by Gerald Raunig and Gene Ray, 29–32. London: Mayfly.

Sholette, Gregory. 2011. *Dark Matter: Art and Politics in the Age of Enterprise Culture*. New York: Pluto Press.

Shore, Cris. 2008. "Audit Culture and Illiberal Governance: Universities and the Politics of Accountability." *Anthropological Theory* 8, no. 3 (September): 278–98. DOI: 10.1177/1463499608093815.

Shore, Cris, and Susan Wright. 2000. "Coercive Accountability: The Rise of Audit Culture in Higher Education." In *Audit Cultures: Anthropological Studies in Accountability, Ethics, and the Academy,* edited by Marilyn Strathern, 57–89. New York: Routledge.

– 2015. "Audit Culture Revisited: Rankings, Ratings, and the Reassembling of Society." *Current Anthropology* 56, no. 3 (June): 421–44. DOI: 10.1086/681534.

Siciliano, Michael. 2016. "Disappearing into the Object: Aesthetic Subjectivities and Organizational Control in Routine Cultural Work." *Organization Studies* 37, no. 5 (May): 687–708. DOI: 10.1177/0170840615626464.

Side, Katherine, and Wendy Robbins. 2007. "Institutionalizing Inequalities in Canadian Universities: The Canada Research Chairs Program." *NWSA Journal* 19, no. 3 (Fall): 163–81. https://www.jstor.org/stable/40071234.

Simpson, Jennifer S. 2014. *Longing for Justice: Higher Education and Democracy's Agenda.* Toronto: University of Toronto Press.

Singerman, Howard. 1999. *Art Subjects: Making Artists in the American University.* Berkeley: University of California Press.

Slater, Graham B. 2015. "Education as Recovery: Neoliberalism, School Reform, and the Politics of Crisis." *Journal of Education Policy* 30, no. 1 (January): 1–20. DOI: 10.1080/02680939.2014.904930.

Slaughter, Sheila, and Gary Rhoades. 2004. *Academic Capitalism and the New Economy: Markets, State, and Higher Education.* Baltimore: Johns Hopkins University Press.

Smith, Dorothy E. 2005. *Institutional Ethnography: A Sociology for People.* Walnut Creek, CA: AltaMira Press.

Smith, Kimberly K. 2000. "Mere Nostalgia: Notes on a Progressive Paratheory." *Rhetoric and Public Affairs* 3, no. 4 (Winter): 505–27. DOI: 10.1353/rap.2000.0019.

Solomon, Deborah. 1999. "How to Succeed in Art." *New York Times*, June 27, 1999.

Sparkes, Andrew C. 2007. "Embodiment, Academics, and the Audit Culture: A Story Seeking Consideration." *Qualitative Research* 7, no. 4 (November): 521–50. DOI: 10.1177/1468794107082306.

SSHRC. 2021a. "Definitions of Terms." Government of Canada. https://www.sshrc-crsh.gc.ca/funding-financement/programs-programmes/definitions-eng.aspx.

– 2021b. "Merit Review." Government of Canada. https://www.sshrc-crsh.gc.ca/funding-financement/merit_review-evaluation_du_merite/index-eng.aspx.

Stacey, Robert, and Liz Wylie. 1988. *Eighty/Twenty: 100 Years of the Nova Scotia College of Art and Design.* Halifax: Art Gallery of Nova Scotia.

Stahl, Matt. 2013. *Unfree Masters: Recording Artists and the Politics of Work.* Durham, NC: Duke University Press.

Stallybrass, Peter, and Allon White. 1986. *The Politics and Poetics of Transgression.* Ithaca, NY: Cornell University Press.

Standing, Guy. 2014. *The Precariat: The New Dangerous Class.* London: Bloomsbury.

Stankiewicz, Mary Ann, and Donald Soucy. 1990. *Framing the Past: Essays on Art Education.* Reston, VA: National Art Education Association.

Statistics Canada. 2018. "University and College Academic Staff System – Full Time Staff (FT-UCASS)." https://www23.statcan.gc.ca/imdb/p2SV.pl?Function =getSurvey&Id=504700.

Stephens, Lindsay Katyana. 2015. "The Economic Lives of Circus 'Artists': Canadian Circus Performers and the New Economy." *Canadian Journal of Communication* 40: 243–60. DOI: 10.22230/cjc.2015v40n2a2817.

Stewart, Anthony. 2009. *You Must Be a Basketball Player: Rethinking Integration in the University*. Halifax: Fernwood Pub.

Stirling, J. Craig. 2006a. "Postsecondary Art Education in Quebec from the 1870s to the 1920s." In *From Drawing to Visual Culture*, edited by Harold Pearse, 47–84. Montreal: McGill-Queen's University Press.

– 2006b. "Postsecondary Art Education in Ontario, 1876–1912." In *From Drawing to Visual Culture*, edited by Harold Pearse, 47–84. Montreal: McGill-Queen's University Press.

Stokes, A. 2015. "The Glass Runway: How Gender and Sexuality Shape the Spotlight in Fashion Design." *Gender & Society* 29, no. 2 (April): 219–43. DOI: 10.1177/0891243214563327.

Stoler, Ann Laura. 2010. *Carnal Knowledge and Imperial Power: Race and the Intimate in Colonial Rule*. Berkeley: University of California Press.

Strathern, Marilyn, ed. 2000a. *Audit Cultures: Anthropological Studies in Accountability, Ethics, and the Academy*. New York: Routledge.

– 2000b. "The Tyranny of Transparency." *British Educational Research Journal* 26, no. 3 (June): 309–21. DOI: 10.1080/713651562.

Strauss, Anselm. 1970. "The Art School and Its Students: A Study and Interpretation." In *The Sociology of Art and Literature*, edited by M.C. Albrecht and J.H. Barnett, 159–77. New York: Praeger.

Suchin, Peter. 2011a. "Rebel without a Course: Peter Suchin on the Academicisation of Art Education." *Art Monthly* 345, April 2011. http://www.artmonthly.co.uk /magazine/site/issue/april-2011.

– 2011b. "More on PhDs." *Art Monthly* 352, December 2011. http://www.artmonthly .co.uk/magazine/site/issue/dec-jan-11-12.

Sullivan, Graeme. 2010. *Art Practice as Research: Inquiry in Visual Arts*. 2nd ed. Thousand Oaks, CA: SAGE.

Susen, Simon, and Bryan Stanley Turner. 2014. *The Spirit of Luc Boltanski: Essays on the "Pragmatic Sociology of Critique."* London: Anthem Press.

Swidler, Ann. 1986. "Culture in Action: Symbols and Strategies." *American Sociological Review* 51, no. 2 (April): 273–86. DOI: 10.2307/2095521.

– 2003. *Talk of Love: How Culture Matters*. Chicago: University of Chicago Press.

Szeman, Imre. 2010. "Neoliberals Dressed in Black; or, the Traffic in Creativity." *English Studies in Canada* 36, no. 1 (March): 15–36. DOI: 10.1353 /esc.2010.0006.

Tannock, Stuart. 1995. "Nostalgia Critique." *Cultural Studies* 9, no. 3 (October): 453–64. DOI: 10.1080/09502389500490511.

Tasker, Yvonne, and Diane Negra. 2008. *Interrogating Postfeminism: Gender and the Politics of Popular Culture*. Durham, NC: Duke University Press.

Tatli, Ahu, and Mustafa Özbilgin. 2012. "Surprising Intersectionalities of Inequality and Privilege: The Case of the Arts and Cultural Sector." *Equality, Diversity and Inclusion: An International Journal* 31, no. 3 (January): 249–65. DOI: 10.1108/02610151211209108.

Taylor, Stephanie. 2011. "Negotiating Oppositions and Uncertainties: Gendered Conflicts in Creative Identity Work." *Feminism & Psychology* 21, no. 3 (August): 354–71. DOI: 10.1177/0959353510386095.

Taylor, Stephanie, and Karen Littleton. 2012. *Contemporary Identities of Creativity and Creative Work*. Farnham, UK: Ashgate.

– 2013. "Negotiating a Contemporary Creative Identity." In *Cultural Work and Higher Education*, edited by Daniel Ashton and Caitriona Noonan, 154–71. London: Palgrave Macmillan.

Taylor, Yvette, and Kinneret Lahad, eds. 2018. *Feeling Academic in the Neoliberal University: Feminist Flights, Fights and Failures*. London: Palgrave Macmillan.

Tello, Verónica. 2020. "What Is Contemporary about Institutional Critique? Or, Instituting the Contemporary: A Study of *The Silent University*." *Third Text* 34, no. 6: 635–49. DOI: 10.1080/09528822.2020.1841409.

Terry, Andrea, and Jayne Wark. 2018. "'Make Some Noise': Precarity, Dialogue, and Professional Development: Introduction." *RACAR* 43, no. 1 (August): 81–4. DOI: 10.7202/1050822ar.

Thévenot, Laurent. 2015. "Engaging in the Politics of Participative Art in Practice." In *Artistic Practices: Social Interactions and Cultural Dynamics*, edited by Tasos Zembylas, 132–50. London: Routledge.

Third, Pamela. 2015. "OCAD University vs Emily Carr University: Toronto Complaining vs Vancouver Complaisance." *Education, Art and Where the World Takes Me* (blog), February 24, 2015. https://pamelathird.wordpress .com/2015/02/24/ocad-university-vs-emily-carr-university-toronto-complaining -vs-vancouver-complaisance/.

Thornton, Alan. 2013. *Artist, Researcher, Teacher: A Study of Professional Identity in Art and Education*. Bristol: Intellect.

Thornton, Patricia H. 2004. *Markets from Culture: Institutional Logics and Organizational Decisions in Higher Education Publishing*. Stanford, CA: Stanford Business Books.

Thornton, Patricia H., William Ocasio, and Michael Lounsbury. 2012. *The Institutional Logics Perspective: A New Approach to Culture, Structure, and Process*. Oxford: Oxford University Press.

Thornton, Sarah. 1996. *Club Cultures: Music, Media, and Subcultural Capital*. Hanover, NH: University Press of New England.

– 2009. *Seven Days in the Art World*. London: W.W. Norton.

Tickner, Lisa. 2008. *Hornsey 1968: The Art School Revolution*. London: Frances Lincoln.

Tight, Malcolm. 1994. "Crisis, What Crisis? Rhetoric and Reality in Higher
Education." *British Journal of Educational Studies* 42, no. 4 (December): 363–74.
DOI: 10.1080/00071005.1994.9974009.

Tinius, Jonas. 2015. "Institutional Formations and Artistic Critique in German
Ensemble Theatre." *Performance Research* 20, no. 4 (July): 71–7. DOI:
10.1080/13528165.2015.1071041.

Tuchman, Gaye. 2011. *Wannabe U: Inside the Corporate University.* Chicago:
University of Chicago Press.

Turk, James, ed. 2014. *Academic Freedom in Conflict: The Struggle over Free Speech
Rights in the University.* Toronto: James Lorimer & Company.

– 2017. "The Landscape of the Contemporary University." *Canadian
Journal of Communication* 42, no. 1 (January): 3–12. DOI: 10.22230
/cjc.2017v42n1a3202.

Tyler, Imogen. 2013. *Revolting Subjects: Social Abjection and Resistance in Neoliberal
Britain.* London: Zed Books.

Universities Canada. 2016. "Membership Criteria." News release, September
23, 2016. https://www.univcan.ca/media-room/media-releases
/statement-proposed-membership-criterion/.

– 2018. *Recent Data on Equity, Diversity and Inclusion at Canadian Universities.*
Ottawa: Universities Canada. https://www.univcan.ca/wp-content
/uploads/2018/11/Data-on-equity-diversity-inclusion-Oct-2018.pdf.

Vosko, Leah F. 2011. *Managing the Margins: Gender, Citizenship, and the
International Regulation of Precarious Employment.* Oxford: Oxford University
Press.

Weber, Max. (1904) 2003. *The Protestant Ethic and the Spirit of Capitalism.*
Translated by Talcott Parsons. Mineola, NY: Dover Publications.

– 1978. *Economy and Society: An Outline of Interpretive Sociology.* Vol. 2. Translated
by Guenther Roth. Berkeley: University of California Press.

Wendt, Fabian. 2018. *Compromise, Peace and Public Justification: Political Morality
beyond Justice.* New York: Palgrave Macmillan.

Whelan, Andrew, Ruth H. Walker, and Christopher Moore, eds. 2013. *Zombies in the
Academy: Living Death in Higher Education.* Bristol: Intellect.

Whitelaw, Anne. 2017. *Spaces and Places for Art: Making Art Institutions in Western
Canada, 1912–1990.* Montreal: McGill-Queen's University Press.

Whittaker, Elvi, ed. 2015. *Solitudes of the Workplace: Women in Universities.*
Montreal: McGill-Queen's University Press.

Wilf, Eitan Y. 2014. *School for Cool: The Academic Jazz Program and the Paradox of
Institutionalized Creativity.* Chicago: University of Chicago Press.

Willis, Rebecca. 2019. "The Use of Composite Narratives to Present
Interview Findings." *Qualitative Research* 19, no. 4 (August): 471–80. DOI:
10.1177/1468794118787711.

Willmott, Hugh. 2013. "Spirited Away: When Political Economy Becomes
Culturalized." In *New Spirits of Capitalism? Crises, Justifications, and Dynamics,*

edited by Paul Du Gay and Morgan Glenn, 98–123. Oxford: Oxford University Press.

Windsor, Howard. 2011. *Time to Act: Report on the Nova Scotia College of Art and Design*. Halifax: Province of Nova Scotia. http://docplayer.net/16598178-Report -on-the-nova-scotia-college-of-art-and-design-time-to-act.html.

Wohl, Hannah. 2021. *Bound by Creativity: How Contemporary Art Is Created and Judged*. Chicago: University of Chicago Press.

Wolfe, Morris. 2001. *OCA 1967–1972: Five Turbulent Years*. Toronto: Grub Street Books.

Wolff, Janet. 1981. *The Social Production of Art*. New York: St. Martin's Press.

Wong, Rita. 2018. "Why Can't We Elect B.C. University Chancellors?" *Georgia Straight*, April 19, 2018. https://www.straight.com/news/1060856 /rita-wong-why-cant-we-elect-bc-university-chancellors.

Woo, Ben. 2015. "Erasing the Lines between Leisure and Labor: Creative Work in the Comics World." *Spectator* 35, no. 3 (Fall): 57–64. https://cinema.usc.edu /spectator/35.2/7_Woo.pdf.

Woodhouse, Howard. 2017. "The Contested Terrain of Academic Freedom in Canada's Universities: Where Are We Going?" *American Journal of Economics and Sociology* 76, no. 3 (May): 618–47. DOI:10.1111/ajes.12189.

Woods, Charlotte. 2010. "Employee Wellbeing in the Higher Education Workplace: A Role for Emotion Scholarship." *Higher Education* 60, no. 2 (August): 171–85. DOI: 10.1007/s10734-009-9293-y.

Wreyford, Natalie. 2015. "Birds of a Feather: Informal Recruitment Practices and Gendered Outcomes for Screenwriting Work in the UK Film Industry." *The Sociological Review* 63, no. S1 (May): 84–96. DOI: 10.1111/1467-954X.1224.

Wright, Douglas. 1968. *Report on the Organizational Structure and Administration of the Ontario College of Art*. Toronto: OCA.

Wunker, Erin. 2015a. "Crisis in Academic Labour Puts Canadian Universities on the Brink." *Rabble.ca* (blog), March 10, 2015. https://rabble.ca/blogs/bloggers/campus-notes/2015/03 /crisis-academic-labour-puts-canadian-universities-on-brink.

– 2015b. "With Toil and Solidarity We Can Solve Canada's Academic Labour Crisis." *Rabble.ca* (blog), March 12, 2015. https://rabble.ca/blogs/bloggers/campus-notes/2015/03 /crisis-academic-labour-puts-canadian-universities-on-brink.

Youn, Ted I.K., and Tanya M. Price. 2009. "Learning from the Experience of Others: The Evolution of Faculty Tenure and Promotion Rules." *The Journal of Higher Education* 80, no. 2 (March): 204–37. DOI: 10.1080/00221546.2009.1177213.

Yuen, Nancy Wang. 2017. *Reel Inequality: Hollywood Actors and Racism*. New Brunswick, NJ: Rutgers University Press.

Zelizer, Viviana A. Rotman. 1985. *Pricing the Priceless Child: The Changing Social Value of Children*. New York: Basic Books.

Zolberg, Vera L. 2015. "A Cultural Sociology of the Arts." *Current Sociology* 63, no. 6 (October): 896–915. DOI: 10.1177/0011392114551652.
Zukin, Sharon. 1982. *Loft Living: Culture and Capital in Urban Change*. Baltimore: Johns Hopkins University Press.
– 1995. *The Cultures of Cities*. Cambridge, MA: Blackwell.

Index